Business Driven Human Resource Management

Business Driven Human Resource Management

D. E. HUSSEY

JOHN WILEY & SONS

Chichester · New York · Brisbane · Toronto · Singapore

658.3
H976

Other Wiley Editorial Offices

John Wiley & Sons, Inc., 605 Third Avenue,
New York, NY 10158-0012, USA

Jacaranda Wiley Ltd, 33 Park Road, Milton,
Queensland 4064, Australia

John Wiley & Sons (Canada) Ltd, 22 Worcester Road,
Rexdale, Ontario M9W 1L1, Canada

John Wiley & Sons (Asia) Pte Ltd, 2 Clementi Loop #02-01,
Jin Xing Distripark, Singapore 129809

Library of Congress Cataloging-in-Publication Data

Hussey, D. E. (David E.)
  Business driven human resource management / D.E. Hussey.
      p. cm.
  Includes bibliographical references and index.
  ISBN 0-471-96969-9 (cloth)
  1. Personnel management.   I. Title
HF5549.H884   1996
658.3—dc20   96–28499
                                              CIP

British Library Cataloguing in Publication Data

A catalogue record for this book is available from the British Library

ISBN 0-471-96969-9

Typeset in 11/13 pt Palatino from the author's disks by Mackreth Media Services,
Hemel Hempstead.
Printed and bound in Great Britain by Biddles Ltd, Guildford and King's Lynn.
This book is printed on acid-free paper responsibly manufactured from sustainable
forestation, for which at least two trees are planted for each one used for paper production.

Contents

Introduction

A strategic approach to Human Resource Management (HRM) has great appeal and, it could be argued, is at the heart of the difference between modern HRM and traditional personnel management. Unfortunately, the lesson from much of the research, and my own experience in and observations of a large number of organisations is that, although the idea is seen as attractive, it is much harder to do than to say.

Many of the books available deal more with the concept than the detail of how to make it work, and this is valuable in gaining awareness, but is of little help to the HR practitioner who has to apply the concept in a particular organisation. In my view it is not enough to cover HRM's strategic role only at the highest level in the organisation, and to assume that a chapter on a strategic planning process will enable HR managers, by some mystical means, to convert all the ideas to detailed HR policies and strategies. Regrettably, some of the books do little more than this.

The main aim of this book is to help with the *how*, as well as giving some space to the *why*. The how is reinforced by some case studies, chosen to illustrate the good and the bad, and includes specific approaches to the whole scope of HRM. It offers detailed step by step approaches, checklists of things to consider, and suggestions that aid the application of the ideas. The whole is reinforced with summaries of some of the key recent research findings about what organisations actually do. It is not part of my argument to suggest that no organisations have a business driven approach to HRM, and if this were the case I should feel less confident in my own advice, and would be able to offer no positive case studies.

I first came to the problem of a strategic approach to HRM in the early 1970s, when I was responsible for both personnel management and strategic planning at Otis Elevators Ltd. Like many of the HR managers interviewed in the various research studies, I believed strongly in the strategic link, and was convinced that closeness to the strategy was enough to achieve this. We did audit our HR activity, but this was against a concept of what was good practice, rather than against the specific strategic needs of the organisation. If asked at the time, I would have claimed that the personnel activity was business driven, and it is only the hindsight gained from a further twenty years plus of experience, research and deliberate attention to the issue that makes me now realise that my answer would have been wrong.

What I gained from this experience was an unwavering belief in the importance of HRM in the strategic process, and an awareness that strategy does not implement itself, which led me to another strand of my subsequent work: the implementation aspects of strategic management.

I believe that the book I coauthored (Hussey and Langham, 1979) was the first to try to link strategic analysis to the people aspects of management. I might add that the book did not sell out its first and only printing for about 12 years. When this happens we authors like to claim we were ahead of our time, so it is never our fault! In retrospect, I think we did quite well in covering the behavioural aspects of strategic management, but did much less well in how this could be related to HRM.

There were some good books on what was then called manpower planning published at this time, such as Bramham, 1975, and which still have value. Although stressing a link with corporate plans, these books tended to focus on forecasts of employee numbers, with some argument about how to ensure that the corporate need was met. This is still important, and I have a chapter on it in this book, but these books did not deal with the proactive role that HRM should play during the formation of corporate strategies, nor did they get into all the many ways in which HR activity could be used to support the organisation's vision, objectives and strategy.

In 1976 I moved into the consultancy with which I was to stay until the end of 1994, when it was sold, and from 1980 I ran the European side of that business. This gave me an unrivalled opportunity to continue my interests in strategic management, particularly the issue of implementation, and the strategic role of HR. Many of our activities were as much about implementation as strategy formulation, and we had a particular interest in tailored management education and training.

In the early 1980s I initiated a research programme, which yielded much useful information, and which led to the development of a number of different concepts by the consultancy, all of which added to my experience, although there are many detailed proprietary methods which I am not able to write about. The mix of experience, research, and much of my own thinking came together in various articles. In Hussey, 1984, an article developed from a paper given to the Executive Club, Singapore a year earlier, I explored the problem of why organisations that claimed to embrace strategic management were continuing to plan their way into oblivion. Among the conclusions were a conviction that much strategic analysis was spurious, and a concern for the implementation of strategies. This was followed by Hussey, 1985, which took the issue of implementation further, and was one of the first articles on the subject of using management training as a means of implementing strategy. This drew on some of the consultancy's own research, as well as experience in this activity in the USA and the UK. The article was inspired partly by research carried out by Peel, 1984, which showed that the majority of management training effort was spent on worthy subjects such as team building which of themselves did little to help UK companies meet the threats they were facing from global competitors. Coincidentally Bolt, 1985, published an article with a similar theme a month later in the USA. In the same year research in the USA (Lusterman, 1985) found a strong movement in the USA to management training that contributed to bottom line results.

All this came together in a book. Hussey, 1988, was one of the first books to offer a strategic approach to management development and training. It was written at about the same time as two other books on the same subject, although their actual publication dates varied (Nilsson, 1987 and Bolt, 1989). Even more information came to hand with the landmark reports Constable and McCormick, 1987 and Handy et al, 1988.

My interest in strategic implementation continued with Hussey, 1991, an edited book which included a chapter by Alexander, 1991, which was based on original research into why strategies did not get implemented. Many of the reasons were related to HRM. Hussey, 1996, explored the problems of strategy implementation in even greater detail.

One lesson I have learned is that the more you do on a subject, the more you find there is to do. I continued to develop the concepts, had the experience of many aspects of strategic HRM through the consultancy, was grateful for the opportunity to talk over my ideas with colleagues and clients, who are all people of the highest calibre, and was able to write about my ideas at some length. My interest expanded from management development to the broader issues of strategic HRM, leading first to a chapter on the subject in Hussey, 1994, and next to an article on undertaking a strategic audit of HRM (Hussey, 1995). The results of this rich mix are the ideas and models presented in this book.

Besides helping to turn concepts into actionable approaches, another purpose of this book is to refute a number of the myths which the research and my experiences suggest have some currency.

- *Myth 1*: If the top HR manager is on the Board, this is enough to ensure that HRM is business driven.
- *Myth 2*: If HRM is allowed to be proactive when new corporate strategies are considered, this automatically means that all HRM activities will become business driven.
- *Myth 3*: Doing things right automatically means that we are doing the right things: therefore it is enough to apply good professional practice.
- *Myth 4*: Because new HR policies and procedures take a lot of time and effort to implement, they will have a long shelf life.

- *Myth 5:* Evaluation and performance measures are too difficult and expensive for HRM activities, and HRM does not need to be subject to such disciplines.
- *Myth 6:* In any case it is not possible to evaluate the results of many HRM actions which should be treated as acts of faith.
- *Myth 7:* Every action we take in HRM is with a concern for the interests of the organisation, which means that we are business driven.
- *Myth 8:* Line management know that HRM is a valuable, value adding strategic partner which plays an irreplaceable role in the management of the organisation.

Try asking line managers about myth 8!

As always, I owe a debt of gratitude to the various authorities from whom I have learned more about this intriguing subject. In particular I should like to acknowledge the part played by my friends and former colleagues at Harbridge Consulting Group, some of whose work is referenced, quoted or described in the book.

I hope that the book will play a part in helping HRM to be a major force in organisational success. At the least, I hope it will make a contribution to thinking that will encourage others to work on the issue. It will be even better if it helps your organisation to develop a business driven approach.

D. E. Hussey

REFERENCES

Alexander, L. D., 1991, Strategy Implementation: Nature of the Problem, in Hussey, D. E., editor, *International Review of Strategic Management*, 2.1, Chichester: John Wiley.

Bolt, J. E., 1985, Tailor Executive Development to Strategy, *Harvard Business Review*, November/December.

Bolt, J. E., 1989, *Executive Development*, New York: Harper.

Constable, J. and McCormick, R., 1987, *The Making of Managers*, London: British Institute of Management.

Handy, C., Gordon, C., Gow, I. et al, 1988, *Making Managers,* London: Pitman.

Hussey, D. E., 1984, Strategic Management: Lessons from Success and Failure, *Long Range Planning,* 17.1.

Hussey, D. E., 1985, Implementing Corporate Strategy: Using Management Education and Training, *Long Range Planning,* 18.5.

Hussey, D. E., 1988, *Management Training and Corporate Strategy,* Oxford: Pergamon.

Hussey, D. E., editor, 1991, *International Review of Strategic Management,* 2.1, Chichester: John Wiley.

Hussey, D. E., 1994, *Strategic Management: Theory and Practice,* 3rd edition, Chapter 21, Oxford: Pergamon.

Hussey, D. E., 1995, Human Resources: A Strategic Audit, in Hussey, D. E., editor, *Rethinking Strategic Management,* Chichester: John Wiley.

Hussey, D. E., editor, 1996, *Rethinking Strategic Management,* Chichester: John Wiley.

Hussey, D. E. and Langham, M. J., 1979, *Corporate Planning: The Human Factor,* Oxford: Pergamon.

Lusterman, S., 1985, *Trends in Corporate Education and Training,* New York: Conference Board.

Nilsson, W. P., 1987, *Achieving Strategic Goals Through Executive Development,* Reading, MA: Addison Wesley.

Peel, M., 1984, *Management Development and Training,* London: British Institute of Management/Professional Publishing.

1
Pressures for Change

Organisations have been subject to enormous pressures over the past few years, with major underlying structural changes in industry sometimes concealed behind the short-term issues of recession. Every generation of managers since the Second World War, and possibly before, has felt that it has had to face more change in a more complex situation, than did preceding generations. For each generation this is probably a true statement, which means that we have faced a trend of increasing difficulty and turbulence, which shows no sign of slowing.

I believe that organisations will face continuing pressures as we move into the early years of the next century, and the problems that managers will have to cope with in the next decade will be even greater than we have experienced in the turbulent 1990s.

There will be no simple solutions, and success will depend, as always, on the soundness of the strategic decisions taken by top management, and the ability of the organisation to implement those strategies. This would push the human resource aspects of the business to the fore, even without the added complication of continued change and the pressures that this brings. Human Resource Management, which is already very professional in many organisations, needs to become even more strategic in the way it operates. In effect it needs to be driven by the business needs of the organisation, but without losing sight of the critical value and importance of people in making strategies become reality. Top management also needs to give greater consideration to HR issues at the strategy formulation stage. These are not easy tasks.

WHY BUSINESS DRIVEN HUMAN RESOURCE MANAGEMENT?

Of course Human Resource Management (HRM) has always tried to contribute to business results. Most HR managers are motivated to play a part in achieving success for the organisations for which they work, and make this concern a driving force in their day to day operations. Like any other area of management, HRM involves setting policies, formulating plans, and trying to make the best decisions possible. All this is done in a context of how the organisation as a whole, and the HR manager in particular, see the role of HRM, the environment of the business, and the situation in which it operates. This creates a perception within which logical actions can be taken. But what if the perception is faulty? What if the world as we see it, is not the world as it really is? Once you change the boundaries of perception, you also may destroy the logic that made sense of previous decisions.

This is the situation in which I believe many businesses now find themselves. The perceptual boundaries to business have changed and with that has come a need to look at HRM from a different perspective, so that it makes a greater strategic contribution to the business. I have used the term 'business driven' to describe the focus which I believe is needed, but which is not yet universally applied. Business driven means being proactive as well as reactive and playing a role in setting the strategy of the organisation. It means using the strategy as the driving force for all HR policies and plans, and ensuring that this thinking becomes a philosophy that stretches to the lowest level of decisions and actions in the HR department. It means ensuring that the human factor is considered by the chief executive and other managers in all important decisions. Above all it means that HRM must add value to the organisation.

Of course there are organisations where a business driven

approach to HR is practised. If this were not so, any book such as this would deal only with theory. There are many more organisations where only some of the concepts are applied. There are others where the need has been recognised, but for one reason or another progress has been disappointing. The research evidence for these statements will be given later.

The aim of this book is to explore practical approaches that will enable an organisation to apply a business driven approach to HRM, and to support this with case studies and examples. Research findings will be used to add emphasis to the points made.

The starting point is to examine some of the forces for change which I believe are making it ever more necessary for organisations to examine the degree to which HRM is contributing to the strategic health of the business. To aid this process checklists of questions will be provided to enable readers to "audit" their current HRM activities.

FORCES FOR CHANGE

Strong forces are shaping the environment in which we operate, and old concepts of management have to be re-examined against the challenge of the world we live in today, and the world we believe we will live in tomorrow. While there will always be many new issues in the external business environment which will affect the organisation from time to time, and which will impact both the corporate strategy and HRM, we can also see some long running trends which have been with us for some years, and which will continue into the future. A feature of these forces for change is that they know no geographical boundaries, and few organisations and few countries are immune to them. Perhaps of more significance than the individual forces described here is the cumulative result: organisations face a period of almost continuous change. There is no escape from this, so the only solution is to learn to live with it, and this makes the people aspects of management even more significant than they have been in the past.

The forces described here are unlikely to surprise the reader, as they will fit the observations of most managers. However, they were not derived by guesswork, but from a number of studies undertaken in Europe and the USA. Those which I found the most useful include Sullivan, 1989, and Barham and Bassam, 1989. The second work was an extension of an earlier study by Barham, Fraser and Heath, 1988. To these references could be added so many articles that the statements made here have become almost part of the body of knowledge which we all share.

- *Competition.* Competition has increased, and for most industries it is no longer possible to define competition within the boundaries of a particular country. There are few places where an organisation can shelter from competitors, and many industries have been shaken up because their competitors have taken a global view of their markets. The demise of the British motor cycle industry was in a large part due to the inability of the British firms to imagine that anyone could gain great production advantages by thinking of manufacture for a global market, instead of the traditional approach of producing for the local market and the exporting of any surplus, mainly to countries of the former Empire where there was a protective customs tariff. More and more organisations are compelled to think of their business in global terms, and most others are subject to more intense competition. The European Union has been one of many factors which have increased competition in member countries, even when the markets themselves are not global.
- *Customers are more demanding.* The life style expectations of the whole population have increased steadily, and continue to rise. Many in the developed countries regard poverty as relative rather than absolute deprivation. With higher expectations, and more choice, it is not surprising that the individual consumer is less tolerant of poor products and service, and more vocal in expressing dissatisfaction. The industrial customer is more demanding, quite rightly so, in order to attain the cost levels and to supply the quality and timeliness of delivery that enable him/her to compete. While the new requirements bring opportunities for the whole supply chain to work in a more cooperative manner than

may have been traditional, there is much less willingness by industrial customers to condone failures. Few can afford to do so, if they are to succeed in their own markets.

● *Accelerating pace of technological obsolescence.* Product life cycles are shortening. This has a positive advantage in that it keeps markets growing: these days we are unlikely to run into the old problem of Singer Sewing Machines who made products that would last for many years, but without the technological advances that would make people want to upgrade to the next level. It also means that the time to exploit a new product or innovation is much shorter than in the past, and if too long is spent in development, the product may be nearly obsolete before it is launched.

Plant and office equipment also becomes obsolete more quickly. Think of how we now process letters and reports. The forerunner of the typewriter was invented in 1843. Some 30 years later Remington began production of a "proper" typewriter. The mechanical typewriter became the office staple until after the Second World War, and still had a use in many offices up until the 1960s. Of course there were improvements but it was not uncommon to expect a 20 or 30 year life from a machine. Around the 1950s electric typewriters began to appear, and had become the norm in modern offices by the 1960s. There were more frequent innovations, but again buyers could expect them to be long lasting. Word processors using punched cards found their way into offices in the early 1970s, but were soon to become obsolete as computer technology developed. Later in the 1970s electric typewriters gave way to electronic machines. The big acceleration in obsolescence came in the late 1970s and early 1980s, when computer-based systems took over, expanding from typing to desktop publishing, and providing the ability to produce graphics and text as well as many other features. Innovation of software and hardware now means that few office systems have a life of more than about five years. Certainly no one could contemplate going back to the long life cycles of the pre-computer age. Businesses which cannot afford to update, or which take too long in launching new innovations have a great competitive disadvantage.

- *Pressure to deliver shareholder value.* Top managements of public companies have always had to balance the needs of shareholders for dividends and share price growth against the needs of the business. What became apparent throughout the 1980s was that many strategic actions taken by organisations reduced shareholder value. Porter, 1987, drew attention to the ways in which the diversified organisation could create value, and pointed out that many did not do so. Conglomerate organisations went out of fashion in the stock market, and evidence of their failure to deliver as much as the sum of their individual parts was provided by high profile acquisitions which led to the sell off of most of the parts, leaving the acquirer with either a handsome profit or retaining the plum business while recovering the full investment from the sale of the other businesses. An example is Hansen Trust's acquisition of Imperial, which meant that they retained the cash-generating tobacco business for a net cost of well below its true value. Hansen's shrewdness helped focus the minds of shareholders and managers on issues of shareholder value. Fuelled by a hostile bid, BAT Industries divested all activities except tobacco and finance. ICI separated its pharmaceutical operation from its other businesses.

COMMON RESPONSES TO THE FORCES FOR CHANGE

The response to these trends has been the triggering off of a number of remarkably similar actions across many organisations and industries. The past ten years have been called a decade of restructuring. Common actions taken by many organisations have included:

- seeking a reduction of costs, with more attention being given to competitive positioning;
- attention to time as a strategic issue, and attempts to reduce cycle times throughout the organisation;
- changing structures to achieve a closer relationship with customers;

- more emphasis, in Europe and the USA, on quality. Japan already had this emphasis;
- attempts to change the culture of organisations to enable them to react faster and more effectively to market requirements.

Before looking at the forces for change, I should like to explore the reactions in more detail. The headings encompass many of the new pieces of jargon which have crept into our vocabulary, and will also emphasise that few, if any, of the new actions can be successfully implemented without careful attention to human resource issues.

Cost Emphasis

Businesses have always been concerned about their costs. The new emphasis has been of costs compared to competitors, and much of the new thinking has been about ways of achieving comparative advantage. One of the manifestations of this was the emphasis on becoming a world class manufacturer. The concept embraces more than costs: it covers also quality and innovation. Hayes, Wheelwright and Clark (1988) define world class: "Basically, this means being better than almost any company in your industry in at least one important aspect of manufacturing" (page 21). For most organisations it was no longer enough to gain an improvement over their own previous year's activities. Long-term success is only possible if organisations do better in some way than their competitors.

Hayes, Wheelwright and Clark argue that "soft" infrastructural decisions, in which they include "human resource policies and practices, including management selection and training policies", are critical to the achievement of a world class position. They argue that it is almost impossible for an organisation to spend its way to world class performance by concentrating only on the hardware, such as new plant and equipment.

The most important thing was the recognition that the criteria for success lay outside the business, and that meeting internally-generated targets was irrelevant unless they happened to be as good as or better than the performance of competitors. In the UK we learned this lesson the hard way, with many previously successful industries disappearing because the competitors offered better products at lower cost.

Also in the 1980s was the rise in popularity of benchmarking (which is described in more detail in Chapter 12). Many organisations misunderstand benchmarking and see it as just a comparison of ratios. In fact it should be a comparison of the processes that caused the ratios. There are many stories of successful benchmarking projects, including companies such as Ford and Xerox. Lessons can be learned from organisations that are not competitors: for example, Motorola was reputed to benchmark against motor racing pit stops, to gain insight into ways of improving changeover time on assembly lines.

Benchmarking does not itself cause change, but it is a means to deciding where changes are needed. Karlöf and Östblom, 1993, argue that benchmarking should be part of an approach to the learning organisation.

Even more fashionable, and much more widely applied, are the sweeping "downsizing and delayering" actions which have swept through most organisations on both sides of the Atlantic. A more recent attempt at a politically correct description is "rightsizing". The aims are usually to reduce costs, to push decision making further down the organisation to the closest possible point to the customer, and to change culture. Despite all the hype, my impression is that most such initiatives are really for cost reduction, and that comparatively few organisations are really serious about the other aims. The human resource implications of "rightsizing" are immense, in terms of dealing with the selection and termination of those who are to leave, the retraining of those who are to stay, minimising the impact on morale of large redundancies, and helping to change culture in the required direction.

The latest concept to hit the headlines is business process reengineering. Again, not all organisations that claim to undertake BPR are truly doing so: many have followed the British habit of renaming existing activities without properly taking on board the changes required by the new concept. BPR is about the complete rethinking of how processes are undertaken, and the result of a successful BPR exercise is fundamental change. Johansson, McHugh, Pendlebury and Wheeler, 1993, describe BPR as "... the means by which an organisation can achieve radical change in performance as measured by cost, cycle time, service and quality ..." (page 15). The change in emphasis is the focus on the business "... as a set of related customer oriented core business processes rather than a set of organisational functions" (page 16). Not surprisingly a BPR initiative has many HR implications, both for the running of the initiative and the implementation of any conclusions.

Time as a Strategic Issue

Time has always been seen to have business significance. Benjamin Franklin's advice to a young tradesman in the eighteenth century was "Remember that time is money", and I am sure that the same sentiment has been expressed by even earlier sages. In modern business, when the development of new products or improvements takes longer than competitors, there is a multiple impact. The opportunity to gain revenue from the product may be considerably reduced by the competitor who can respond quicker, costs are likely to be higher than when the product was conceived, and customers may feel let down because expectations are not met. Töpfer, 1995, quotes an Arthur D. Little analysis which showed that to exceed launch time by 10% causes a reduction of revenue for innovative products of 25–30%. Exceeding production costs by a similar 10% would reduce total revenue by 15–20%. The underlying issue is not just about keeping to schedules, but reducing the overall time on a continuing basis. Töpfer illustrated this with some comparisons. For example in 1980 Brother took four years to develop a new printer: in 1990 it took only two. Honda's development time for cars over the same period came down from eight to three years. In 1986 Sony needed two years to develop a television set, but by 1990 only took nine months.

No doubt similar successes could be observed across a wide range of high technology industries. The pressure is not just to improve, but to improve enough to get ahead of competitors. Typical steps taken by organisations to achieve this include new approaches to project management, closer working relationships between internal functions, the involvement of suppliers and customers in the development, and simultaneous engineering. All of these steps have considerable HR implications, for culture, working methods and attitudes.

Closeness to the Customer

The more exacting demands of customers have led to a new industry: consulting and writing about customer focus. For many this has been no more than using a few words of the new jargon, or making some other cosmetic change. For example British Rail started calling us customers instead of passengers in their station public address announcements, but it was hard to find any accompanying improvement in customer service.

Carlzon, 1987, triggered a revolution in thinking with the "moment of truth" concept. This was each moment when a customer came into contact with an employee. At SAS where he applied the ideas of customer focus when he became president in 1980, he calculated that there were twenty-five million such moments each year, as there were five million customers who each made contact on average with five SAS employees. In fact the concept was not invented by Carlzon, and had previously been published in Normann, 1978 and other articles by this author. What Carlzon had done was to apply it very successfully through a mix of restructuring and training so that the front line people were seen as the most important, with the rest of the organisation as backup support. In order to give the front line greater ability to maximise the value of these moments of truth, levels of bureaucracy were removed, the rule book which had previously required matters to be passed upwards for decision was scrapped, and decision-making power was delegated to the front line people to enable them to act in the interest of the customers.

Many organisations have followed this lead of seeing the organisation as an upside down pyramid, with the people who face the customers at the top, and everyone else, including the chief executive, being there to enable them to work effectively. A natural result was to remove blockages in the organisation to communication and decision making; blockages frequently identified as layers of middle management which were removed because in theory the role they played was now being undertaken by the people who shared the moments of truth with the customers. What we will never know is how many of the organisational restructures, ostensibly undertaken for this reason, were in fact a straight cost reduction measure with little thought about how the organisation would function in the future. If fashion is on your side, do you need to think? I would say yes.

There is another trend in responses which applies to industrial organisations. This is the tendency for suppliers and buyers to work closer together, partly because this can reduce overall costs in the chain, and partly to take time out of development projects. Moving from an antagonistic relationship to one of cooperation is also one of the ways in which overall quality can be improved. As a result, there has been a trend to preferred suppliers, who understand each other, which gives both sides the opportunity to plan production more effectively, schedule investment, and work on quality and value. The preferred relationship is great if it is your organisation that is preferred, but tough on the former second and third source suppliers who do not make it to the first division. But it is only great as long as you stay in the preferred position, and to do this requires considerable attention to customer needs, and the many "moments of truth" that are the result of this sort of relationship. There are numerous structural, attitudinal and cultural factors which have to be appropriate for the success of the new approach.

Emphasis on Quality

Another approach taken up by numerous organisations has been TQM (total quality management), and for many this has been the only approach which has used training which has cascaded from top to bottom of the organisation.

> "Total quality management is an approach to improving the effectiveness and flexibility of business as a whole. It is essentially a way of organising and involving the whole organisation; every department, every activity, every single person at every level."
>
> Oakland, 1989

There are variations on the theme, depending which authority inspired the approach, but all TQM approaches have a number of things in common. These include:

- moving responsibility for quality to the people who do the work;
- creating an immutable objective for the improvement of quality throughout the organisation;
- establishing a culture which makes quality a priority;
- achieving widespread cooperation in quality matters, which crosses the functional and departmental boundaries within the organisation (and sometimes the boundaries outside between buyers and suppliers);
- using project teams to solve quality problems;
- finding ways of measuring quality and reporting back to the quality teams;
- creating an attitude of team and self control, rather than control through supervision and inspection.

Although many have walked this road, and spent vast sums on TQM to try to achieve the necessary changes, not every organisation has travelled the full journey. Many have underestimated the length of time that such major changes take, and many have not given the amount of management time needed to make them work (partly because managers underestimated the time they should spend on the initiative in the first place).

The other universal approach to quality has been BS 5750 (ISO 9000), which is endorsement that the organisation has the procedures in place to produce quality, but does not by itself create a quality culture, or ensure a quality product.

There is some empirical evidence that in the long run superior quality leads to superior profits. This comes from the PIMS database (Profit Impact of Market Strategy), which showed that businesses in the top third on relative quality received prices that were 5–6% higher than those in the bottom third (Buzzell and Gale, 1987). What is not revealed in these figures is the steady loss of competitiveness of those organisations which fall behind competitors in quality. We have already seen that customer expectations continue to rise.

My expectation is that increasingly organisations will find that TQM can not deliver when it is applied in an organisational vacuum, which asks people to behave differently on quality matters than they do on any other aspect of the business. Perhaps the secret for the future will be to move more towards a concept of the learning organisation within which TQM will be an element. Mayo and Lank, 1994, state: "A Learning Organisation harnesses the full brain power, knowledge and experience available to it, in order to evolve continually for the benefit of all its stakeholders". There is clearly much here which is of concern to business driven HRM management, and the learning organisation is something which we will explore later.

Culture Change, Flexibility and Fast Reaction

Earlier we looked at one aspect of the strategic importance of time. There is another, which is the ability of the organisation to respond quickly to unforeseen events. Although some of the delayering initiatives have been intended to serve this purpose, there are also accompanying trends. One which has come to the fore in the last decade is the announced intention to change culture. The reasoning seems to be that a chief executive recognises a mismatch between the existing culture, which reflects the behaviours needed for the success patterns of the past, and the business situation the organisation now faces. One of the pioneers of this route was General Electric in the USA, where Jack Welch took action to make the whole organisation "lean and agile". Leanness might come from delayering, but agility is a cultural attribute. BP's now famous *Project 1990* was inspired by a new chief executive elect, who assembled a small team to assess the gap between existing culture and organisation and that needed for competitive success. When he took up office he was in a position to embark immediately on a high profile, and to a large degree public, culture change initiative. It is not possible to be more public than to invite a leading business journalist to the board meeting where the need was debated and the intention to change culture confirmed.

The search for flexibility and fast response has taken other forms. Flexible working has become more than a minority activity, giving the employer the ability to turn costs on and off like a tap. There are many consequences of this, and it has become a subject in its own right. Similarly one of the reasons for outsourcing activities may be cost, although for many organisations it is to give greater flexibility, as it leaves someone else with the problem of adjusting capacity to a decline in work. There are also ideas, particularly those of Ansoff (see Ansoff and McDonnell, 1990) about matching the way an organisation is managed to the degree of turbulence in the environment. At present these are used consciously by comparatively few organisations, so can hardly be considered to be a trend. However, this is an area of strategic importance to organisation and to HRM, and is something which will be explored later.

The picture I have painted is one that shows a business arena where human resources management is critical for strategic success. This, of course, is the general background before any consideration is given to the human resource implications of the particular strategies of individual organisations. The following chapters will move from the generalisation that HR should have a greater strategic role to the ways in which this can be achieved.

REFERENCES

Ansoff, I. and McDonnell, E., 1990, *Implanting Strategic Management*, Hemel Hempstead: Prentice Hall.

Barham, K.A. and Bassam, C., 1989, *Shaping the Corporate Future*, London: Unwin Hyman.

Barham, K.A., Fraser, J. and Heath, L., 1988, *Management for the Future*, Ashridge Management College and the Foundation for Management Development, UK.

Buzzell, R. D. and Gale, B. T., 1987, *The PIMS Principles*, New York: Free Press.

Carlzon, J., 1987, *Moments of Truth*, New York: Ballinger.

Hayes, R.H., Wheelwright, S.C. and Clark, K.B., 1988, *Dynamic Manufacturing: Creating the Learning Organisation*, New York: Free Press.

Johansson, H.J., McHugh, P., Pendlebury, A.J. et al, 1993,

Business Process Reengineering, Chichester: John Wiley.

Karlöf, B. and Östblom, S., 1993, *Benchmarking*, Chichester: John Wiley.

Mayo, A. and Lank, E., 1994, *The Power of Learning: A Guide to Gaining Competitive Advantage*, London: Institute of Personnel Development.

Normann, R. et al, 1978, *Utvecklingsstrategier for svenskt servicekunnande*, Stockholm: SIAR.

Oakland, J.S., 1989, *Total Quality Management*, Oxford: Heinemann.

Porter, M. E., 1987, From Competitive Advantage to Corporate Strategy, *Harvard Business Review*, May/June.

Sullivan, P., 1989, *Managing in the 1990s*, unpublished research, Harbridge House Inc, Boston, MA.

Töpfer, A., 1995, New Products—Cutting the Time to Market, *Long Range Planning*, 28.2, April.

2
Strategic Management— The HR Element

WHAT DO WE MEAN BY STRATEGY?

It would be pleasant if it were possible for a human resource manager to pick up a copy of the strategic plan, and immediately have all the information needed to develop a comprehensive strategic HR plan. In theory there would have been full consultation with HR as strategy was formulated, and all the detailed plans would have considered every HR issue in considerable depth. This may happen in some organisations, but one reason why we should not expect it is that there is no single, universal approach to strategy formulation and planning. Even the words are overworked and used in different contexts by different people. Let me start by saying what I mean by three terms:

- *Strategy* is the means chosen to reach a predetermined objective. However, what is seen as strategic will vary with level in a company. For example strategy at the level of a multi-divisional company might be to choose the divisions where investment will be made, and the geographical scope of activities. It may also be how to add shareholder value by creating synergy between businesses. At the level of a business unit, strategy might be more concerned with competitors, markets and manufacturing policies.

- *Strategic planning* is the process of determining the objectives (ends) and the strategies (means) and ensuring implementation. If done well it will give consideration to sound analysis, will encourage creative, entrepreneurial thinking, and will be concerned with the human problems of applying the strategies. It will also cover all areas of the business in an integrated way: marketing, manufacturing, technology, human resources and finance. Increasingly more people believe that they should look at these as if they are all equal partners in strategy formulation, rather than what might have been construed as an earlier philosophy that marketing comes first and all other strategic considerations are consequential.

- *Strategic management* has become a term of common usage and mis-usage. Too many people see it only as a more fashionable term for strategic planning, rather in the way that a large number of people regard human resource management as no different from personnel management, except that it must be smarter because it is an American term. The true concept of strategic management is another of Ansoff's major contributions to the way we approach strategy (see Ansoff, Declerk and Hayes, 1976). The important emphasis is that it is about managing the strategy. This means placing as much emphasis on implementation as on formulation, and an equal concern with the "soft" behavioural issues as with the "hard" analytical matters. Strategic management embraces a greater concern for the whole process of strategic change. Implementation is not the bone tossed to line managers to worry over after the plans are formulated. It is an integral concern when strategies are formulated, and of the whole way in which the organisation is managed. Some of the differences are shown in Table 2.1.

Thus strategic management may be seen as a more complete way of managing a business, concerned not only with markets and decision making, but with social developments, implementation, and the "fit" of strategy with organisational structure and climate.

The way in which organisations choose to approach strategic

Table 2.1 *Differences between strategic planning and strategic management.*

Strategic Planning	Strategic Management
External linkages (e.g. products, markets, environment)	Adds internal elements (e.g. organisation, style, climate)
Strategy formulation to solve problems	Adds implementation and control
Focuses on the "hard" aspects of the external environment	Also concerned with social and political aspects

formulation and management is immensely variable. Apart from situational differences caused by the nature of the business and the style (or should I say whim?) of the top management, there has also been an evolution in approaches. Gluck, Kaufman and Walleck,1980, concluded that there had been four phases in the evolution of formal strategic planning. Approaches to planning tend to co-exist, which means that it is possible to find all forms in current use. Gluck and his co-authors noted that at the time of their work only a few companies were managing strategically, and that all of these were multinational and diversified companies. The starting dates shown below are my own interpretation, based on experience, and cannot be blamed on the researchers.

Phase 1, which was popular from the 1950s to the mid-1960s could be described as extended budgeting, and the approach is based largely on projecting the figures in the budget for a few more years. This tends to emphasise the existing aspects of the business, and allows little room for major changes in strategy. In these companies any new strategic thinking occurs outside of the planning system. My observation is that these methods are not strategic, there is little concern with implementation, and their main intent is to project future financial requirements. Some organisations have not progressed beyond this, although later we will look at some more work of Ansoff's which suggests that for organisations in certain situations this is the best way they could manage.

In **Phase 2**, which I date as starting around 1965, the key driver is forecasting. It tries to match the company's strategies to the perversities of the real world. The feeling is that more accurate forecasting would lead to better planning, and the emphasis in this approach is on forecasting techniques and models. Operational research techniques were high on the list of the planner's tools when this approach was at its most popular, and one was invited to attend seminars with titles such as *Corporate planning, the control of company destiny*. The Gluck study observes that one benefit of this approach was greater attention to resource allocation, and the growing use of portfolio analysis techniques to aid this.

Repeated frustration resulting from the discontinuity of world events created a realisation that accurate forecasting was not possible. I suggest 1970 as the time when **Phase 3**, externally based planning, began to appear, but for the majority of companies the trigger was the 1973 oil crisis, which overnight put the world into a situation of unexpected turbulence. Externally based planning was characterised by more attention to markets and the dynamic causes of market change, and much closer examination of competitors. Resource allocation took a more dynamic part, and the approach was accompanied by the formal grouping of businesses with like strategic characteristics into strategic business units. Planners were expected to produce alternative strategies, an action which, under the forecast based approach, would have been seen as indecisiveness. According to the Gluck study the weakness of externally based planning is that it imposes a burden of choice on top management which is too heavy, with the consequential result that many major decisions by default end up being taken by the planners rather than the managers.

Phase 4 melds strategic planning and management into one process of strategic management, and I put the start of this around 1975. The main difference between **Phases 3 and 4** is one of management philosophy rather than technique, and more emphasis is placed on the "soft" internal aspects of management such as values and culture. As this phase developed, beyond the period studied by the authors, increasing emphasis came to be placed on the development of a vision by the leaders of the organisation, this vision becoming the motivation for structural and cultural change, as well as for strategies relating to markets and the supply of goods.

If I had to put a label on what, had the research been undertaken in 1990, might have been found as the current fifth stage, for which I cannot offer research based support, I would suggest strategic change, and would date its origins around the second half of the 1980s. It embraces strategic management, but considers this in a global context, it emphasises the need for flexibility, continuous change and adaptation, and it recognises that for many organisations there will be a need for almost continuous change in the future. Three driving concepts are vision, core business/core competencies, and recognition that resources do not have to be owned to be effective (it is the era of strategic alliances and virtual organisations).

STYLES OF STRATEGIC MANAGEMENT

Anyone who has been employed in more than one large organisation will probably have observed differences in the way the planning process is applied in each. There may be some universal principles, but there are many differences in how chief executives choose to apply them. Goold and Campbell, 1987, published an important research based study of styles of strategic management. They saw the styles as arising from the attempt by top managers to determine the appropriate role for the corporate office *vis-à-vis* the business units, during which process trade-offs have to be made. The desire to give strong leadership from the centre conflicts with the desire to encourage entrepreneurial activity at the business unit level. Styles arise as a result of the way in which the group chief executive determines where the trade-offs have to be made.

A number of possible styles were identified on a matrix of planning influence from the corporate level (high, medium and low), and corporate control influence (flexible, tight strategic and tight financial). Of the nine possible positions on that matrix, three were found in the sample of companies studied. These were labelled *strategic planning*, with a high planning influence accompanied by flexible control, *strategic control*, which has medium level planning influence and tight strategic control, and *financial control*, with low planning influence and tight financial control.

There are strengths and weaknesses to each style, and the head office can both add and subtract value under each style. The authors conclude that the appropriate style is one that fits the situation of the business, and that appropriate matching is an important determinant of business success. In this way it is something like leadership, where the right style is relevant to the situation in which the leader operates. Business factors fall under two headings: those related to the business nature, and those related to the resources in the organisation. Among the former are issues such as the ferocity of the competitive environment, size and length of payback of investments, and the shape of the corporate portfolio. Among the latter are the financial health of the company, the personality of the chief executive and the skills of senior management.

The Goold and Campbell contribution is important, but in my opinion it raises two issues. The first is whether the research on the evolution of planning, and that on styles of planning are in fact intertwined in some way. Is the evolutionary argument as straightforward as it seems, or are some of the successive steps reflections of differences in style? There is an interesting area for further thought here.

My second issue concerns the chief executive, and a query about whether or not it is the individual in this slot who is in fact the most significant factor affecting style, and that this will override all but extreme situations among the other factors. The research covers 16 companies and by chance I had a professional consulting relationship with two of them. One, a strategic control company, was an assignment where I helped formulate corporate level strategy and design a planning process. The only reason the process is more strategic control than strategic planning is because of the deep-seated beliefs of the chief executive in delegation of autonomy to the people closest to the "coal face". The other company is a strategic planning firm. My association with that company began in 1978 and was continuous to 1993, involving many planning assignments, although none to do with the process. Over this period I have observed three changes in planning style, which I believe have again been the result of chief executive preference rather than a change in business circumstances.

Whatever the driving force behind the differences, we know that they exist, just as there are also differences in the degree to which different organisations centralise or decentralise human resource management between head office and the businesses, and the way responsibilities are divided between line managers and the HR function. There are no answers which are always right, and even those which might be thought to be wrong can often be made to work. What is important is the awareness that the application of ideas in any book, and this book is no exception, should be interpreted in relation to the specific organisation. Principles should be more easily transferable, but as we will see many of these are also situational. We know what side of the road to drive on in the UK, but only a fool would deliberately apply the same rule when motoring in France.

ENVIRONMENTAL TURBULENCE

I mentioned earlier in this chapter that the organisation that stuck to extended budgeting could be right. The evidence for this statement comes from some 15 years of research work led by Ansoff (see Ansoff and McDonnell, 1990; Ansoff, 1991 and Ansoff et al, 1993). He has been researching and developing the concept that the way in which an organisation should undertake strategic management should be related to the degree of environmental turbulence in which it has to operate.

The Ansoff approach sought to identify the different environmental conditions under which various organisations were operating, and to match these to appropriate approaches to management and strategy. This resulted in a scale of turbulence (see Table 2.2).

The scale moves from level 1, low turbulence, to level 5, very high turbulence. The approach to strategic decision making is different under each. It follows that the optimum approach to strategic management should also vary with the turbulence level. Ansoff suggests that for level 1 the appropriate system is management by procedures, since nothing is changing, and the

Table 2.2   *Ansoff's scale of turbulence.*

	Environment	Strategic Aggressiveness
1	Repetitive	Stable, based on precedents
2	Expanding	Reactive, incremental, based on experience
3	Changing	Anticipatory, incremental, based on extrapolation
4	Discontinuous	Entrepreneurial, based on expected futures
5	Surpriseful	Creative, based on creativity

best guide to the future is the past. In this situation short-term budgeting as the main approach to planning could be appropriate, as the success criterion is "stay the same as you are". However it is doubtful whether many commercial organisations currently operate in level one situations.

The optimum level two approach is what Ansoff terms financial control, where the emphasis is on control through budgets, rather than seeking new strategies. This is where an extended budgeting approach could still be appropriate.

At level 3 the approach is extrapolative, and termed long range planning: the emphasis is on sticking to the historical strategies of success, since the future is a logical extrapolation of the past, and this implies understanding markets and competitors.

At level 4 it is no longer safe to assume that tomorrow will be a continuation of the trends of yesterday, and the appropriate process is strategic planning. Ansoff defines this as being "... focused on selecting new strategies for the future and redirecting the firm's energies and resources to follow the logic of the new strategy development ... Thus strategic planning repositions the firm for success in the future environment".

Ansoff argues that even before level 5 is reached, forward looking strategic planning is not adequate to ensure a speedy response to future events. This is particularly true when future changes are both violent and difficult to foresee. He suggests two "real time" system responses: issue management, which can begin to supplement strategic planning from level 4, and surprise management. Issue management attempts to anticipate and respond to threats and opportunities. There is a link here with the scenario planning approaches which are used by some organisations.

By level 5 an increasing number of issues confront the organisation without prior warning. To cope with these the firm needs to add a further management system to deal with surprises. He suggests an emergency communication network, with a top level strategic task force to cross organisational boundaries to deal with the issue. The key to success is to plan the surprise management organisation, and to train people in operating it. In other words, while issue management is a form of contingency planning for a predicted possibility, surprise management is a planned framework to deal with contingencies that cannot be foreseen.

The appropriate approach may vary in different parts of the same organisation. Thus it is quite possible for an organisation to have one strategic business unit operating under level 3 and another under level 5. The approach to strategic management should be varied by strategic business unit to take account of this.

In theory, although there are organisations operating under each level of turbulence, there has also been an evolutionary movement from the lower to the higher levels. Thus there are more organisations in levels 4 and 5 now than there were in the 1970s. It is reasonable to suggest that this increase in uncertainty will continue in the future, and by the end of the next decade someone might have defined several even higher levels of turbulence. However it is also possible to move the other way. Ansoff, 1991, used the example of Apple, which was at level 5 when founded, but moved to level 3 after a few years. (Market conditions have probably moved it back again to at least level 4 since he wrote this statement.)

Although not a specific part of the Ansoff model, from observation I would suggest that organisations make temporary changes to higher levels of turbulence from time to time, sometimes reverting back to their old position when the period of turbulence is over. It is reasonable to suggest that in severe economic recession even organisations that are normally at level 3 will for a period find themselves operating at level 5.

The importance of fitting the right approach for the level of turbulence is demonstrated in the research. Consistently Ansoff has found that those organisations which are managing in an appropriate way for the level are the most profitable, and that those whose approach is wrong by two levels will be losing money. Those out by one level will not be doing as well as those that have an appropriate fit.

At this stage the levels of turbulence concept has been used to demonstrate that there should be differences in the way different organisations tackle strategy formulation and implementation. I will return to the ideas later when I explore the role that HRM should have in overall strategy formulation. The concepts help us to see one reason why an organisation might fail in its strategies. There are other reasons which require exploration, particularly the failure of many organisations to implement strategies.

FAILURE TO IMPLEMENT STRATEGIES

Conventional wisdom in some of the first books on planning (and one or two of the more recent ones) was that plans would be implemented if line managers were involved in setting the strategy. A consequence of this was the development of planning systems, largely bottom up, which tried to involve the whole organisation. What was missing from this concept was an understanding of the fit with the level of environmental turbulence, whether the culture of the organisation could tolerate such an approach, and the fact that commitment alone is not enough to implement strategy. In many organisations still there is an almost implicit faith that if the strategy is good, it will get itself implemented. If only it were true.

The first point is small but important. It is the tendency for the plans themselves to overestimate the speed at which things can be done. I am sure many readers have noticed what I long ago defined as the two *laws* of planning, which all written plans seem to follow. They are as noticeable in the project plans which support requests for capital expenditure as they are in strategic plans, and I have noticed little difference by function. Even HRM is not exempt!

1 *In any written plan, everything comes right in the third year.* This does not mean that it will come right, only that the plan says it will. The third year is close enough to appear to have meaning, but far enough away to escape retribution. The underlying psychology is that three years is long enough for things to work out.
2 *The third year never comes.* My second law of planning is that the bounty of the third year is never delivered. Somehow the cornucopia expected three years ago when the plan was made is as empty in the third year as it was in the first two.

Of course things can come to pass as the plan suggests.

However, knowing that so many plans show two lean years followed by a time of plenty makes me want to probe very deeply into any plans which follow this pattern. This usually means exploring the information on which the plan was based, as well as studying the strategy itself.

Much of our information on implementation failure comes from research by Alexander (see Alexander, 1991). What is interesting for human resource management is the number of causes which relate in some way to people. In the list that follows the problems are summarised from Alexander's research, but the comments are my own interpretation.

1   *It took longer than expected.* This could be due to several causes, varying from failure to identify all the key actions to failure to build commitment.

2   *There were major unidentified problems during implementation.* On the surface this appears an analytical issue, or possibly in some cases a realisation that we are not always able to anticipate everything. It may also be an involvement issue, in that often wide participation can bring in people whose special knowledge helps the organisation to identify problems and actions that would otherwise be missed. Thus HR issues might not have been foreseen, because no one involved HR in the formulation of the strategy.

3   *Implementation activities were not coordinated effectively enough.* This is most likely to be a failure in management. Many of the modern writers on transformational leadership stress the need to give attention to both the behavioural, motivating tasks and the management, administrative planning and control tasks.

4   *Management were distracted by other activities and crises and did not implement.* This may have been appropriate if priorities changed. Just as likely is the possibility that management was not committed to the plan: a behavioural issue.

5   *The capabilities of managers involved in implementation actions were inadequate.* This may be a recruitment or training issue. Those who make plans should not assume that everyone is competent to fulfil all necessary actions or to work in a different way.

6 *Inadequate training and instruction were given to lower level employees.* It is easy to assume that the factory workers can operate new plant without help, that clerks will easily change to a new procedure, or that sales people will change priorities. Such assumptions may be damaging.

7 *Events in the outside world impacted on the plan.* This could be poor planning, or the fact that there will always be some unpredictable changes.

8 *Departmental managers did not provide enough leadership.* This again is a behavioural problem, which could have been caused by ignorance or poor management.

9 *Key implementation tasks and activities were not defined in enough detail.* If people do not know what has to be done, they are unlikely to do it.

10 *The information systems were inadequate to monitor performance.* Clearly if you do not know whether or not an action has been implemented it is difficult to manage the process.

Of course responsibility for implementation of strategy lies with the chief executive and line management, but it is an area where HRM could play a much larger role than is the common practice. Strategies may bring about two types of change. The first is incremental, when the intention is to do more of the same. The organisation may become bigger as a result of this, and there may be issues of recruitment and structure to deal with, but by and large this sort of change is exciting and non-threatening. Most people are very happy if they feel that the organisation is growing.

The second type of change is fundamental (in some of the literature the words *transformational* or *strategic* might be used instead). Under this type of change the strategies can change the whole shape of the organisation, both in terms of what it does, and how it sets out to do it. This sort of change can be complex and threatening.

HRM has a role in both types of change. Without being too dogmatic, it is possible to argue that for incremental change the main emphasis is planning to deal, in good time, with the consequences of the strategies (for example training or recruiting to obtain the right numbers of employees at the right time, or reviewing reward policies to ensure that they are appropriate for the new circumstances). With fundamental change it is much more important to be an equal partner with management when the strategies are considered, as well as developing plans to deal with the consequences of the strategies. Put simply, HRM should be in both a leadership and a support role when strategies require fundamental change, but the emphasis may be more on a support role when the strategies lead only to incremental change.

Sometimes strategies are apparently implemented but do not bring the results expected. This could be because the strategies are inappropriate, either because of ineptitude, or, frequently, because of what I have called the problem of perceptual boundaries. By this I mean that the strategic situation the organisation faces is not seen in an appropriate way, and logical strategies are developed which provide solutions to the wrong problem. In a sense the strategic situation is perceived as a neat, small box, when it is really much more like a very large, untidy ink blot. This is how the companies in the UK motor cycle industry lost dominance and then disappeared through the 1960s and 1970s. They saw the world through very different eyes from the leading Japanese competitor, Honda, and claimed a foul when Honda was able to manufacture at a lower cost than they were. It did not occur to them that the answer was not dumping, but the cost advantages gained by looking at the markets on a coherent global basis.

If the strategic boundaries to markets and competition are perceived as single country, when instead the organisation should be taking a global view, the resultant strategies will not fit the real problem. If all the strategic issues are perceived as external to the organisation, when in fact many of them are really internal issues, again the wrong solutions will result. They may fit the problem as it is seen, but not the problem as it really is.

A further point is that much of the evidence about strategic success and failure is ignored. Research over several decades shows that more than half of acquisitions are divested because they are not successful, yet few companies take much notice of the lessons in either the pre- or post-acquisition strategies (see Kitching, 1967, 1973, 1974; Porter, 1987; Coopers & Lybrand, 1993).

I am not implying that HRM should somehow consider itself a critic of the strategic decisions in the organisation, any more than I believe that issues to do with people are reserved for HRM and nothing to do with line management. But the senior HR manager may be in a position to play a part as a member of the management team in debating the overall plans, and certainly has the duty to ensure that the plans of the human resource function are set up to deal with the right problems.

In the next chapter we will explore in more detail whether it is possible to establish some principles to help ensure that Human Resource Management is driven by the business.

REFERENCES

Alexander, L.D., 1991, Strategy Implementation: Nature of the Problem, in Hussey, D.E., editor, *International Review of Strategic Management*, Chichester: John Wiley.

Ansoff, H.I., 1991, Strategic Management in a Historical Perspective, in Hussey, D. E., editor, *International Review of Strategic Management*, Volume 2.1, Chichester: John Wiley.

Ansoff, H.I., Declerk, R.P. and Hayes, R.L., editors, 1976, *From Strategic Planning to Strategic Management*, Chichester: John Wiley.

Ansoff, H.I. et al, 1993, Empirical Support for a Paradigmic Theory of Strategic Success Behaviors of Environmental Serving Organizations, in Hussey, D.E., editor, *International Review of Strategic Management*, Volume 4, Chichester: John Wiley.

Ansoff, H.I. and McDonnell, E. 1990, *Implanting Strategic Management*, Hemel Hempstead: Prentice Hall.

Coopers & Lybrand, 1993. Detailed reference not available.

Gluck, F.W., Kaufman, S.P. and Walleck, A. S., 1980, Strategic Management for Competitive Advantage, *Harvard Business Review*, July/August, Boston: Harvard.

Goold, M. and Campbell, A., 1987, *Strategies and Styles*, Oxford: Blackwell.

Kitching, J., 1967, Why do Mergers Miscarry?, *Harvard Business Review*, November/December.

Kitching, J., 1973, *Acquisitions in Europe*, Geneva: Business International.

Kitching, J., 1974, Winning and Losing with European Acquisitions, *Harvard Business Review*, March/April.

Porter, M.E., 1987, From Competitive Advantage to Corporate Strategy, *Harvard Business Review*, May/June.

3
A Model for Business Driven HR Management

The aim of this chapter is to introduce a model which can be used as a framework for human resource planning, and to show how this links with corporate strategy. The first steps towards the use of the model will be discussed, and will be taken up again in more detail in subsequent chapters, when selected specific aspects of human resource management are considered. In the previous chapter there was considerable discussion of strategic management, and because the whole concept of business driven human resource management is that it should relate to the corporate strategies, the starting point will be the components of a strategy.

COMPONENTS OF STRATEGY

Figure 3.1 offers a generalised outline of the components of a business plan. This does not mean that all strategies result from the carefully crafted approach implied by the diagram. In many organisations strategy may be developed incrementally, building on success and knowledge, rather than through the formal planning approach implied by the diagram.

Nevertheless it is valid to examine the components of a plan, because for better or worse these do affect what is possible and what is likely to succeed. Management will use the components, although in different ways, whether they attempt to plan strategy through a formal system, apply the "logical incrementalism" approach described by Quinn, 1980 (under which strategies emerge over time), or work entirely through judgement based on knowledge of the industry. The last, of course, can be the most dangerous as it is more likely to lead to the problems of misperception of the strategic situation

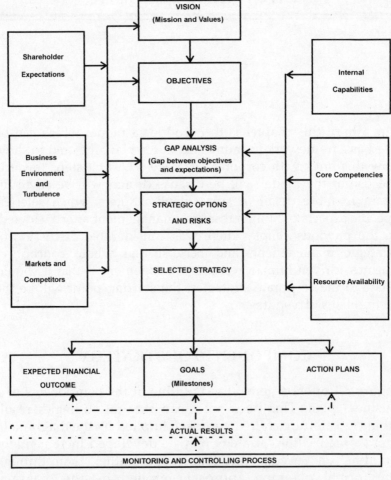

Figure 3.1   *Outline components of a business plan.*

which were discussed in the last chapter. Obviously if the strategy is poor, HR attempts to support it may help to compound any lack of success that results. The assumption made here is that whether the organisation is planning formally or informally, the key managers are considering the components shown in Figure 3.1 when strategies are decided. If this is not true for your organisation, perhaps the first step that should be taken to achieve business driven HRM would be to arrange some workshops to train managers in strategic thinking.

The boxes running down the centre of the figure represent things the organisation has to do to formulate and implement a strategy. But it is a little more complicated than this, and later it will be necessary to look at the mix of analytical and behavioural processes that go on in all organisations. The three boxes on the left in Figure 3.1 refer to things external to the organisation, while the three on the right deal with internal issues. These six boxes illustrate matters which should influence the strategic decisions, and provide most of the hard data on which the decisions are based. At the bottom of the diagram there is a monitoring and control process which feeds back information on whether strategies were implemented, and whether the outcome was as hoped.

The centre boxes begin with the concept of vision, which has become an important element in approaches to the management of change. It is top management's expression of what the organisation is striving to become, and incorporates values as well as what, in earlier writings, had been called mission statements. The vision may result from the drive of one person, or a small team, or if the culture of the organisation is appropriate, may result from a more widespread involvement of others in the organisation. To be useful, the vision has to be credible and inspiring, and eventually must be shared by the whole organisation. It is very easy to slide from a clear view of the future the organisation intends to create, into the abyss of nightmare and fantasy.

Objectives are more specific targets that derive from the vision. They should be limited to the things the overall organisation is seeking to achieve, and become a critical component of the vision. An example might be quantitative measures of shareholder value, or some other form of financial target.

Gap analysis can be expressed simply as the difference between where we are and where we want to be. In the broad corporate context it defines the gap that has to be bridged in order to achieve the vision and objectives. The concept is useful at all levels of planning, and is built into the models which will be suggested for HR planning.

The fourth box identifies the strategic options and the risks associated with each, enabling the decisions to be taken as the next step, where strategies are selected. Some organisations, including many of the oil companies, develop the option box into a complex process of scenario planning (see, for example, the description of strategic planning at Royal/Dutch Shell given by Schoemaker and van der Heijden, 1993). This is a minority approach to strategy, although many organisations will look at sensitivity when they consider the risks of various options.

To move towards implementation it is necessary to quantify the expected outcome of the strategies, both for the period of the plan, and for the immediate future, to establish goals (such as standards of performance, market share, and quality) which can act as milestones against which progress can be assessed, and to develop detailed action plans for implementation. Action plans may be a mix of budgets and project plans, but must be worked out in enough detail for the strategies to be turned into action.

The left hand elements of the model start with shareholder expectations. In a family-owned company it would be possible to argue that this box should shift to the right hand side, and be seen as internal to the organisation. For most large organisations, except those in the public sector, shareholders are so divorced from management that they are external, and their decisions are influenced not only by what the organisation does, but what else is going on in the stock market and the other investment opportunities available. The growth of institutional investors has led to a different form of external shareholder influence on the organisation, where dissatisfied shareholders can more easily band together to put pressure on the organisation to act in a certain way. It is not enough to increase profits and dividends. The organisation has to satisfy shareholder expectations which are based on comparisons with other investment opportunities. Growth may look good on internal criteria, but be unacceptable to shareholders making external comparisons. Shareholder expectations are also influenced, of course, by the business environment, which is the next box for consideration. The issue of turbulence was discussed in the previous chapter, but what are also important are the issues and trends which impact on strategic success. Figure 3.5, which will appear later in the context of human resource strategy, gives a list of headings which should be considered, although the importance of various trends and issues under these broad headings will vary between organisations, and countries, and will change over time.

There is another aspect of the business environment which is both important and capable of more detailed consideration than are some of the general business environmental issues. This is the nature and trend of the markets, including the requirements of customers and the positioning and strategies of competitors. Overlooking one environmental issue of importance will rarely bring disaster: getting the market assessment wrong, or failing to detect the new actions of competitors can collapse the entire strategy.

On the right hand side of the model, the three groups of internal factors that need consideration are the internal capabilities, core competencies and resource availability. The internal capabilities are the strengths and weaknesses of the organisation, the things it can do well, and the things that are not so well done. This can become something of a shopping list if care is not exercised. In many consulting assignments I have found that the organisations have found it extremely difficult to assess their true strengths, often falling back on platitudes such as "an excellent chief executive" and "a loyal and competent management team". Weaknesses become an enormous list of faults, but few of them are prioritised and many are not significant for strategic decisions. The real capabilities of the organisation, and the real strategic weaknesses often escape definition.

Core competencies are one way of viewing the shopping list to identify what really matters. The word competency is used here with a different meaning from the normal human resources concept of competencies, for we are not talking about the capabilities of the individual but of the organisation. The concept of core competencies described here is drawn from Hamel, 1994, who argues that a competence has to pass a number of tests before it can be considered core:

● It is not a discrete skill or technology, but a bundle of constituent skills and technologies which combine into something critical for the strategic success of the organisation.
● It is not an asset in accounting terms, such as a factory, but it may be an aptitude to manage that asset in a particular and special manner.
● It "must make a disproportionate contribution to customer perceived value". This means the competence must be both visible by and important to the customer.
● It must deliver competitive advantage. A competence which is held by all competitors in an industry may be important, but cannot be considered core.

The idea behind the core competency approach is to build strategy around those strengths which make a strategic difference. It does not imply that everything which is not core is unimportant, but that only those that are core should be maintained or developed as a key element of strategy. The danger is that the core competencies of today can become the white elephants of tomorrow, if customer needs or competitor actions create a situation that means that one or more of the above tests cannot be passed. Thus the concept should be seen as something dynamic, not as a recipe for complacency. The importance of HRM in helping to maintain and develop the management and other capabilities and skills that support the core competencies is self evident, as is the difficulty of doing this if HRM is unaware of what the core competencies are.

The availability of resources is also critical in developing a strategy. The organisation can define, from purely internal sources, the resources it currently has, whether these are people, plant or finance. Assessing whether additional resources can be obtained to support a strategy requires a consideration of factors from the left hand side of the model shown in Figure 3.1, as well as the purely internal issues, and the strategic decision process needs to consider resource availability very seriously. Inability to command the required level of resources can frustrate a strategy, or tilt the balance to strategic alliances. Where additional resources can be obtained, the timing of implementation may extend beyond the original estimates, and an objective assessment of this may be vital. Delayed implementation sometimes means failed implementation.

STRATEGY IS MORE THAN ANALYSIS

It is easy to gain an impression from a model such as this that strategy is mainly about facts and analysis. These are critical dimensions of good strategy making, but there is more to it than this for there is a strong behavioural element. Figure 3.2 sets out in diagrammatic form some of the characteristics of the two dimensions of strategy.

The analytical aspects have been discussed already, in a slightly different way, and as we have seen there are areas here where HRM should have a strong involvement. The behavioural aspects, and I have not tried to list them all in the diagram, should be considered by all managers, but often elements will be overlooked unless specialists remind management to deal with them. HRM has a key role to play here during the formulation and implementation tasks.

The centre boxes in this diagram are areas which in theory could be wholly based on analysis and rational argument, but very rarely are in practice. I still see much truth in a quotation made long ago by one of the early writers on strategic management (Steiner, 1972):

> "The decision-making process in a company is infused with political, social and other considerations. To think that it is a completely rational process, in the sense that any fair-minded person would come to the same conclusion with the inputs which were used, is to misunderstand not only the decision-making process but the human mind."

The left hand boxes in the diagram show some of the factors which influence the boxes in the centre, and the degree of success the organisation will have in implementing its chosen

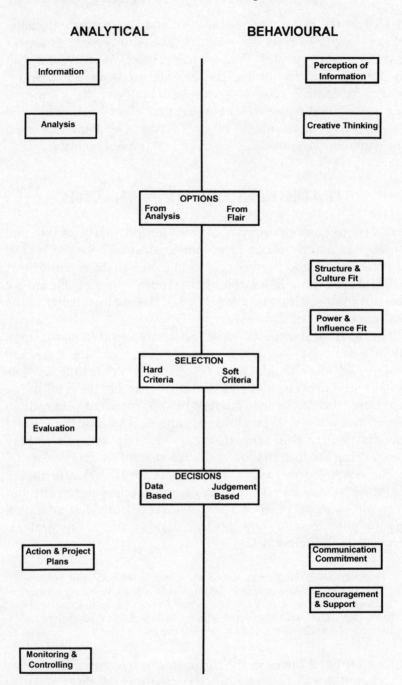

Figure 3.2   *Two dimensions of strategic decisions.*

strategies. An analytical process begins with information, but the behavioural influence may be the selection of what information should be considered, and how it should be interpreted. Because of the biases we all have, it is possible for different people to view the same data, and reach a completely different view of what it means, something we see every day in the way politicians of different parties interpret economic statistics. The screening processes we use to decide what information is important are even more subtle, relating to the perceptions of the strategic arena, and were discussed in the previous chapter.

There is another reason why the same data can yield different answers, and this is the creative flair of those looking at the data. One person may see a great opportunity, while others are still ploughing the furrow of trying to use the data to reinforce yesterday's strategies. Differences in creative thinking are obvious when one looks at different organisations. There is some evidence that the problem is not always a lack of creative thinking, but an inability to manage the process so that the creative idea becomes an implemented innovation. It is a matter of some concern that the majority of training given by organisations in this area is concerned with encouraging creative thinking: much less addresses the larger problem of how the person or team with the bright idea can turn it into an innovation.

Another behavioural aspect is the fit of the strategy with the culture of the organisation and its structure, which is closely allied to the next box, the fit with current patterns of power and influence in the organisation. Although senior managers may not give conscious thought to power and influence, decisions may be taken in a way that excludes options which do not fit the current power structure. When decisions cut across the current lines of power, implementation may be harder because those whose power is reduced may resist the changes. Many organisations do not think through the implications of a change of strategy on the structure and culture of the organisation, although there are numerous examples (such as SAS, BP and British Telecommunications) where top management has realised that there have to be changes if the strategy is to work. In fact culture change has almost become an industry in its own right.

No vision can be shared, and no strategies implemented until there is understanding and commitment. Communication, both in terms of the mechanisms, but even more importantly tone, style and content, is a key ingredient. The final box illustrates the need to encourage and support those involved in implementing the plan.

RELATIONSHIP OF HUMAN RESOURCE MANAGEMENT AND CORPORATE STRATEGY

We will need to return to some of these behavioural issues from time to time. At this stage they give some credence to the view that HRM should be involved in the strategy decision processes, an argument reinforced by the need to consider the effects of planned changes on employees. Who better than HRM could advise on the time required, the costs, and the impact on morale, of a major redundancy exercise?

Figure 3.3 sets out a philosophy which stands behind many of the approaches to business driven HRM which will be discussed in the book. The centre ring stresses that it should all begin with the vision, values, objectives and strategies of the organisation. This should cause few surprises as it restates a point of view already made, and which no doubt will be made again as we go into more detail.

The thin shaded ring also refers to a concept just discussed, which is the broader role of HR in the strategic process. Enough has been stated already about this to make my view clear: the pity is that not all organisations observe it.

When we come to the remainder of the diagram, we are looking at the strategic management of the HR function itself. Some of the activities in the little triangles may not fall inevitably under the human resources department: for example communication is sometimes grouped under public relations; others may have been devolved to line managers. However all of them are linked to the people task, and I should expect HR to play a role in the development of coordinated policies and strategies, even if responsibility fell outside the function.

The headings in these triangles are examples, and I have not tried to produce a definitive list. Also there is variation in

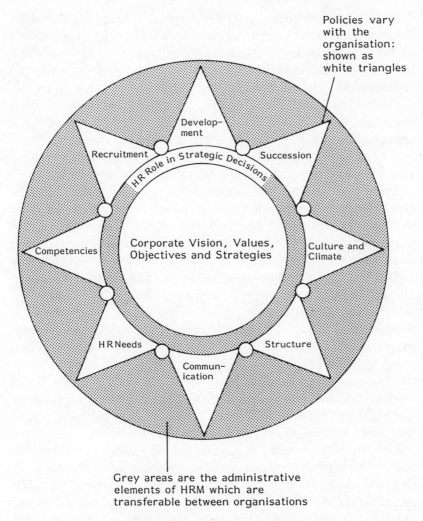

Figure 3.3 *Relationship of HRM and corporate strategy.*

priorities between organisations. In London Underground, industrial relations (not on my chart) is an area of considerable importance, but this is of much less significance in the professional environment of one of the "big six" accountancy firm.

What is important is that the triangles represent areas of potential strategic concern, and the grey areas represent the "good practice" administrative activities that "should" support the strategic areas. The word "should" is used deliberately, because a common problem I have seen in the HR departments of many companies, is that the good practice is given more importance than whether what is being done is right for the organisation. A common theme has been "we are HR professionals", and concentration on good methods has often been at the expense of questioning what priorities the organisation needs. In fact in some of these organisations there has been highly professional activity applied to the wrong priorities, and many things the organisation really needed were not covered at all. An example is the financial services organisation which put all of its training budget into lower level management, and did not tackle the task of training senior managers, despite the fact that the vision and strategy required them to manage in a very different way than previously. This sort of problem is not always the fault of HR people. If you are in an organisation where you are starved of strategic information, and rarely consulted on the policy issues, the only thing left is to do the administrative tasks to the highest professional standard. In the case of the financial services company quoted above, what was done was done very professionally, but it could have little impact on the success of the organisation unless the other higher priority training needs were tackled. It is the difference between being efficient, which they were, and being effective, which they were not.

Perhaps one way to visualise the difference between the policy/strategy aspects, and the supporting administration, is that the decisions on the former will be different for each organisation. An HR manager who left one company and joined another, would be foolish to expect that all the policies developed for the original organisation would have equal validity in the second. Good administrative practice is transferable to a much larger degree, and can be transplanted to many more situations, although even here there are some limitations imposed by the sophistication and culture of the organisation. However there is a strong common core, and most HR specialists would feel familiar with good administrative practice in any other organisation.

This leaves only one part of Figure 3.3 to explain, the little circles between the triangles. Apart from the fact that they make the diagram look more attractive, they serve a symbolic purpose as nodes through which every triangle may be connected to every other triangle. None of the elements of HRM described in the triangles exists in isolation: they all integrate with each other. So while the business drives all of them, each has a relationship with all the other elements. An example is that development may be an alternative to recruitment in some circumstances, is certainly influenced by the forecasts of supply and demand considered in the HR needs triangle, and has close links with competencies and succession. A training programme, which is part of the development element, may be designed to communicate, and to impact on climate. A change in structure may put a completely new slant on development needs.

A FRAMEWORK FOR PLANNING HRM

It is easier to talk about business driven HRM than to apply it, and the rest of this chapter begins a journey, which will continue in later chapters, to try to turn the broad concepts into an approach which can be applied in practice. I should like to begin this journey with Figure 3.4, which gives a broad approach which will be made more specific when we look at some of the elements of HRM activity in detail.

In this figure there is a sequence of steps which, with modification, can be applied to various aspects of HR activity. All the steps are described in plain English, although behind them stand the more complex descriptions, including the jargon, which were discussed earlier.

- *Step 1: What the organisation needs*. What requirements does the organisation have that HR should meet through its own policies and plans? To complete this we need ways of understanding the vision and strategies in HR terms, and converting this to priorities that must be met. How the information might be obtained will be discussed later in this chapter: how it might be analysed and applied will be explored in chapters showing how the concepts can be applied to certain HR activities.
- *Step 2: How the environment affects HR*. The importance of the

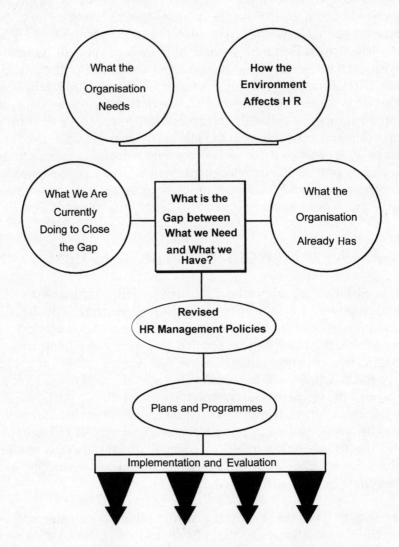

Figure 3.4 *A framework for planning HRM.*

business environment when assessing the overall strategies of the organisation was discussed earlier. Here we are concerned with matters that have a specific effect on HRM, and matters pertaining to the people side of the business. Because each environmental issue may affect several of the

key HR activities, methods for considering the environment
will be suggested later in this chapter.

- *Step 3: What the organisation already has.* In all organisations
many of the HR requirements will already be being met.
There is a core of people who have certain competencies.
There are policies in place, which may or may not be
relevant to the tasks that need to be undertaken. There is a
culture, even if we have made no previous effort to define it.
There is a structure, which may or may not be appropriate
for the strategic tasks the organisation has set itself. This step
is about assessing what exists, so that it can be related to
what is needed in a later step in the process. To do this may
require a strategic audit of HR activity, and/or special
surveys, such as climate surveys, or training needs
assessments focused on business driven requirements. It
needs an open, questioning attitude, and a hefty dose of
common sense.
- *Step 4: What we are currently doing to close the gap.* There are
always initiatives in progress. Thus there may be training
programmes under way, or we may be taking action to
recruit more people. These too should be identified, and
scrutinised against the strategic priorities.
- *Step 5: What is the gap between what we need and what we have?*
In theory, by this stage we can contrast what the organisation
needs against what it is being given, factor in the impact of
environmental issues, and identify where the gaps are, and
where we are doing things that perhaps should not be done
in that way or even at all.
- *Step 6: Revised human resource management policies.* From all
the above information it is possible to assess priorities and
the resources HR needs to deliver what is needed, and to
revise the policies that drive HRM activity.
- *Step 7: Plans and programmes.* This is the action planning
phase that converts the plan into numerous projects and
tasks that can be delegated and monitored so that they really
do happen. Objectives should be defined clearly for each
plan or programme, so that the reason for it is understood,
and the expected results made specific.
- *Step 8: Implementation and evaluation.* This step is about doing
what was planned, monitoring that it has in fact been done,

and evaluating whether it achieved the objectives. Again this is a lot easier to say than to do, and evaluation is ignored more often than it is done.

In concept the steps outlined are straightforward and easy to understand. Complexities come from the size of organisations, difficulty in obtaining the right information, and problems in applying the strategic information to a real situation. It would be wrong to underestimate the problems, but it would be equally wrong to make them seem too difficult.

THE ENVIRONMENT AND HUMAN RESOURCE MANAGEMENT

The business environment should be considered by all the sections in HR on a common basis. This is partly on grounds of economy, as there is little sense in having several people collect and interpret the same information, and partly because the various elements of HR need to use the same assumptions. Clearly it would be wrong for the person developing a business driven approach to succession to be using a different set of forecasts of external trends from the person forecasting overall supply and demand. Figure 3.5 shows how I like to think about the business environment. At this stage this is a general planning model, but it will be followed by an outline checklist which applies the concepts specifically to HRM.

The three circles in the centre represent the industry, which I have shown as suppliers, competitors and customers. Although not directly relevant to HR planning, it is worth mentioning that the classic text for analysing an industry is Porter, 1980. Information on the application of industry analysis and other relevant analytical approaches will be found in Hussey, 1994.

Every industry is affected by the general business environment, which in the diagram is represented by the octagon, at each point of which is a heading to aid thinking about what factors are important for the individual organisation. Although all competitors in an industry are affected by events and trends in the environment, they are rarely affected equally. It is not sensible to ignore a trend or

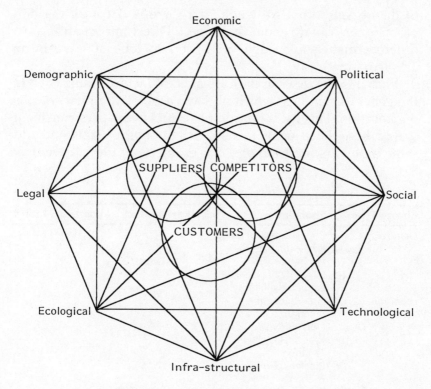

Figure 3.5   *The integrated environment.*

issue on the grounds that every one is hit equally hard. Apart from differences in manufacturing processes, location and mix of products, which can affect the impact of the external pressures, many competitors may be from other countries where there are different issues to contend with.

Lines connect the points on the diagram, indicating that few things happen in isolation, and that what happens to the economy, for example, may have a direct influence on social attitudes, change political pressures, and lead to new laws. Technology can, and has, sent thunderbolts to all the other headings in the model.

It goes without saying that the multinational organisation is concerned with the environments of many countries.

How does any of this affect human resource management? Indirectly HRM is impacted by anything that affects the success of the organisation as a whole, but there is not a lot that HR practitioners can do about that aspect. Direct impact areas are a different matter, and Table 3.1 begins to look at these in an action oriented way.

What this shows is an indicative list of factors, under each of the general headings, which all have a possible impact on the organisation. This list is not complete, and every person using it will want to delete some items which are not relevant, and add some more specific headings. For example, in the UK we may

Table 3.1   *Environmental issues and HR activities.*

Change Type	Examples	HR Implications	Importance Rating
Demographic	Population structure		
	Migration patterns		
	Population size		
	Diversity of population		
	Labour availability		
Economic	Growth/decline		
	Inflation		
	Unemployment levels		
	Wage/salary levels		
	Taxation		
	Black economy		
	Exchange rates		
Legal	Employment law		
	EC Employment law		
	Health & Safety		
	Specific Industry Regs.		
	Information disclosure		
	Equal Opportunity laws		
	Case law (eg stress)		
Technological	Information Technology		
	Manufacture: process		
	Manufacture: methods		
	Product life cycle		
	Cycle time		
Infrastructure	Education: schools		
	Education: higher		
	Education: post exper.		
Ecology	Pressure groups		
	Smoking attitudes		
Social	Ethical issues		
	Work attitudes		
	Cultural differences		
	Educational values		
Political	Government changes		
	Industry specific concerns		

feel that the black economy is not a factor that affects us: however operations in another country may have a number of very specific issues arising from this. Similarly there may be no industry specific regulations for some industries, while others, such as financial services, may have to undertake specific training and proficiency testing of certain employees because of legal requirements.

The next step is to look at the HR implications column of the table. This was drawn to suit the page rather than the problem, and in practice you may need more space both to write in the implications and allow for multiple implications under each heading.

Judgement comes in again in the last column, the importance rating. The aim of this is to focus concentration on the things that matter the most. It is possible to use this column in a simple way, by rating each identified HR implication as high, medium or low. If preferred, it is possible to use a scoring system, such as treating importance as impact × probability of occurrence. Using a 1 = low to 5 = high scoring system for both impact and probability, it is possible to get a numerical weighting for what is important. However this is indicative only, and relies on assessment skills and judgement.

There are also some factors we should consider about the competitors and the industry as a whole. I have treated these separately from the general environment, but they could easily be added to the bottom of Table 3.1 if this aids thinking. They include factors such as:

- competitors' wage levels;
- competitors' employment practices;
- comparison of industrial relations issues between competitors;
- specific industry norms and practices;
- study of competitors who have broken away from the norms and practices (as for example Rupert Murdoch did in the newspaper industry).

There is a practical issue about how to undertake such an assessment as has been described. It needs information, which may come partly from the specialist HR functions which have kept up to date with developments in their area, partly from whatever sources the company uses for general planning, and partly from collecting environmental information on a regular basis. There are also specialist services that can be subscribed to, such as information on social trends from the Henley Forecasting Institute. Information services for wage levels and trends, and periodic analyses of specific issues like demographic trends are among the other information that may be purchased.

My experience is that the most effective consideration comes from a mix of hard analysis and the harnessing of individual thinking. One way to provide this is to have someone analyse all the information that can be obtained to produce a first draft of the sort of list that appears in Table 3.1, but of course with background notes and forecasts that explain the headings so that they can be used.

This information can provide the agenda for a team consideration of the factors, where the background information is shared, and the list of factors discussed and expanded if necessary. The HR implications of each factor are an ideal subject for a team exercise, because the mix of knowledge and experience, plus the individual focus of each person, is likely to lead to a greater understanding of what each factor means to the organisation. Similarly the importance rating is a good group exercise, because differences in perception of a factor's importance may lead to a greater overall understanding of that factor. It is possible to expand Table 3.1 in the group work with one more heading: "What might we do about it?"

The aim should be to increase the level of shared understanding of the trends and issues that constrain or offer opportunities for the organisation, to develop some possible courses of action which will be fed into the next stages of the process, and to ensure that top management is aware of any implications which may impede the success of the overall company strategy.

MOVING FORWARD WITH A BUSINESS DRIVEN HR STRATEGY

It would be possible to examine the HRM implications of the business environment without any discussion with the rest of

53

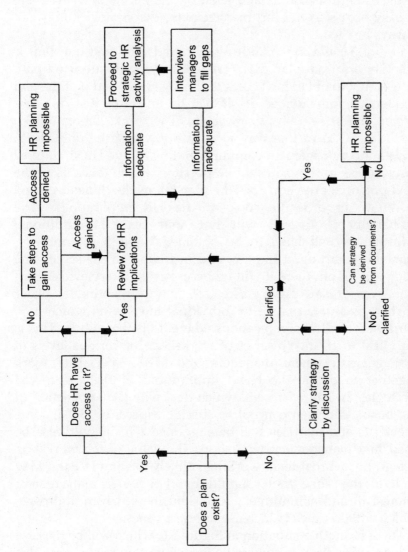

Figure 3.6 *Getting started on HR strategy.*

the organisation, as this aspect of planning lies within the domain of the function. The linkage of HR policies and strategies with corporate vision and strategy cannot be undertaken in isolation, and even in organisations where there is easy access to the top management, the strategies may not always be clear.

Figure 3.6 is about how to get started. The first question is whether a formal plan exists. Where it does, the decision path moves first to obtaining access to this by HRM, and if at the end access is totally denied it should be accepted that business driven HRM is hardly possible. The organisation which excludes HRM in this way would in any case be unlikely to have a top management commitment to effective HRM. In most cases access to the plan will be possible, which takes us to the next potential problem: does the plan tell us the things we need to know in order to look at the HR implications? The probability is that it will not, and that the additional information will have to be obtained through interviewing managers, starting at the top, and including all the senior line managers. From there it will be necessary to interview selected managers who are playing a key role in implementing the plan.

There is an alternative to individual interviews, which may work very well in organisations where it fits the culture. This is for HRM to arrange a series of workshops, at various levels of management, where managers and HRM specialists work together to define the HRM implications of the vision and strategies. In later chapters, which deal with the application of the business driven concept to specific aspects of HRM, some checklists and matrices will be suggested which could also be used in a management workshop. The value of the workshop lies in the fact that team working is likely to stimulate thinking and, at the same time, should build a wider management interest in and commitment to the business driven approach, which will do much to increase its effectiveness.

There is another situation in Figure 3.6, which will be the case in many organisations where no formal written plan exists. This rarely means that there is no strategy, although one route through the diagram deals with the situation where, either because there is no strategy, or because of top management attitudes it cannot be clarified, we are back to the situation where business driven HRM is almost impossible. The positive route follows a process of defining strategy through discussion and examination of available documents like Board minutes and position papers, to take the organisation roughly to the same state as if there had been a formal plan. This path joins the path where a plan exists at the review of HR implications, and will go through the same sequence of interviews or workshops which have already been discussed.

As is always the case, the way in which the suggested approach of Figure 3.6 is applied will vary with the structure of the organisation. Multi-divisional, multi-business organisations are not all structured identically, nor are the roles of HRM at the centre and in the businesses always defined in the same way. The principles will be relevant, but how they are applied should be adjusted to the realities of the situation.

WHERE TO NEXT?

There is still much to be considered in order to move from the outline concepts of this chapter to the implementation of business driven HRM. Later chapters will explore how the concepts can be applied to some particular aspects of HRM, such as management development, and for completeness will deal also with the forecasting of requirements and issues through what used to be called manpower planning. But moving from concept to concept without relating things to the real world may not be the most helpful approach, so before going deeper I should like to look at some good and bad examples of what real organisations have done, and share some of the research findings on the degree to which business driven concepts have been applied. These are the topics of the next two chapters,

REFERENCES

Hamel, G., 1994, The Concept of Core Competence, in Hamel, G. and Heene, A., *Competence-Based Competition*, Chichester: John Wiley.

Hussey, D. E., 1994, *Strategic Management: Theory and Practice*, 3rd edition, Oxford: Pergamon.

Porter, M. E., 1980, *Competitive Strategy: Techniques for Analysing Industries and Competitors*, New York: Free Press.

Quinn, J. R., 1980, *Strategies for Change: Logical Incrementalism*, Homewood, Illinois: Dow Jones Irwin.

Schoemaker, J. H. and van der Heijden, C. A. J. M., 1993, Strategic Planning at Royal Dutch/Shell, *Journal of Strategic Change*, 2.3, page 157.

Steiner, G. A., 1972, *Pitfalls in Comprehensive Long Range Planning*, Oxford, Ohio: Planning Executives Institute.

4
Some Examples from Experience

It is one thing to look at conceptual models in isolation from the hurly-burly of real life situations. It is quite another to see how real companies approach the business driven concept. The purpose of this chapter is to examine a few case histories, which may be used later to help us consider more detailed, practical concepts. Most of the case histories described here illustrate one aspect of the business driven approach, and this does not imply that this extends to every other area of that organisation. In fact it is extremely difficult to develop case histories that look in depth at every aspect of business driven HRM that could be discussed. Discussions held with those at the top of organisations very often lead to answers that sound right. Most chief executives know what the "right" answer ought to be, and may genuinely believe that what they describe is what really happens in their organisations, but finding out how deep the concept goes requires in-depth investigation. No doubt the chief executives in the first case example which will be covered here would have *talked* a good strategy and the way HRM supported it: after reading the case, you may feel that there was neither a sound strategy nor strong HRM support. Armstrong and Long, 1994, discuss a number of named organisations that they believe apply a strategic HRM approach. While it is no doubt true that some of these do, and possible that they all do, I am not convinced that the world inside all these organisations is as described. Read the book for yourself, and make up your own mind.

At this point we should also challenge an implied assumption of my first three chapters: that to practice business driven HRM you need an HRM function. There is a trend to decentralise HRM responsibility away from specialist departments to line managers. All the concepts discussed in this book could be applied without a separate HRM function. My own feeling is that although line managers should take on board more HRM responsibility than has been traditionally the case, it is not a good long-term solution to do away with the entire function. I will continue to write as if the organisation possesses a Human Resource Department. However, one of the case examples used here, besides being a good example of business driven HRM, also involves the diffusion of more HRM responsibility to the line, and is partly about making this happen in an effective way.

The four case examples discussed are my own summaries and analyses of papers by others (a full reference is given in each case). I have some personal knowledge of three of the four organisations. Any distortion of the facts from the published papers is of course my responsibility, and the original authors are not responsible for what I say here. My debt to them is considerable, as their work takes us a long way forward in our study of business driven HRM.

TIMEX DUNDEE (after Martin and Dowling, 1995)

Successful business driven HRM depends on the attitudes and abilities of the chief executive, and of those responsible for HRM. In this example we look at the strategic choices made by Timex Dundee over a long period, and the HRM issues that these brought. Many readers will remember that Timex closed its Dundee operations in August 1993, after a particularly acrimonious industrial relations dispute. The problem went much deeper than it might have appeared on the surface, and to blame it on intransigent unions or stubborn management is to oversimplify. With hindsight we can see where strategic decisions went awry, and where HRM strategies were not brought in line with what the organisation was trying to achieve.

The Dundee activity was established in 1947 to manufacture mechanical watches for Timex internationally. In the 1970s the labour force reached a peak of 6000: in 1975 it had fallen to 4200. By 1985 it was down to 1000, dropping to 580 by 1990, and in 1992 was under 500. This sort of decline, for whatever reason, would tax HRM skills and management abilities, but was more difficult as it was accompanied by a total change in the activities of the business.

Until the 1970s, Timex Dundee with its three plants was a manufacturing satellite of Timex internationally. Its task was to produce watches under a cost leadership strategy, with all product development centred in the USA, manufacturing long runs of mass-produced watches which carried reasonably high margins. The evidence was that it did this job well, and was a cash generator for Timex as a whole.

Historically, Timex Dundee faced an aggressive trades union, and the story of Dundee was of adversarial relations, with a history of compromise and accommodation, anything to prevent disruption of production which would have affected Timex markets throughout the world. Management appeared to manage its industrial relations with only short-term objectives in mind. As a result, the union became very powerful, not only in wage bargaining, but also in taking over much control of how labour was organised to undertake the various activities in the factory. In this the local management was typical of many other organisations in the UK at the time, where even communication by management to employees passed by default through the filter of the shop stewards. During this period, and until about 1980, Timex had a reputation as a good employer, offering career prospects, training and good conditions.

Timex internationally appears to have been taken by surprise at the decline of mechanical watches and their replacement by electronics. When it did respond it set up new plants in other countries to make watches under the new technology, and the importance of Dundee to the international watch marketing strategy withered to nothing. Nevertheless, there was a sentimental attachment to the Dundee operation at the top of Timex USA, and a willingness to try to maintain an activity there, even though it was not for the reasons that it was originally established.

As mechanical watch volumes declined, Dundee had moved into subcontracting assembly of electronic products, initially the

Sinclair ZX computer and a Japanese designed camera. This incremental strategy appeared to be a logical way of making up for the under capacity utilisation, and to be compatible with overall Timex expertise because the parent company was involved in manufacturing related products.

Dundee suffered a triple blow. The Sinclair ZX computer manufacture was transferred to IBM, the camera operations moved to Japan, and the remaining watch manufacture was relocated to France. This resulted in compulsory redundancies of 1900 people in 1983, and a worker sit-in aimed at preventing the transfer of work out of Dundee. Management fought the sit-in, and insisted on the compulsory redundancies and on changes in flexibility for those that remained.

Discussions took place between the USA and local managements about the future of Dundee. Although it was recognised that the Dundee cost structure was too high, the decision was taken to keep the business going as contract assemblers of electronic equipment. A new general manager was brought in by the USA management team to strengthen local management's electronics knowledge. The business continued to develop in contract manufacture and related services for original equipment manufacturers in the electronics industry, and by the late 1980s the company had secured a place in the electronics industry.

In their insightful analysis, Martin and Dowling, 1995, suggested that the problems that led to the final demise of the business went back to this decision. The only options that appeared to have been considered were contract assembly or closure, and management were blind to other possibilities. This is illustrative of the behavioural aspects of the way information is selected for strategic analysis (see previous chapter).

In one of my attempts to grapple with the failure to see a strategic issue clearly, (Hussey, 1984) I wrote:

> "All managers are prisoners within the boundaries of their own perception, and although corporate planning is supposed to move those boundaries it does not always do so. It is thus possible for a company to achieve better results because of the coordination and motivational impact of its planning processes and yet to be still following the wrong strategic path. This has certainly happened in the UK, and in many companies planning has failed to change these perceptual boundaries, through failings of managers and planners."

By the boundaries of perception I meant the way in which a strategic situation was defined. Centuries ago most people knew beyond doubt that the world was flat. Their strategic decisions wisely took account of this and they tended to avoid sailing their ships too close to the edge in case they fell off. This was a very logical decision. But we now know that the world is not flat, and that making decisions as if it were is not wise but instead is very stupid. The strategic problem has not changed, but our perception of the problem has.

There is a direct parallel with the way managers often perceive the strategic arena in which they operate. In the past I have had long discussions with managers who refused to accept the increasingly global nature of their industry and the competition: the Japanese entrants to their markets were seen as freak events offering unfair competition and not as evidence that the competitive arena was enlarging.

It may be because of this perception that strategy often follows fashions. In the 1980s financial service companies competed frantically to acquire estate agents: in the 1990s there was a headlong rush to divest these businesses. Airlines round the world saw hotels, car hire and other services for travellers as the businesses to buy in the late 1970s and 1980s. By 1990 most were preaching the virtues of concentration on the core business, had sold off the peripheral businesses, and talked of segmentation as the way forward.

In the Timex situation there was a belief that the company had the necessary manufacturing strengths, expertise and experience to succeed in contract assembly. Because local management was totally focused on manufacture, there were no insights from functions such as product development and marketing, and the only external thinking came from US managers who were blinkered by their perceptions of the role of Dundee as something of an anomaly in the current international strategy.

It is interesting to speculate whether the company might still have succeeded had it related in strengths and competence to the requirements of the market they were now going to concentrate on. There is of course a vital difference between taking on some contract assembly to help absorb the overheads and keep skilled workers (the Sinclair situation), and running a total business which is wholly focused on such contract work. The competency requirements of the new business included:

* great flexibility, with the ability to change economically between products;
* ability to work as an extension of the customers' businesses;

- low cost base to enable success in a lower margin business;
- greater unpredictability of products and volumes;
- all customers would be external to Timex;
- continuous attention to technical skills, to keep up to date with new or different products.

These competencies appeared to be absent at the outset. The cost problem was known, and additional top management knowledge and experience was brought in, as described, and some attempt made to increase the flexibility of working methods. What appears not to have been done was to undertake an exhaustive analysis of all the human resource issues and needs, and the development of a human resource strategy as an integral part of the business strategy. At this stage a hard-nosed examination should have been made of whether it would even be possible to bring about the necessary changes, particularly changes in culture.

During the 1980s the electronics markets expanded rapidly. Timex invested substantially in new plant, and by 1993 were one of the big six contract electronic assemblers in the UK. Redundancies, mainly voluntary, occurred throughout the period, as the company strove to remove its cost disadvantage of 20–30% compared with competitors. IBM was one of the major customers, and had installed electronic control systems which gave it instant access to production information. Dundee managers had little influence over sourcing or scheduling as these decisions were taken by IBM, who also controlled price and conformance to specifications.

In 1990 an attempt was made to change the culture of the organisation in the *Fresh Start Change Programme.* This was initiated from the USA, and the aim was to break with past industrial relations traditions, agree more redundancies, and concentrate all production into one factory. There was a buy out of some of the restrictive contract terms. Employees who survived the redundancy received a payment of £2000 to accept the new contract terms. In addition a share ownership scheme was introduced.

Culture change had begun to be a management fashion at this time but, as many organisations have found, it is not a simple undertaking. This particular programme, which one could fairly argue was at least ten years too late, was probably doomed from the start. It was driven by American managers who had little understanding of or empathy with the culture they were trying to change, and many local managers were not committed to the process. With hindsight the appearance is more of a one-off intervention rather than a step in a carefully thought out HR strategy. The costs of the change programme and other restructuring contributed to accumulated losses of £10 million between 1987 and 1993. It is probable that the perceptual boundaries of those involved in HR matters, both line and staff, were founded on the belief that a culture change had to take place on the shop floor, forgetting that a large determinant of culture is caused by how managers manage and, because of the adversarial industrial relations tradition, as much effort would be needed to change management attitudes as was devoted to the workforce.

Martin and Dowling, 1995, suggest that management failed to understand that compliance in a forced situation does not mean commitment, and the fact that the workers did what was expected did not mean that the culture had changed. A further point was that culture change requires an understanding by the change agents of the culture they are trying to change, and the intensity with which current values are held. Timex USA managers as change agents did not have this understanding: they knew the destination they were trying to reach, but not the point of departure. Local management were not committed to the change.

In June 1991 a new person was recruited to manage the Dundee plant and turn it around, in what was frankly described as the last throw of the dice. He introduced a number of well received efficiencies, but did not establish a rapport with the union officials and representatives. They saw him as an aggressive dictator, who saw every concession they made as their weakness. This was hardly conducive to the furtherance of the fresh start initiative. The closing events in the drama occurred in late 1992, when IBM cut back on their scheduled requirements. Local management developed a cost-cutting scheme in conjunction with two USA-based vice presidents, which involved lay-offs and wage reduction. Initially the workers rejected the scheme and went on strike, then accepted under protest. The general manager said that grudging commitment was not good enough, and sacked 340 workers who he replaced with non-union workers from outside the district. This led to mass and aggressive picketing over a four month period. Ultimately a peace plan was put to the strikers, involving even worse terms than they had previously accepted. This was rejected. The general manager resigned suddenly, and the US management decided to close the plant. There is now no Timex operation in Dundee.

Poor transformational leadership skills undoubtedly contributed to the ultimate failure. It is fair to question the validity of the strategy followed, but the failure owed much to the lack of a coherent HR strategy. The blame for this must lie with top management, line management and HR managers, and the degree to which each is to blame is not really relevant. The lesson is that underlying people problems, particularly the soft issues such as those which are culture related, will rarely solve themselves. We will never know whether the chosen strategy could have worked had it had a stronger HR component: we do know that without this component it never had a chance to succeed.

The next three case examples all have happier outcomes.

PREMIER FOODS EUROPE (after Cannon, 1995a)

This case study is of a real company under an assumed name. I am pleased to be able to cite it because although I was not personally involved, the work described was performed by Harbridge Consulting Group Ltd while I was managing director, and I have knowledge of both the work and the identity of the client. The organisation is the European operation of a global company. The European organisation is a multibillion dollar international food company which employs 30 000 people, operating in many countries and product areas, and achieved its present form through a variety of acquisitions and mergers.

No attempt has been made to separate the role played by the organisation from that of the consultants. The relevance of the example is in what happened, but what is important is that throughout the whole process the champion role of top management was critical for success.

The organisation's mission is to be the most successful branded food company, and this is underpinned by four clearly defined strategic priorities. The value of these sorts of statements lies less in the words that they use, than the degree to which the organisation lives and breathes them. Perhaps because of this, top management placed a high priority on people and their development. Making the people priority real should neither be a matter of the empty rhetoric found in many annual reports, nor should it be a doctrinaire commitment of a do-gooder type. Instead, it should be a sound, business driven commitment which realises that the priority on people has to be focused on business needs. Empty rhetoric provokes cynicism and acts against the business interests.

The do-gooder approach may satisfy employees, but does not do much to improve corporate performance or develop competitive advantage, and will frequently fall prey to cost-cutting initiatives. Companies are not in the management development business, unless they happen to be consultants or colleges, but they are in the business of using management development to achieve the main mission of marketing product and delivering profit.

The first phase of creating a business driven approach began with an audit of what was currently going on in management development across the whole organisation. This phase included an extensive survey of managers, which achieved a 97% response rate. The factual base of information was critical for knowing where changes should be made, and created an agenda of critical issues which could be brought to top management attention.

As a direct result of the findings, the organisation set up a task force of senior HR professionals from many countries and areas, with the objective to develop a strategy to change the role played by management development in the business. The task group used a change model developed by Beckhard and Harris, 1987:

- Define the desired future state (the vision for management development).
- Obtain consensus on what is the current reality (the results of the audit).
- Make a plan on a sensible timescale for transition from the current to the desired state.

A description of the end result of this phase leapfrogs the process itself of building consensus within the task force and changing a group of disparate members to a team committed to the success of the change. In fact, so great was the ultimate commitment, and so successful the outcome, that the task force later received the annual Chairman's award for the most significant contribution to the organisation's progress.

Cannon ascribes the success of this phase of the work to the personal dedication and conviction of this small group of people, to the overwhelming factual evidence from the audit, and to the existence of a top management champion for the initiative.

A vision for management development was defined and issued by the president and CEO:

"We believe that outstanding people, more than physical assets, financial resources or brands, make the difference in achieving superior business results.

The continued development of people must therefore be a top priority for all Premier Foods Europe managers."

Nice words: were they rhetoric or a genuine description that would guide actions in the organisation? Read on before you make up your mind.

In addition to the definition of the vision, the task force defined the critical success factors that would support the overall business mission and strategy, and from this information developed 13 management competency headings, which were considered essential for the success of the business strategy. Under these headings management behaviours were defined for the various levels of management, creating a situation where there was variation within a consistent framework.

The broad headings were:

- Ideas leadership
- Handling complexity/judgement
- Superior execution
- Drive for results
- Influencing and negotiating
- Attracting and developing talent
- Team leadership
- Professional maturity
- Business acumen
- Risk taking
- Adaptability
- Building and sustaining relationships
- Customer focus.

What makes these work is, of course, the detailed definition by level.

A third output from the task force was the development of management development principles, to guide the way in which management development actions were implemented. Again only the headings can be given here:

- Business driven
- Leadership and technical expertise
- Shared responsibility
- International perspective
- Appointments from within
- On the job learning
- Diversity

- Management competencies
- Entrepreneurism.

Vision, competencies, and principles were derived from the business vision and strategic priorities, all of which were (and are now regularly) assessed for HR implications. Everything could be tied back to what it was the organisation was trying to achieve.

However well founded the above elements were, they could not work unless communicated to the organisation at large, and integrated into the day to day aspects of management. In order to move from sound words to sound actions something else was needed. This was a process which was known internally as GOLD. The acronym stood for Gaining Organisational Leadership through Development.

The main elements of GOLD were:

- communication of the vision
- building commitment to the vision across all levels
- achieving consistency across the organisation
- translating the ideas into personal action plans
- integrating the action plans into the performance management system.

One element of GOLD was a four day training programme, more details of which will be given later. The programme itself would not constitute a process, and companion elements were the retention of a smaller task force to help address organisational blockages to the changes, a feedback mechanism which fostered organisational learning and built motivation by passing details of success to the organisation. The whole approach was seen as a partnership between line management, HR and the individual. Senior management took responsibility for maintaining the right climate for development, specific variables were defined to measure improved performance, and business success was measured by progress towards achieving the mission.

The training programme was intended to help line managers understand and be equipped for their own roles in the HR development process, and performance based action plans for personal improvement and for the development of employees on the job were developed by participants during the event. Top management was involved through their own participation in the first four day event, and thereafter by holding an open forum session when the event was repeated for line managers. Some of the features of the programme are:

- It cascades top down through the organisation.
- Delivery is by a mix of internal and external faculty, some from line and some from HR.
- Business based case studies written around Premier Food situations link people development to the business itself.
- Vision and management development principles are presented by a member of the executive team.
- A feedback mechanism (peers and subordinates) is used to enable participants to see their own performance on the 13 management competencies. Feedback for the boss is part of the appraisal process and is taken outside of the training event.
- Training is provided in core skills such as coaching and teamwork, and there are practical issues around succession planning, performance management and professional development.
- The organisation's commitment to on the job training as the primary development method underlines the role of line managers.

The action planning components of the programme have already been mentioned. The course itself was first delivered in English, and subsequently in a number of other European languages.

Cannon states that at the time he wrote his article (early 1995), a critical mass of 650 managers had been trained. Premier's parent company has taken up the GOLD concept for the rest of its global activities and is extending it beyond Europe. Many of the planned benefits in succession planning, career development and people development have been realised. The link between business strategy and people management is better understood, and the HR implications of strategies are now specifically defined. The whole management development climate has changed, becoming business driven and more effective.

OTIS ELEVATORS AND CENTRAL EUROPE: MANAGEMENT TRAINING TO ACHIEVE RESULTS (after Coast, 1995)

Many organisations who have taken up positions in Central and Eastern Europe have found that they needed to provide training for local managers. The need for such training often becomes apparent when it is realised that there is a lack of experience in many of the management concepts which are commonplace in the West. Recognition of this need, and doing something about it can legitimately be called business driven, but there is a difference of degree between an initiative which provides routine training or education, and one which is also designed to improve bottom line results.

It is also very easy to cause resentment among managers in the countries concerned, because they feel that their existing knowledge and past experience count as nothing, and that in some way they are seen as second class citizens. If you add to this the fact that many good managers in those countries do not speak the languages of the West with great fluency, but often receive training delivered in English despite this, there is a recipe for disaster, the seasoning of which may be a refusal by those providing the training to take account of the national cultural differences between those receiving the training and those providing it.

From my personal observations through work in Hungary, I would suggest that much of the training provided to local organisations through international aid programmes has done more harm than good, has alienated participants, and done little to change management behaviour. It is too easy for parent companies to fall into a similar trap, when providing training to their Central/Eastern European operations.

In this context, business driven training is a question of seeking enhanced business performance through the way training is designed, and in taking particular care over how it is applied. The case study described by Coast is interesting because the aims of training were directly related to the needs of the parent and local business, and because the story shows the need for great flexibility in the adjustment of the training methods to the local situation. It is very easy to overestimate the English language fluency of nationals of another country, and much harder to do what Otis did and be flexible in how the programme was delivered once the language problem becomes apparent.

Coast describes how management training was used to help Otis Elevators implement its joint venture strategies in Central Europe. Here the need was to help the top management teams of these businesses to develop business plans and to implement them. Both aspects were seen as equally important. The European headquarters needed to apply its planning approach to the new businesses, but in a way that was effective. Implementation is a critical aspect of planning, as has been seen in the earlier chapters of this book.

The programme was designed and managed by a steering board of senior line managers, and an external consultant. The line managers were the area director for Central Europe, the managing directors of each of the three companies for which the training was being provided, the director of planning from the European headquarters, and Colin Coast who was responsible for management development. At a later stage the finance director for Central Europe was added to the board.

Participants on the programmes were the senior management teams from the three country companies, and the aim was to help each team to develop and implement a business plan. The design of the programme followed the business planning process. It was intended to consist of seven modules, each of three days duration. The decision was taken to develop each module, within the guideline framework, as the programme rolled out, so that there was maximum flexibility to adjust to new situations, and to meet emerging needs of the participants.

This flexibility proved to be very important, and the steering board had to be even more flexible than planned. By the end of the first day of the first programme it was clear that the English language fluency of the participants was lower than believed, and the group worked late into the night to modify the teaching approach for the remaining two days. How this was done, and the detailed design elements of the whole programmes, are described in the reference, but are not significant here.

Apart from its desirability anyway, the language problem forced a low reliance on lectures, and a high use of group and project work. All the projects were actions that the teams themselves planned to improve the performance of their companies. The timing of each module was set to coincide with the business planning timetable so that the training initiative became an extension of the business. External consultants helped with some aspects of the programme, but 70% was taught by Otis managers.

This programme would have cost no more than a more traditional approach to teaching managers the skills they lacked. Tying it to business performance, including an almost seamless link between management tasks on the job and the programme meant, firstly, that the learning of participants was enhanced, because the value of the programmes was clear. This meant that the training was more effective. In addition it led to many actions inside the businesses, and the preparation of what should be effective business plans. Only time will tell the true extent of the business improvement that the training produced, but the signs are that it has been very effective.

ASPECTS OF BUSINESS DRIVEN HRM AT PREMIER BANK (after Cannon 1995b)

This is another case study where the company name has been disguised. It is also another situation where I have privileged information, and know the true identity of the organisation. The similarity of name with Premier Foods does not imply any connection between the two organisations (there is none), and says more about the preferences of Cannon, who wrote up both cases, than anything about the organisation. The facts are derived from Cannon's article, although again the summarising, interpretation and comments cannot be blamed on him.

The real organisation is the UK operation of a USA financial services organisation of substance, which has operated in the UK for some 20 years. It has 150 branches throughout the UK, a direct banking operation, and credit card and insurance divisions. Some of these business areas are new to the organisation.

The environment for banking changed as the economy moved from boom in the 1980s to recession in the 1990s. The competitive environment steadily became fiercer, with an increase in the number of organisations moving from one financial area, such as banking, into others, such as insurance. Regulatory pressures increased. Technology enabled many changes to be made in the way financial services were organised: examples are 'hole in the wall' cash dispensers, and direct banking over telephone lines. Particularly from 1990 many firms in the industry have gone through a process of rationalisation and cost reduction, as technology and the changing market modified the role of branch offices and the levels of staffing in these.

In 1990, at a time of severe recession, the Premier Bank identified four critical strategic challenges. Two were directly related to the bottom line: returning to profit, and the related issue of managing credit quality and expense. Two others were of equal importance, but less direct in their impact: these were improving employee morale and motivation, and achieving the bank's customer service vision. There were obvious human resources implications, and a need to ensure that the right HRM actions were taken to aid the implementation of the overall strategy.

The business driven HRM approach began with a survey of the organisational climate, and an analysis of the strategic situation of the organisation. Put simply, climate is the employees' perceptions of how it feels to work in the particular organisation. The approach used had two components. One part established employees' perceptions of the climate. The second measured their views of their own managers' behaviours. The questionnaire used was developed from a sound research base by consultants Harbridge House Inc. It measures climate through how managers manage, on six dimensions:

1 *Structure:* The extent to which employees feel they are organised and have clarity of purpose.
2 *Standards:* Pressure to improve performance and the degree of pride employees have in doing a good job.
3 *Responsibility:* The degree to which employees feel empowered.
4 *Recognition:* The feeling of being rewarded for a good performance. It measures whether the emphasis is on positive or negative incentives (for example, praise versus criticism).
5 *Support:* Feelings of trust and mutual support in the organisation
6 *Commitment:* Feelings of pride in belonging to the organisation, and the extent to which there is commitment to organisational goals.

The part of the report which measures management behaviours under these headings is based on the research findings that a major part of climate is caused by the way managers manage those under them. Because the survey generated good quantified data, it allowed managers to see their own profiles (on a personal and confidential basis), and provided aggregate information on the whole organisation and its key components. Overall, the information enabled an assessment to be made of where changes were necessary to support the strategies, while the emphasis on management behaviours meant that it was possible to see where action could be taken to change the climate.

Responses were compared with an extensive data bank of management behaviours in other organisations. This changes the view of where action is needed: for example a raw score of 3.5 out of a total of 5 for any one of the behaviours measured could be seen as a good result, until, that is, it is compared with all other organisations in the database which might show that 3.5 was in the bottom decile for all organisations, and that in comparative terms much improvement was needed.

In broad terms the findings showed that current emphasis on sales success and individual performance created barriers to the achievement of the vision of customer service. Management practices in some areas were perceived to be directive and punitive, restricting individual responsibility and creating a risk-averse culture. The culture was inward looking, although the competitive situation required an external orientation.

The results of this first phase led to a number of areas of HRM that required attention.

- The performance management process had to change from a short-term orientation, with little qualitative criteria, that was sales driven and stressed target-linked pay. What was needed was a service culture approach, which was concerned with quality of work as well as quantity, and put weight on how results were achieved, as well as the results themselves.
- Internal communication needed attention, and required to be two way. Attention has to be given to both formal and informal communication.
- The service approach required more cross functional teamwork, which the management practices of the time made almost impossible.

All of these issues required managers to manage in a different way, and this included senior managers who, through their actions, had to emphasise that those values which were critical for customer service were seen as being as important as those which were critical for sales success. The climate survey put a quantitative dimension to many of the management behaviours that needed to change, as well as indicating where changes had to be made.

Many of the changes identified training needs, both in terms of learning how to manage differently, and in acquiring the skills needed to support some of the changes. Premier Bank had hitherto taken a fragmented approach to training. The information that had been collected and analysed enabled a training needs analysis to be completed. In turn this led to some new principles for management development, and a number of particular initiatives.

The principles were:

- Training must be part of the business plan.
- All training must contribute directly to business performance.
- It must start at the top to provide a visible change in leadership behaviours.
- Training initiatives must be sustained, evaluated and followed up.

Five major training initiatives were identified for implementation over a two year period. Measures were determined in customer service orientation, workforce quality and employee motivation so that the effect of the training could be monitored. In addition a decision was taken to repeat the climate survey after a reasonable time to measure the changes that had taken place.

The repeat survey was undertaken in 1994. A comparison of the scores of the two surveys is given in Table 4.1.

Cannon, 1995b, sums up the results:

"Analysis of the results shows that significant improvements in management practices were a major impact on the organisational climate change. This change could not have been achieved without a concerted and business-focused commitment of the executive team."

This case study shows how the business driven approach impinged on a number of aspects of HRM, and it is reasonable to assume that other aspects not specifically mentioned by Cannon were also changed as a result of the work. What is covered in the case study is culture change, performance management, management behaviours, management training principles, and management training itself. However the concept was not just about being business driven: it was also about being businesslike in HRM, with attention to measurement and evaluation of HR initiatives. It also made HRM pivotal to the changes that had to take place in the organisation.

Table 4.1   *1991 and 1994 climate surveys (percentile scores).*

Climate Dimension	1991	1994
Structure	40	56
Standards	70	84
Responsibility	46	57
Recognition	29	47
Support	18	48
Commitment	35	66

SOME PRINCIPLES FROM THE CASE STUDIES

The case studies illustrate different aspects of what it means to
have business driven HRM, or in the case of Timex, what it
means not to have it. The Timex case, analysed with the benefit
of hindsight, shows the many problems that arise from a lack of
strategic vision and the HRM approach to support it. The lesson
here is not that in the calm of a *post mortem* we can all see the
things that went wrong, particularly when the corpse has been
dissected as well as it has been by Martin and Dowling. It is
that in the normal pace of management life any organisation
can make errors of equivalent magnitude, unless it gives equal
attention to where it should be heading, and the actions
(including HRM actions) needed if it is to get there. The fresh
start initiative, as described, makes an interesting contrast with
the quieter and sounder approach of Premier Bank, although
admittedly the bank did not have to cope with the legacy of an
adversarial relationship with trades unions.

The Premier Foods case focused on only one part of HRM
activity, but showed how the business driven approach changed
both the perception and reality of management development
from something that made little difference to a force which
affected the competitive positioning of the organisation. The
additional lesson here is the role of top management, which
championed the initiative. It would probably have been
impossible to achieve such significant results if top
management were neutral and certainly impossible if they were
hostile. The importance of careful analysis of the organisation's
strategy, and the collection of good information both to enable
an appropriate course of action to be defined, and also to build
the commitment of others, is a feature of both the Premier case
studies, although they illustrate different methodologies.

Otis shows the value of taking a business driven approach to
the design of an individual initiative. This is not to imply that
Otis either do or do not take this approach into the policy areas
of HRM: the case study does not tell us. But it shows that even
in the absence of a broader approach, it is possible to apply
some of the concepts to particular initiatives, and that this in
itself adds value to the organisation.

All three of the successful cases illustrate also the value to the

HR function of being able to demonstrate how its expenditures have added value to the organisation. The HR survivors of the future will be those functions that make a positive difference, and can show this. Those that are simply good administrators will be forever vulnerable. And so they should be.

REFERENCES

Armstrong, M. and Long, P., 1994, *The Reality of Strategic HRM*, London: Institute of Personnel Development.

Beckhard, R. and Harris, R. T., 1987, *Organisational Transitions*, Reading MA: Addison Wesley.

Cannon, F., 1995a, Developing Competencies that Drive Business Performance, *Journal of Strategic Change*, 4:3, May–June.

Cannon, F., 1995b, The Role of Education and Training in Organisational Climate Change: A Case Study, *Journal of Professional HRM*, 1:1, October.

Coast, C. R., 1995, Central Europe—Management Training, *Team Performance Management*, 1:2.

Hussey, D. E., 1984, Strategic Management: Lessons From Success and Failure, *Long Range Planning*, 17.1, February.

Martin, G. and Dowling, M., 1995, Managing Change, Human Resource Management and Timex, *Journal of Strategic Change*, 4: 2, March–April.

5
What the Research Tells Us

Research provides an insight into the issues of business driven HRM, and gives an impression of the interest in the approach and the extent to which it is practised. In this chapter some of the research findings will be examined, but some notes of caution must be sounded.

- There are timing differences in when the various surveys were undertaken, so one cannot be certain that the jigsaw puzzle assembled from the findings of different researchers is made up of pieces from the same box. Information valid in 1991 may not still be valid when combined with that from a later survey.
- The surveys have different sample frames and sample sizes. In any case there are significant problems in sampling in this type of industrial market research, which means that information should be treated as indicative, rather than precise. The fact that a certain percentage of respondents did a certain thing, does not automatically mean that the same percentage would have applied to all organisations in the country. In some cases the surveys focused on a specific segment of the universe, and did not sample organisations from other segments.
- Even if the sample is totally representative, the results can

still be affected by the person in the organisation who answers the questions. This is a particularly complex issue in large decentralised multi-business organisations, where the view from the centre may not reflect the view from a business unit, and vice versa.

● Terms in questionnaires may not have the same meaning to all respondents. Thus someone might honestly believe that there is (or is not) a human resource strategy, whereas another in the same situation might have interpreted the questions differently and stated the opposite. For this reason I prefer surveys that probe what actually happens, rather than relying on a commonality of definitions.

Even with these cautions, the surveys provide evidence that is helpful in shaping perceptions of the general state of affairs, and stimulate thought about some of the issues.

What is possibly the largest scale survey of HRM is that of the Price Waterhouse Cranfield Project, which has undertaken a series of surveys since 1990. The figures quoted here come from the 1991/2 survey (Brewster, 1993).

In the 1992 survey questionnaires were completed by 123 organisations (compared to 1503 in the 1991 survey). The sample size differences make it difficult to determine whether the small movements detected were a trend, or just due to sampling differences. Because the movements were relatively small, I have only quoted from the 1992 survey, but have referenced the earlier survey for those interested (see PWC, 1991). In any case the real conclusion is unaffected: that many organisations do claim to take a strategic approach to HRM, but a very large number do not.

If the organisation were committed to a business driven approach, one manifestation might be expected to be that the head of HRM was on the main board of directors. In the UK the percentage of organisations where this happened was 49%. It may be a coincidence, but this is roughly the number of organisations that can be inferred from the survey as possibly having a business driven approach.

A little over 50% claim to have a direct involvement in the development of corporate strategy from the outset, with a further 9% having an involvement in implementation. This leaves 7% who had no role, and about a third who claimed to have had a consultative role. Consultation may mean a number of possible things, but to me it implies a minor involvement, and it is therefore unlikely that these organisations have a business driven HR strategy. Even where there is an involvement, we cannot assume that this always leads to a fully integrated strategy, since not all HRM managers carry that involvement through to the next logical stage. What we can say is that it is among these organisations that we are most likely to find a business driven approach.

Another question which is relevant asked whether there was an HRM strategy. Half the UK respondents claimed to have a written strategy, about a quarter claimed an unwritten strategy, and the rest had no strategy, did not know, or did not answer the question. The existence of a written strategy again is only indicative, as it could be defined in a way that had little relationship to the needs of the business, but once again we have about half of the organisations who might have a business driven approach. Those organisations with unwritten strategies are very doubtful contenders, purely because of the complexity of the components of HRM, and the difficulty, in all but the smallest of organisations, of coordinating the various specialisms without a written strategy.

My interpretation of the survey information is that the proportion of organisations with a strategic, or business driven, approach to HRM is unlikely to be more than 50%, but could be much lower. Certainly I know organisations where the HR manager is on the Board, takes part in all the discussions of corporate strategy, and has a written plan, but still does not have a business driven HR strategy. Three essential ingredients are present, but in these cases two are missing: knowledge by the HR manager of how to do it, and lack of awareness of the value of doing it by the chief executive.

Brewster, 1993, produced a grouping of the level of integration of HRM with corporate strategy for all the countries covered by the survey (14, including the UK). On a scale of one, most integrated, to four, least integrated, the UK was placed in group three along with Denmark, Ireland, Portugal and Turkey. Only two countries fell in group four, Germany and Italy. At the other extreme, Sweden, Norway and France were placed in group one, and Switzerland, Spain, Finland and The Netherlands in group two.

Harbridge Consulting Group, while under my direction, undertook a regular stream of research from 1983 to 1993. Each survey examined a specific area of HRM, with many concentrating on aspects of management development (including all its supporting processes). This gave an opportunity to probe behind some of the broader statements, to gain a deeper impression of what actually went on. The two surveys referenced here are Tovey, 1991 and Mason, 1993. The cautions about sampling apply to these surveys, and although percentages are given, please treat them as indicative only. Tovey's survey was of organisations from the Times Top 150 companies, and equivalents in areas such as finance which are not included in this listing. The sample was 57 organisations. Mason's survey was of 49 organisations in the £200–700 million turnover range. Extracts from these surveys are used with the permission of Coopers & Lybrand, who now own the copyrights.

The Mason survey had the benefit of the knowledge of issues gained from the Tovey survey, and includes figures for both surveys. Section two of the Mason report stated that it:

> "....seeks to ascertain the degree of commitment and interest of senior executives to management development and its use as a competitive weapon. To what extent is management development linked to business objectives and strategies? What are the current business trends and how well are companies prepared for these? What are the emerging management development initiatives?...."

This statement is a fair description of the similar intent of the Tovey report.

In addition to asking straight questions about the business link, the surveys explored how organisations were using management development to deal with major strategic forces. This gave some indication of the gap between what was said about strategic linkages, and what really happened. Although management development is only one part of HRM, it is reasonable to assume that what might be termed the quality of the linkage reflects the quality of the overall HRM linkage. An organisation which had a weak or superficial approach in one area of HRM, in organisations of the size sampled, might be assumed to have a similar manifestation in the overall linkage. The insight given from the surveys is interesting, and potentially helpful for organisations that accept the logic of a business driven HR approach, and are struggling with how to make it effective.

In the survey of large organisations 55% of respondents claimed that there was a link between training and development, and corporate objectives and strategy, and a further 12% were trying to improve the link. Medium-sized organisations showed almost the same degree of awareness, but only in 41% was the link established and working. The percentage trying to improve the link was 23%. Of all the organisations interviewed in both surveys, only one respondent felt that there should be no such linkage. It is possible to look at the results optimistically, and argue that around two-thirds of organisations have a link, or pessimistically, that around one-third have no link at all, and that the link is perceived to be effective in only about a half of the organisations.

The survey of medium-sized organisations included this note of caution:

> "The responses were the opinions of the individual respondents and it was not possible to test the quality of the linkage. For example, of those who felt that the link was specific, there was a handful who had answered every question in the context of business objectives and strategies as this was the reason the training department existed. Similarly there were others who needed time to think of the answer which indicates that the link may have been less effective than stated."
>
> (Mason, 1993, p. 17)

In both surveys around two-thirds of all organisations had at least one member of the Board who was involved to some degree in the formulation of the training policy. However there were a number of organisations where this interest did not continue to the implementation of the policy. Tovey, 1991, page 83, found that many respondents qualified the nature of Board interest by indicating that it was only a question of sanctioning the policies, and not being involved in their formulation. Only about 10% of the large companies had established a top level steering or executive committee with responsibility for management development matters, but where this occurred at least two of the members were on the Board. Mason, 1993, page

93 found that although there was Board involvement in two-thirds of the organisations, only in half of these (that is one-third of the total sample) did it include the formulation of policy. In the remainder it was only to sanction a policy, or in some cases the ability to present a paper to the Board should HRM think this necessary.

In both surveys respondents were asked whether certain strategic forces were relevant to their organisations, and whether they had resulted in any management development action. The selected forces, which have been described in Chapter 1, and the response are shown in Table 5.1. The results of the survey of medium-sized companies are contrasted with those of the larger companies, which are shown in brackets.

What is interesting about the results of these questions is:

- Each of the strategic forces identified was seen as relevant by between 80% and 100% of respondents in both surveys. They may in fact be relevant to more organisations than the respondents perceived, but this could not be deduced from the surveys.
- In all but the quality area, the proportion of those who see a force as relevant, but who have either not taken any management development action to help the organisation cope with it, or do not know whether action has been taken, is higher than might have been expected. It implies that the link between management development and the business needs is less perfect than many of the respondents might have thought. The figures of Table 5.1 are recalculated in Table 5.2 so that only those that see a factor as relevant are included.
- In many situations the action taken is relevant, but at a surface level: in other words the issue might be covered but not its consequences. A good example is delayering and downsizing, where few organisations appeared to have realised that the impact on the way organisations manage is very significant, and that the transition to the new organisation could be eased by training of both those who manage and those who are managed.
- For some of the forces the action taken should be qualified as

Table 5.1 Management development responses to key issues and changes.

KEY ISSUE	Action Taken		Relevant (%) Don't Know		No Action Taken		Not Relevant (%)	
	Medium	Large	Medium	Large	Medium	Large	Medium	Large
Global Competition	37.0	59.0	0.0	7.7	43.5	25.6	19.5	7.7
Demographic Change	28.3	50.0	0.0	0.0	63.0	47.2	8.7	2.8
Information Technology	52.2	87.5	0.0	2.1	47.8	10.4	0.0	0.0
Mergers/Acquisitions	34.8	60.7	0.0	3.6	50.0	25.0	15.2	10.7
Quality/Service Pressure	89.1	98.0	4.3	0.0	6.6	2.0	0.0	0.0
Managing Strat. Change	63.0	87.0	0.0	0.0	37.0	13.0	0.0	0.0
Strategic Alliances	21.7	57.1	2.2	3.6	60.9	25.0	15.2	14.3
Delayering & Downsizing	28.2	72.2	0.0	8.3	54.3	5.6	15.2	13.9
Cross Functional Team	52.2	58.6	0.0	7.3	47.8	34.1	0.0	0.0

Note: Medium organisations see Mason, 1993: sample 49 organisations. Large organisations see Tovey, 1991: sample 57 organisations

Table 5.2 Management development responses to key issues and changes by those seeing the issue as relevant.

KEY ISSUE	Action Taken (%)		Don't Know (%)		No Action Taken (%)	
	Medium	Large	Medium	Large	Medium	Large
Global Competition	46.0	63.9	0.0	8.3	54.0	27.7
Demographic Change	31.0	51.4	0.0	0.0	69.0	48.6
Information Technology	52.2	87.5	0.0	0.0	47.8	10.7
Mergers/Acquisitions	41.0	68.0	0.0	4.0	59.0	28.0
Quality/Service Pressure	89.1	98.0	4.3	0.0	6.6	2.0
Managing Strat. Change	63.0	87.0	0.0	0.0	37.0	13.0
Strategic Alliances	25.6	66.6	2.6	4.2	71.8	29.2
Delayering & Downsizing*	33.3	83.9	0.0	9.6	64.0	6.5
Cross Functional Team	52.2	58.6	0.0	7.3	47.8	34.1

Note: Figures calculated from Table 5.1. *Delayering & Downsizing medium companies % do not add up to 100 in Table 5.1.

spasmodic and very limited. For example, the survey of larger organisations commented on strategic alliances:

"Only a minority of those who have taken action appear to have done so on a coordinated and regular basis. Many spasmodic actions, for example workshops run by a business school for senior management; an initiative which 'seemed to die a death for some reason'; reliance on the fact that the topic would be included in the external business school programme on which a small minority of managers were sent; or occasional coverage in broader training programmes to create awareness. A minority were treating the subject more seriously, with, for example: training that incorporates the identification of possibilities and methods of expansion that will become available in Europe; or making the issue a significant element in an executive programme."

(Tovey, 1991, p. 26)

Management development is by no means the whole of HR activity, and it may be that a more strategic approach was being undertaken over other elements of the HR mix. Yet if you believe, as I do, that all elements of the HR mix should be both business driven and coordinated, the implications from these research studies are that many organisations do not understand what it means to be business driven, and are deluding themselves over the extent to which management development is reinforcing corporate objectives and strategies.

Although the percentages varied somewhat, the general findings of the two surveys in respect of the strategic forces were very similar. The Mason survey reflects the tone, if not the precise detail, of the findings of the Tovey survey, and includes some comparisons of the two. The following extracts, which omit areas which the majority of organisations claim to be covering, are taken from this report, which has added value because some examples of the topics that organisations might have considered are included. The report also describes each issue, but these passages have been omitted as they duplicate issues already covered in Chapter 1.

EXTRACTS FROM MASON, 1993*

Global Competition

Of the sample group of companies 37% said that a number of measures were being taken to address the issue. The majority of these said it was

---

*Reproduced by permission.

covered at the more senior end of the management scale. Forty-four per cent said that, although it was acknowledged that it was an issue relevant to the company, they felt no training was necessary. Nineteen per cent said that they believed it was not of relevance to their company.

Two companies who do not currently provide such training said that it is likely to be incorporated into the future management development programme. Of those currently providing such programmes, all said that it would continue to be addressed on a similar scale.

A common reaction to the issue was that managers have grown up with it due to the company's current global environment. A few respondents who had taken action had only addressed competition at a European level but not, as yet, on a truly global scale.

The issue appears to be seen as less urgent by companies in this survey than we found in the survey of large companies where nearly 60% had taken management development action. However the issue is not related to company size.

Sample Topics where Management Development Needs Might Change to Address the Issue

- Global strategy analysis and formulation
- Multinational marketing
- Technology strategy
- World class manufacturing
- Managing change
- National cultural differences
- Culture, structure and strategy.

Changing demographics

Twenty-eight per cent of the sample group stated that they regarded changing demographics as an issue relevant to the organisation and that they had taken some action. Sixty-three per cent said that it was relevant but no action had been taken, while 9% believed it to be irrelevant to them.

The most significant factor emerging from this issue is that a large majority of organisations believed it to be an issue which would impact on them in the future—some in the near future—yet did not regard it as something that needed to be addressed at all in training or as anything more than a low priority.

The most common response to the issue was "you can't train people in that"; others said that because everyone was aware of it already, training was unnecessary. On further questioning, however, several admitted that although managers know what the issue is, few really understand it and the possible implications of not addressing it.

Of those who said action was being taken, most were addressing the issue towards all managers and were relating it specifically to how it may affect the company as opposed to what the issue means generally. The skills gap "time bomb" was most often seen as the most urgent issue although there were instances of others being addressed. For example, one organisation spoken to was one of the companies to commit itself to the Opportunity 2000 campaign which aims to increase the quality and quantity of women's participation in the workforce.

Sample Topics where Management Development Needs Might Change to Address the Issue

The neglected issue is how managers might manage in the expected demographic situation. Topics might include:

- Outsourcing
- Supplier/company network relationships
- Empowerment
- Performance management
- Diversity management
- National cultural differences.

Strategic Alliances

This was the issue that was least pursued in terms of training and development. Only 22% said that initiatives had been taken. Sixty-one per cent felt that the issue was relevant to their organisation but did not address the issue in their programme, while 15% thought it was not relevant. Two per cent did not know whether the issue was covered.

Of the 61% who did not address the issue, the majority said it was a day to day issue. The common reaction, however, was bewilderment as to why anyone should train managers on such an issue: even those who did cover the issue tended to cover it only as part of a wider programme.

Sample Topics where Management Development Needs Might Change to Address the Issue

- National cultural differences
- Strategic analysis
- Pre- and post-alliance planning
- Understanding company cultures
- Creating networking organisations
- Task force management
- Project management.

Delayering and Downsizing

Twenty-eight per cent of respondents stated that training and development initiatives of some description had been pursued. Fifty-four percent said that the issue was relevant but did not address it on their programmes, while 15% felt that it was not an issue relevant to their organisation.

Of those that did address the issue, a large majority directed it at senior managers. Four respondents said it was an issue important to the organisation and that it was covered fully in their programme. However the rest said it was covered to a very limited extent.

Of those respondents who said no initiatives had been taken, most said that there was a certain level of awareness among managers already. Many said that the organisation had downsized already but very few said there had been any attempts to delayer within the organisation. Many people viewed the issue with amusement ("Sacking people? Done that!").

The point that most respondents have missed is that both managers and subordinates have to operate quite differently in smaller, flatter organisations, if they are to be effective.

Sample Topics where Management Development Needs Might Change to Address the Issue:

· Empowerment and delegation
· Performance management
· Continuous improvement
· Communication skills
· Transformational leadership
· Networking organisations
· Outsourcing.

My interpretation of the research is that there are undoubtedly organisations who have a business driven approach, and who are doing what is necessary to sustain this. However, there are others who believe they have such an approach, but have not yet got to grips with the implications of the strategies their organisations are following. This may be because they are not as close to top management as they should be, or it could be because no one in the organisation has thought through the issues in implementing these strategies. Percentages of people who do this or do that are of transient interest, and do little more than to give comfort to those of us who are relieved to find some evidence that our ideas do find their way into what organisations actually do, while proving that there is a need for such a book as this because so many people still have a long way to go. The abiding lesson is more subtle. It is the need to think through what strategies and other changes mean to the things people have to do in the organisation. If the old competencies on which we relied have passed their sell by date, what must replace them? Only when we do this can we have some hope of increasing the success rate of acquisitions (where 50% fail), of matching the vision for the organisation to what happens on the ground, and at a more basic level, of removing stress from the many managers who in too many organisations are left to sink or swim after an organisational change.

The issues explored in the Harbridge Consulting Group surveys were taken from a composite of surveys about those topics which were seen as most important by senior managers. Some are external trends, but others are in effect strategies in response to external issues.

Tovey, 1996, carried out a survey of HR practitioners (mainly directors), specialist consultants, and journalists in HRM which asked respondents to identify what they saw as the five most critical issues in HRM over the next five years: fieldwork was undertaken in 1995.

The results are shown in Table 5.3, and although few of the issues themselves are surprising, only one issue, the flexible workforce, is a concern of a majority of respondents. This may be because respondents were restricted to five, or because they felt an issue was already under control and would not be critical in the future, or because they had not thought of it. Although closer alignment of the HR function with the business was listed by less than a third of the 35 respondents, a majority of the issues could fairly be described as strategic. To me this is a much more hopeful sign than if the finding had been that all organisations were at exactly the same stage in dealing with an issue. Whether all the organisations who responded will deal with the strategic issues in a strategic way is another question, about which we can only speculate.

One of the issues identified in Tovey, 1996, was the trend for more services to be devolved to line management. The causes of this trend are many, including the cost drive that has led to a reduction of size of many HR departments, and the desire by many line managers to control everything that affects their bottom line results. There is also something else going on, which is the changing shape of organisations with the trend to flexible employment systems, and a greater movement to outsourcing and concepts of the virtual organisation. All this is important to the discussion of business driven HRM, but only

Table 5.3   *Most important HRM issues for the next five years.*

Human Resource Issues	No. of Mentions	Percentage
Flexible organisation & workforce	24	70
Management of change & organisational development	16	47
Changing shape of HR function/devolution	16	47
Globalising & the influence of Europe	12	33
Greater investment in training and development	11	32
Reassessment of approaches to compensation	11	32
Closer alignment of the HR function with the business	10	29
Motivation, commitment & employee loyalty	10	29
HR impact of internal/external communication	10	29
Increase in the use of technology	8	23
Downsizing and career management	7	20

Source: Tovey, 1996. Reproduced by permission of Coopers & Lybrand
(Original research by Laura Tovey and Sharon Matthews)

in the context of who should be responsible for various initiatives, not what should be done. The Premier Foods case in the preceding chapter shows how the business driven concept was applied in an organisation where much responsibility was so devolved. As many of the functions of HRM are also capable of being outsourced, the debate on who should be responsible for what aspects of the strategic tasks takes on a new dimension.

Hutchinson and Wood, 1995 undertook a survey of 27 UK organisations for the Institute of Personnel and Development, to examine the trend. (Brewster and Mayne, 1995, in the same publication, provided a view of the experience of a number of European countries.) In 22 of the organisations there has been a trend towards greater line responsibility over the last five years, and in most of these the change was from a centralised and controlling mode of operation.

The researchers found that both line managers and HR specialists had some difficulty in adjusting to the new situation. Usually the nature of the devolution has left the HR function responsible for policy. In many organisations this is formulated in consultation with line management, and it is possible to develop a convincing argument for expanding this practice. The conclusion of the researchers is that the strategic, proactive and consultancy role of HR will expand, although responsibility for much of its implementation will pass to the line.

If this conclusion proves to be correct, and it seems a reasonable assumption given the extensive evidence from the research, HR will find it increasingly necessary to apply methods of strategic analysis and decision making which can be explained to and debated with others, which are rooted in an understanding of both the business and the HR implications of various options, and which call for additional competencies from HR specialists. It is one thing to be familiar with employment law and advise on procedures and actions which keep the employer out of the court room. It is quite a different competency to be able to look at an issue such as delayering, with an understanding of how the change will affect what managers and people have to do, and then translate the issue into matters of training, performance management, reward systems, and the like. It is this task of understanding the difference between an old and a new situation in all its human aspects, and developing proactive HR strategies to help the organisation to succeed that I saw as the area of relative failure in many of the organisations in the Tovey, 1991 and Mason, 1993 surveys. Yet it is this type of ability which will determine whether HR is a value adding activity in the organisation of tomorrow, and to a large degree whether the organisation of today survives long enough to have a future.

REFERENCES

Brewster, C., 1993, *The Integration of Human Resource Management and Corporate Strategy*, paper presented to the British Academy of Management Conference, 1993.

Brewster, C. and Mayne, L., 1995, European Comparisons, in *Personnel and the Line*, London: Institute of Personnel Development.

Hutchinson, S. and Wood, S., 1995, The U.K. Experience, in *Personnel and the Line*, London: Institute of Personnel Development.

Mason, A., 1993, *Management Training in Medium-sized U.K. Business Organisations*, London: Harbridge Consulting Group.

PWC, 1991, *The Price Waterhouse Project on International Strategic Human Resource Management*, Bedford: Centre for Human Resource Management, Cranfield University School of Management.

Tovey, L., 1991, *Management Training and Development in Large U.K. Business Organisations*, London: Harbridge Consulting Group.

Tovey, L., 1996, The Changing Business Environment and its Impact on Employer/Employee Contracts, *Croner's Journal of Professional HRM*, 1:4, July.

6
A Strategic Approach to Competencies

A business driven approach to HRM is more than a matter of muttering the right sounding words in the boardroom. To work properly it has to apply detailed and practical approaches to various aspects of HRM. The case studies of Chapter 4 gave examples of some of the detail. The next few chapters will offer guidance on helping to make the application of the business driven concept a practical reality. The starting point is an approach to competencies.

Competencies themselves are an enabling tool: they do not do anything unless they are related to other aspects of management or HRM. They can provide an underpinning for such things as recruitment, development, assessment, reward and performance management. They may help an organisation to maintain or change culture.

Starting here, therefore, makes sense, although I do not wish to imply that a business driven approach *must* build on the foundations of competencies. I think the jury is still out on whether they offer the right approach in practice, for they also bring disadvantages. However I would argue very strongly that if competencies are to be used, they will only be fully effective if they are based on the strategic situation of the business. Any other approach to competencies may prevent HRM from becoming business driven.

WHAT ARE COMPETENCIES?

Tovey, 1992, defines a competency as *the application of a blend of knowledge, skills and behaviours in the context of individual job performance*. The concept is not new, although it has gained a new emphasis in recent years. Accelerated interest began in the UK with the publication of an extensive and careful report into management development by Constable and McCormick, 1987. This stimulated much debate and action, some of it beneficial, and provided the stimulus for the formation of a new organisation called the Management Charter Initiative (MCI). This organisation put much of its efforts into developing the competency approach, and has published books of competencies for various levels of management. These competencies are intended to "provide a basis against which managers may be assessed, their performance improved, and their skills more effectively utilised".

I believe that the MCI have done much good work in demonstrating the use of competencies, and making the concept more widely known. However the main thrust of their work, the definition of competencies on a generic basis for various levels of management is, in my opinion, misconceived. There are too many situational factors which are specific to an organisation and which affect the key competencies required for success.

MCI have published a number of competencies for levels of management, of which those referenced are examples (Management Charter Initiative 1991a, 1991b and 1992). The generic approach is useful for persons designing open educational programmes, although even this can bring problems unless students are also taught the flexibility needed to adjust for specific situations. There may also be value in a generic approach for the lowest level of management, supervisory, on the grounds that the situation of the organisation has much less impact on how the job is done at this level. Even this assumption may be threatened by flexible work practices and trends to greater empowerment. For example an organisation which embraces the concept of self-managed teams will require different competencies from its supervisors, than one that operates in a more traditional manner (see, for example, Manz and Sims, 1993).

The five headings MCI uses to define competencies have considerable usefulness.

1 *Units of competence:* the broad descriptions of what is expected from a competent person at each level.
2 *Elements of competence:* a breakdown of the units.
3 *Performance criteria:* which specify the outcomes which have to be achieved for competent performance.
4 *Range statements:* which describe the range of instances and circumstances in which the element is applied.
5 *Evidence specifications:* the evidence which is required to show that competence is achieved.

WHY COMPETENCIES SHOULD BE BUSINESS DRIVEN

Even when two organisations are of roughly the same size and operate in the same industry it is most unlikely that the management competencies will be the same for them both. The differences will tend to get bigger, the more senior the level of management. Some examples may help make these points clear.

● Two consulting firms offer strategic management services. One operates in the traditional way, defining the problem, collecting the information, analysing, and producing a detailed report with recommendations for solving the problem. Staffing is usually with a large team that may work full time for several weeks on the project. The other firm works in a knowledge transfer way. Some of the steps that have to be gone through are similar, except that where possible the client's employees will be shown how to undertake the tasks and helped to do this. No recommendations will be written up, as a report, but the top management team will be helped to work through the evidence collected, and reach its own conclusions, the consultant's role here being to ensure that all the critical issues are considered. The project is likely to be staffed with one or two people, and may extend over many months but in a part-time role. It is not only what the client is offered which is different, it is the way in which each consultancy has to deal with the management of its own operations.

- Two grocery firms operate across Europe. One uses a concept of country companies, each of which is totally responsible for all aspects of the business, makes its own decisions about products and how they are marketed, and operates its own factory. Head office coordinates and exercises financial control. The second manages Europe as one market, and most of the product and marketing concepts are decided centrally. Production for the whole of Europe comes out of three plants in various countries which are seen as one strategic unit. Country managing directors have less strategic freedom than those of the first company, and are responsible for the local management of the central concepts. Would you expect the senior managers in Head Office and each country to need the same competencies to do their jobs?

- One engineering company involves employees at all levels. It follows a team briefing approach to aid two-way communication, it has a successful, cross functional, team approach to continuous improvement, and has created a culture which encourages innovation throughout the organisation. The other company believes that managers should manage and that others should be involved as little as possible. It manages by a carrot and stick approach, and the chief executive will not tolerate any questions about his decisions. Innovation is the role of the Board. The company has a phobia about sharing information on its results and plans, disclosing only what is legally necessary, and works on the philosophy that if employees want to know the results they can turn up the annual report when it has been lodged at Companies' House. Here totally internal preferences for the way each of these companies manage mean that a manager who changes employment between the two companies and tries to apply the competencies that had hitherto brought career success, would probably be dysfunctional in the new job.

There are many other reasons why competencies will vary between organisations. These include the degree of turbulence the organisation faces in its business environment (an issue already discussed), the extent to which the organisation operates internationally, and the position on the life cycle of its products.

If you believe in the generic approach, you will not accept my next point. One of the potential weaknesses of the competency approach is that the critical competencies are not static. As the organisation and its competitive situation changes, so there is a need to revisit the schedules of competencies which were defined for an earlier situation.

Conceptually this is not a problem. The reality comes in practice, in that defining the competencies in the first place will have been relatively expensive in management and staff time, and may have involved the use of outside consultants. What the organisation wants is a period during which the competencies can be used, and a return obtained on the effort that went into defining them. However what is desired, and what the real situation is, may be two very different things, and wishful thinking will not create reality. Some form of regular review of the competencies is therefore essential, for failure to do this can mean that all the internal HR processes are driving people to manage in a way that is no longer appropriate for the success of the organisation. Of course the competencies will rarely be totally wrong, and it may be that only a few should change. But those few may be critical for the organisation.

DEFINING BUSINESS DRIVEN COMPETENCIES

Deciding that competencies are a good approach is the easy part of the problem. The hard task is to define competencies in a way that makes sense for the organisation. The feature of a business driven approach is that it should start at senior level and cascade down the organisation. Figure 6.1 offers a model to show how to set about this task. It is a modification of Figure 3.4 (page 46), amended to fit the task in hand. A brief description of the model will be given, to be followed by more detail on how the key elements in the second level of the model might be approached in practice. The methods for the first level of the model were discussed in Chapter 3, and

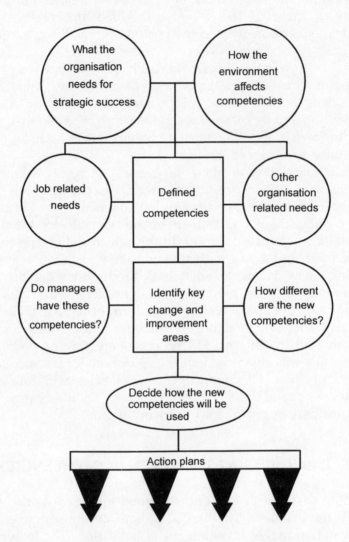

Figure 6.1   Business driven competencies

those for levels 3, 4 and 5 will either be picked up later in the book, or are a matter of common sense which need little elaboration.

The starting point is the vision and strategy of the organisation. This is an issue which was fully discussed in

Chapter 3, and does not need to be repeated here, except to make the point that the impact of the strategic elements may vary between areas of the organisation, and is certain to affect the various management levels in different ways. Although there will be a lot of common ground, the process described here has to be repeated for each level and area, so that we end up identifying what is relevant both for the business and for the jobs of the managers concerned.

In the general strategic HR model of Figure 3.4, the environmental step referred to issues which would impact on HR policies and strategies. This aspect will become important as we begin to use competencies, but for the definition of competencies we are concerned with another aspect of the environment. This is the amount and rapidity of change that the organisation must cope with. It is advisable to ensure that the competencies include those that enable managers to deal with this degree of change, even though the specific changes themselves cannot be forecast. In Ansoff's terms (see Chapter 2) we should be concerned about how the organisation's position on the scale of turbulence affects the competencies needed to manage the organisation in the most effective way.

With the information so far analysed we are ready to move to the next level of the model. The heart of this level is the definition of competencies, but we cannot get to these without going through the two steps shown in the circles on either side, and even when we have the draft definitions there will be some necessary review steps before we can feel confident that they are not only sound, but also meaningful to key people in the organisation.

It would be unrealistic to imply that every element of every job was a) affected by what the organisation was trying to do, and b) could be defined by a top level analysis of business needs. There is a need therefore to bring into the equation knowledge about each job for which we are trying to define competencies. This is what is indicated in the left hand circle. There are four elements to the job-related needs: professional, technical, personal and managerial. I will return to these, and to methods that can be used to work through this step after I have described the whole approach.

The right hand circle shows some of the organisational

influences on the competencies. One of these is the culture of the organisation, and this box may be particularly important if the competency initiative is related to changing the culture. It remains important even if the intention is to maintain the culture. The Premier Bank example in Chapter 4 illustrated the impact of climate on the way managers manage those under them, and also that when it is important to do so, the management behaviours can be measured. A second important area is the levels in the organisation that are to be covered by the competency exercise. This may increase in importance if the organisation is delayering, because information from those who understand the current jobs may have little relationship to the way jobs have to be performed after delayering. It follows that the organisation-related needs circle may hide a large number of tasks in some situations, and be relatively simple in others.

The centre box holds three subtasks:

- Assess the strategic areas of competence which emerge from the first level of our model. This is a critical part of the whole task.
- Produce composite definitions of competency from the job requirements, the strategic needs, and the organisation-related needs.
- Establish a way of reviewing the composite competencies with senior managers, so that the resultant definitions are owned by management and not just by HRM.

In level three of the model the core task is to assess the key change and improvement areas which emerge from the newly defined competencies. The simplest task which is to assess how the new competencies differ from the previous ones, is shown in the right hand circle. There are two key considerations here.

- If there are some competencies which are new and important, but which do not fundamentally alter the way people are expected to fulfil their jobs, there will probably be a need to consider some company wide training to ease them into the new requirement.

- If jobs are dramatically different from in the past, there will be a strong case for mounting a full scale change programme, both to build commitment to the new concepts, and to ensure that the managers have both the understanding of what is required and the capability to deliver it. This situation is particularly likely if there has been a major change of direction by the organisation, such as a complete shift of business concept as in the new NHS, a major delayering exercise, or a new emphasis, such as a stronger commitment to customer satisfaction.

The left hand circle asks whether the managers possess the competencies that have been defined. This is a multilayered question. For competencies which are new to the organisation, it may be enough at this stage for a panel of senior managers to make an assessment which is based on a collective view rather than one built up from an aggregation of more objective assessments of individuals. Or it may be desirable to ask the groups of managers used in earlier phases of the work to give their opinions. If quick, usable data is needed it may be worth undertaking a survey among managers of the extent to which they feel proficient in the key competency areas for their jobs.

Other methods of assessment, such as links with the performance management system, or the use of assessment centres, are longer term in their impact and relate to the decisions on how competencies are to be used.

More attention will be given to assessment in Chapter 7, which deals with management development.

The box in the centre of this level calls for identification of the key change and improvement areas that should be considered in the next stage of the model. It will not be possible to identify everything at this point in the proceedings, but it is essential to have some order of magnitude ideas about how the competencies will impact the organisation. In this task I should also include looking at whether any HR or management policies act against the effective use of the competencies, such as a pay system which rewards behaviour which would run counter to the competencies (for example rewarding individual success while demanding teamwork through the competencies).

The next level, illustrated by the ellipse, should not be completely new thinking. One would hope that some thought had been given to the purpose for which competencies were being defined before committing to a lengthy exercise. However, the aims and what eventually emerges are not always the same, and in any case new factors may arise from the study itself, such as realisation that the original intention to use competencies for management development purposes would not be viable unless attention were also given to some of the other HR procedures. This level of the model is concerned with the policies which will lie behind the final level: the setting of detailed action plans to enable the defined competencies to be properly applied.

COMPETENCY DEFINITION IN MORE DETAIL

Level 2 of Figure 6.1 showed three blocks of activity in the definition of competencies. In a real situation these broad headings have to be brought to life. Not only is there a lot of work to be done, but there are also alternative approaches that could be used for some of the phases. The concern with what the business needs should pervade each of the three phases shown on this level of the figure.

Job Related Needs / Organisation Related Needs

I start with the left and right circles at the second level of Figure 6.1. For practical purposes, a large part of the work under these two headings can be undertaken simultaneously, and the detailed methods described below do this. However, there are some additional issues to establish about the organisation-related needs, which are described before the common elements are considered.

You will recall that the right hand circle of level 2 of Figure 6.1 was meant to cover some rather specific organisational needs, such as those related to the structure and the culture of the organisation. There is of course a strong link with the strategic needs which emerge in the centre box at this level of the diagram. In most situations a useful starting point is the structure of the organisation. Published organisation charts give some information, but these need to be probed by discussion with senior managers, to establish the following:

- Whether the charts are about to be changed. There is little point in starting the analysis from the basis of the chart, if the intention is to remove layers from the organisation, which will affect jobs and alter the levels for which competencies should be established.
- The degree of formality in the organisation, and the nature of the various mechanisms for linkage across organisational units. How the lines and boxes on the paper are converted to day to day working relationships is closely related to the style of management, and the culture of the organisation. Trying to assess competencies without understanding the implications of the organisation's structure will lead to the omission of key areas of competency.
- The scope of the various business units within the organisation.

Culture can only be assessed in a crude way through discussion with managers. Very often it is easy to test the degree to which the culture and value statements issued from the top are seen as meaningful throughout the organisation, but getting beyond this in objective terms requires harder evidence. The issue is more important when there is a gap between what the top management believe the organisation needs, and what the culture really is, and when this happens evidence, in some form of survey, may be very important, and not only for the competency exercise. When British Petroleum began its change initiative, *Project 1990*, it was clear that the existing structure and culture would be altered. In a situation such as this, any competencies defined would only be meaningful if they were related to the planned new BP. What managers said about their jobs could only be established through a knowledge of both the old and the new.

An early decision in the competency exercise is whether this part of the work should begin with a survey. It is not sensible to be dogmatic, and argue that it always should begin in this way, because much depends on the situation inside the organisation. When the competencies are being defined during a major change situation, the need for objective information about both the old and the intended cultures may become imperative. In another organisation, where there is a more stable situation, managers may have a very good feel for the culture, and survey data may be an unnecessary luxury.

Figure 6.1 shows what the organisation needs to achieve for strategic success, and any specific environmental influences should be taken into account in the tasks described here. The business driven concept flows through the detailed descriptions that follow.

The next few pages are not my own work, although I had a role in what is described here. The section consists of extracts from a report by Tovey, 1992.* This was one of a series of research studies which I instigated during my spell as managing director of Harbridge Consulting Group Ltd. The extracts are used with the permission of Coopers & Lybrand, who now own the copyright.

Laura Tovey organised her description around two methods, first discussing what they are, and then going on to show a series of tools and how these might be used with each.

EXTRACTS FROM *COMPETENCY ASSESSMENT: A STRATEGIC APPROACH* (Tovey, 1992)*

There are two main approaches for identifying [job related] competency requirements: Job Analysis and Repertory Grid.

JOB ANALYSIS (the steps are shown in Figure 6.2)

Job analysis is a structured interview approach which identifies job related competencies through a process of breaking a particular job down into its principal tasks.

---

*Harbridge Consulting Group Ltd, London, 1992. Reproduced by permission from Coopers & Lybrand.

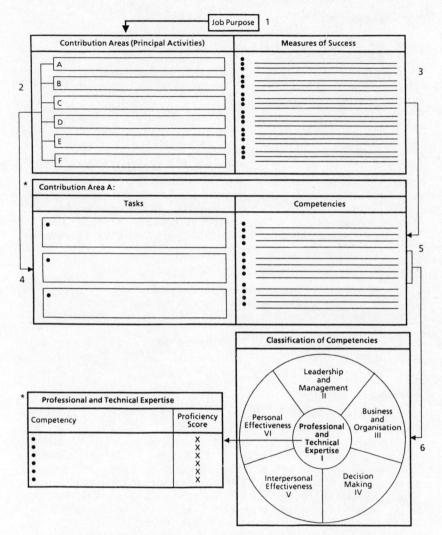

*Each contribution area and competency classification is expanded separately.

Figure 6.2 *Job analysis approach.*

Job purpose

Step one is concerned with defining the purpose of an individual's job, in no more than one or two sentences. It should be specific to the job and say why that job is essential to the activity and hence the company.

For example:

- **Job position:** regional director, Tax Operations
- **Job purpose:** To manage the relationship between Tax Operations and National Tax managers in order to realise the overall tax objective of minimising tax liability, thereby maximising shareholder value for the organisation.

Contribution areas

At step two, the contribution areas are identified. The contribution areas are the principal activities which together ensure the achievement of the job purpose. There should not be more than 4–6 of these in any one job. If appropriate, they can be categorised into core areas and support areas.

Using the example of the position of regional director, Tax Operations, the contribution areas making up the job might include:

A. *Compliance:* for countries within the region.
B. *Advisory:* to local and international businesses.
C. *Team resource planning/management:* for regional international team.
D. *Budgeting and planning:* of regional plans as input into overall tax plan.
E. *Lobbying:* of international tax authorities with regard to company and industry related interests.

Measures of Success

Step three in Figure 6.2 is about identifying measures which indicate success. They can be quantitative or qualitative in the form of standards, although it can sometimes be difficult to identify quantitative measures for certain types of job. A quantitative measure might be "meeting a business development target of £300,000", while a qualitative measure might be (in the case of a tax department employee) "Business people seeking the advice of the tax department at the outset of a project".

By defining contribution areas with measures of success specific objectives can be established. As an example, the contribution areas for the position of regional director, Tax Operations in one particular organisation are shown below, in parallel with possible measures of success.

Contribution Areas	Measures of Success
A. *Compliance*	- The quality/accuracy of the computations. - Meeting compliance deadlines.
B. *Advisory*	- Client problems are solved.

- Clients come back to the regional team to ask for advice.
- Tax liabilities within this region are prioritised.

C. *Team resource* *planning/management*
- Specific and meaningful objectives for national tax managers.
- Equitable allocation of regional resources.
- Team works together to achieve region's objectives.

D. *Budgeting and planning*
- Challenges for region are properly identified.
- One-year and three-year forecasts are accurately made.
- Plans provide correct direction and input into planning process for world-wide tax function.

E. *Lobbying*
- Positive contacts with the right people are established.
- Company and industry maintains a high and positive profile

Tasks

In step four each contribution area is taken in turn and its constituent tasks—those which need to be performed to meet the objectives—are specified. Two examples using the same job position are provided below:

Contribution Areas

Tasks

A. *Compliance*
- To assume ultimate responsibility for all compliance work in each country under the region's authority.
- To allocate sufficient resources to accomplish compliance.
- To participate as a member of a number of international tax teams giving the benefit of personal knowledge when necessary.

B. *Advisory*
- To provide advice to international businesses within the region on issues such as the structure of projects and companies, joint venture agreements, mergers and acquisitions.
- To set up advisory teams and assign team responsibilities.

Competencies

The final step (stages 5 and 6) involves deriving the knowledge, skills and behaviours required to perform each of the tasks listed for the job. The essential and desired competencies required for the job can thus be clearly stated. They need to be specific to both the organisation and the job ("Decisiveness", for example, may be seen differently in different organisations). Specific definitions should be given so that the employee understands exactly what is needed to perform the job at the level required.

The task-related competencies can be grouped under appropriate headings such as:

- Professional and Technical
- Leadership and Management
- Business and Organisation
- Decision Making
- Interpersonal Effectiveness
- Personal Effectiveness.

The above examples will vary from organisation to organisation as will their interpretation. Individual competencies should be classified into clusters which are meaningful to the organisation concerned. Examination of different companies' classifications reveals that similar competencies are often grouped under different headings or may well appear in more than one category.

The key point to make is that the classification should follow the systematic identification of competency requirements and that these should be grouped in a way that reflects common patterns and makes sense for the organisation concerned. In particular, too much complexity and over-detailed descriptions should be avoided to ensure that individuals can easily relate to the end result.

In our work with clients in this area, and based on our review of other contributions, it is apparent that business-related competencies have tended to be underemphasised compared to personal and managerial competencies. Expressing such competencies in behavioural terms may be more difficult but is certainly as important as the latter, around which much of the general work has been undertaken.

REPERTORY GRID

Repertory grid is a popular and highly adaptable method of deriving data for analysis through interviews or questionnaires. Its usefulness in competency assessment stems from its rigorous elicitation structure which is designed to get to the heart of particular issues and behaviours. The repertory grid itself is a matrix containing "elements" on one axis and "constructs" on the other.

Elements

Once the situation under investigation has been defined (in this case, an example might be "What are the key competencies required to succeed in job X in company Y?") a number of elements must be identified. An element in repertory grid terms is any thing or event which can be evaluated. In the competency assessment example given above, suitable elements might be "Someone who does job X well", "Someone who does job X badly", "Someone who used to do job X but has now moved on" and so forth. It does not matter if each respondent thinks of a different individual when presented with these elements: the important thing is that Element A, for example, is always "someone who does job X well".

Constructs

A construct is an individual's abstract concept of the way in which people, things and events are different from or similar to each other. In order to be meaningful, a construct needs to be "polar" in nature: in other words, to say someone is "a good timekeeper" could mean different things to different individuals, depending on their own standards of timekeeping. If an individual was asked to define someone who was not a good timekeeper, they might identify someone who was consistently half an hour late; another individual might identify someone who was occasionally five minutes late for a meeting. It is this opposite pole which creates a construct that is meaningful in individual terms. We have here created two distinct constructs: "Good timekeeper—Always half an hour late" as distinct from "Good timekeeper—Occasionally late".

One way of eliciting constructs is to ask the interviewee to compare two elements and think of a way in which they are similar to each other, but different from a third element. The interviewer must ensure that the interviewee carries out this process in the context of the original situation definition (which in our example is "What are the key competencies required to succeed in job X?"). The interviewee might compare "Someone who does job X well" and "Someone who used to do job X" and decide that they are both good communicators, whereas "Someone who does job X badly" is not.

To arrive at a polar construct, the interviewee would be asked to define the way in which the latter individual is not a good communicator. The response might be that he or she is lacking in confidence. Provided the interviewer has been rigorous enough in enforcing the company context in which the constructs are elicited, we now have a competency construct: "Good communicator—Lacking in confidence", which tells us more about communication skills as they are perceived in this particular company than would the broad competency requirement "Good communication skills".

STRATEGIC AREAS OF COMPETENCE

The interviewing technique required for generating meaningful constructs is as much an art as a science. The interviewer, as mentioned above, needs to be alert to the potential usefulness of the constructs being generated, and in particular how relevant they are to the strategic areas of competence. One interviewing technique for deriving this information is a technique known as "laddering", in which a series of Why? questions are asked in a process which aims to uncover corporate values.

So an interviewee offering the example competency "Good communicator—Lacking in confidence" would be asked: "*Why* is it important in Company Y to be a confident communicator?" When the interviewee gives a reason, the interviewer can again ask "and *why* is that important?" and so on. For example, good (or, in this case, confident) communication skills ultimately might be important because the company wants to project an "upbeat" image to visitors and external customers. This is getting close to a core value of the company, and could, with further clarification, be identified as a strategic area of competence.

Competency Requirements

If the constructs generated during the interview do not seem specific enough—that is, they do not seem to strike at the heart of the key behaviours observed in job X—a further interviewing technique known as "pyramiding" can be employed. In this technique, the question is not *why?* but *how?* or *what?* The interviewer might ask: "How do you get to be a good communicator?" or "What would I see you doing if you were communicating well?" This line of questioning can elicit more specific examples of the knowledge, skills and behaviours required to perform effectively in job X or job category X.

TOOLS USED TO AID JOB ANALYSIS AND/OR REPERTORY GRID

There are a number of tools which can aid the process of job and repertory grid analysis and therefore help to clearly identify and define the competency requirements.

1. Structured Interviews

Job Analysis

These can be conducted on a one-to-one basis using a structured interview guide to ensure consistency across the sample population.
The interview guide might include, for example, the following areas:

- Background to the assignment.
- The individual's understanding of the organisation's mission and strategic direction.
- External factors which are likely to have an impact on the business in

the foreseeable future, such as:

—environment
—industry
—competition.
● The individual's perception of the critical success factors in his/her industry.

Repertory Grid

The structured interview is the heart of the repertory grid process. It is the primary method of eliciting the constructs which will form the basis of an overall competency assessment. A competency audit using repertory grid might start with approximately ten face-to-face interviews, which would each produce perhaps ten constructs. Laddering and pyramiding techniques would elicit further information as previously described.

Following the interview the consultant, in conjunction or consultation with the client, must review the constructs produced from all the interviews and decide if any can be combined or superseded. This final list of competency constructs would then be taken to the next stage of the assessment process.

2. Focus groups

Job Analysis

A focus group is defined as a facilitated discussion between a number of individuals around specific issues. In competency assessment its purpose is:

● to understand the impact of the strategic areas of competence on an individual's job;
● to identify common perceptions about organisation and job-related requirements;
● to compare and contrast individuals' responses concerning the identification of competency requirements and clarify the reasons for any differences.

It should be noted that the success of a focus group is determined by a number of factors. These may seem simple and obvious, but their importance should not be underestimated:

1   *The size of the focus group.* Between six and eight individuals is the ideal size. Larger groups of individuals are often ineffective. If there are too many people in a group too many issues may be raised, making it harder to control the discussion.
2   *The calibre and commitment of each individual.* An understanding of the project's purpose and a willingness to participate are all important. Particular care should be taken when communicating the

purpose of the assignment to avoid any misunderstandings. Participants must feel that the end result will benefit both the individual and the organisation. This results in a willingness to provide information.

3   *The logistics*:
—Meeting rooms should be located away from the managers' own offices.
—A round table, in a suitably sized room, helps to encourage non-confrontational discussion.

4   *The amount of preparation undertaken.* Both the consultants facilitating the discussion and the participants should prepare for the event:
—The more thought the participants have given to the issues, the more productive the discussion.
—The better the planning of the focus group by the consultants, the more relevant the information that is gained.

Well organised and professionally facilitated focus groups can be an effective and cost-effective vehicle for gaining information about job and organisation related requirements.

Repertory Grid

If time is short, or a large organisation is being studied, the process of construct elicitation described earlier can be carried out within focus groups containing a representative sample of the employee population. The process of construct elicitation is essentially the same, but each construct requires agreement by the team as to its relevance. This provides a simultaneous process of validation which may allow the consultant to reach faster decisions on which competency constructs are most meaningful to the organisation.

Focus groups can also be used to prioritise competencies already derived from face-to-face interviews. For example, presented with a grid containing elements representing different jobs within the organisation, and the competency constructs generated in the interviews, the group can be asked to rate each construct in terms of its relevance to each element. This allows competencies to be clustered in a way which illustrates how general or specific the organisation's requirements for them are.

3. Structured Workbooks

Job Analysis

The purpose of the workbook is to aid the individual interviews and/or the focus group. Depending on the nature of the assignment, it will not always be necessary. Issued in advance, the workbook helps to prepare individuals for the forthcoming discussions, as many of them will be unaccustomed to thinking through the precise way they carry out their jobs, and the demands the organisation places on them.

A large number of managers take many of the tasks they perform on a daily basis for granted, and therefore may have a tendency to overlook some of them. For example, asking candidates to list the main internal and external relationships in their job focuses attention on the nature of the tasks they perform and can provide detailed information.

The workbook also provides detailed back-up information for analysis both before and after the interview or focus group. The workbook may be structured to encourage employees to think about some of the following areas:

- *Organisation requirements*
  —The organisation-wide or corporate requirements in the context of the mission
  —Organisation-specific or company requirements.
  —Key contribution areas and competencies required by the activity to which the individual belongs.
- *Job requirements*
  —Job title and grade
  —Job purpose
  —Key contribution areas
  —Measures of success.
  —Input analysis: what are the main inputs (information, resources, etc) provided by other people or activities (boss, subordinates, colleagues, other departments, external etc)?
  —Output analysis: what are the main outputs, (verbal advice, reports, information etc) produced for other parties, (internal clients, other departments, businesses etc)?
  —Task analysis
  —Career pathing
  —Qualifications and experience.

The contents of the workbook will depend on the culture of the organisation and nature of the assignment.

The workbook can be used for additional purposes, for example:

- Testing employees' perceptions about certain job roles.
- Identification of organisational or cultural blockages which may inhibit either the fulfilment of specific individuals' job specifications or the effective implementation of change and management development programmes.

Repertory grid

A structured workbook, or questionnaire, can be used as the final stage in a competency assessment based on repertory grid analysis. Once the constructs have been finalised, and the elements decided upon (for example, are respondents being asked to compare different individuals doing the same job, or the same competency being used in different jobs?) respondents can be sent a standard workbook asking them to complete one or more grids.

The results of this can be used in a focus group, or analysed by

114

Table 6.1 Part of a matrix analysis of competencies needed (illustrative only).

| Strategic Sources | | Broad Areas Of Competency | | | | | |
Type	Need	Market Planning	Cultural Differences	Negotiation Skills	Alliance Management	Performance Management	Project Management
Vision	Global	X	X				X
	Customer Responsive						
Strategies	European Expansion	X	X	X			X
	Delayering		X				X
	Strategic Alliance			X	X		
Values	People Centred				X		
	Integrity				X		
	Empowered People				X		
Objective	Double Market. Share	X					
	25% P.A. Revenue Growth	X					
	25% Return on Capital Employed	X					

computer (depending on the size of the sample) to provide such information as: How important is a particular competency to a particular job? How many people perceive the competency to be important? To what extent is a particular competency perceived as essential in more than one job or area of the organisation? The answers to these questions can be represented diagrammatically, allowing discrete competencies to be evaluated at a glance in terms of relevance or applicability.

Defined Competencies

The methods here are easier to describe, but this simplicity conceals the need for careful interpretation and thought. A suggested approach is given for each of the three steps.

Assess Strategic Areas of Competency

I find it helpful to construct a matrix, which has strategic drivers on the vertical axis, and competency implications on the horizontal axis. Table 6.1 gives an illustrative example of such a matrix. At this point the horizontal axis shows broad clusters of competencies, which will require expansion.

The example is deliberately short, and I have shown only one or two items from each strategic source. Sources are the organisation's vision, the specific strategies, the values of the organisation (which could have been part of the vision, and in effect are a partial definition of actual/desired culture), and specific objectives. The item core competences is a little confusing, as it relates to Prahalad and Hamel, 1990, and the concept that strategic success is based on the ability to apply a bundle of technologies and skills to a corporate competence that gives the organisation leadership. They argue, for example, that Honda's core competence is know-how in engines. In HR terms there may be many management competencies which lie behind the core competences of the organisation. An alternative, and older concept, is the idea of the critical success factors for the organisation: the things it has to do well in in order to continue to succeed. This forms part of the approach described in Tovey, 1992.

Where possible, the terms used in the vertical axis should relate to those used in the organisation in its strategic thinking. There is no value in insisting on the word *vision*, if inside the organisation the word used is *mission*. If the organisation does not subscribe to the concept of core competence, it might be better to use the critical success factors approach. If values and vision are combined in whole or part under the heading culture, it makes more sense to follow this heading.

In a complex, multi-business unit organisation, particularly if the businesses are unrelated, it would be necessary to repeat this exercise for each business unit, as it would be extremely complicated to show the whole organisation on one comprehensible matrix. Before doing this, it would be useful to develop a matrix to cover the things which are common to the whole organisation. For example many of the values may apply to all, as well as certain underlying principles such as a determination to be a world class operator.

Table 6.1 will also be used in the next chapter where its application will be developed further.

Produce Composite Definitions of Competency

The next step, once the main strategic elements have been captured, is to relate this matrix to the detailed definitions of competencies which are emerging from the parallel activities. Initially this requires a comparison, starting at the top levels, of the provisional competencies and the strategic matrix. What has been omitted or underemphasised, and what amendments appear to be necessary to these competencies? Again a matrix analysis may be useful, this time listing the specific competencies that fall under each of the broader headings of the initial matrix.

This needs to be repeated for each of the levels for which competencies are being defined. It is useful at this stage to assign priorities to each competence for each of the levels. This can be done by a simple rating on a 1–3 scale. It becomes useful to help focus any actions based on the competencies to the areas where they have the most impact.

Although the person conducting the competency exercise should extract as much as possible through analysis, this should not be the final source of judgement and information. I recommend the use of focus groups of senior managers to validate and add to what the analytical process suggests. If several focus groups are used, there may well be some differences of judgement where a choice still has to be made, but these differences can be identified for attention in the review stage.

Establish a Review Procedure

Review with senior management is a critical stage, but needs to pass through various steps. The first is to gain agreement to the competencies required for the highest levels of the organisation. This is a precondition for reviewing the lower levels, as these are influenced by what senior management sees as the business imperative. To review the lower levels first, and then find that what is seen as critical for business success has changed, could cause a loss of credibility. Ideally the review of the proposed competencies should be undertaken by a meeting of all the top level managers, although in a large organisation it may be necessary to delegate this task to a smaller steering group.

Once the higher levels have been agreed attention should be given to reviewing the lower levels through a series of panels of managers drawn from the level being reviewed and from their direct managers.

After completion of this process, the whole package should be presented to the top management group for approval.

REFERENCES

Constable, J. and McCormick, R., 1987, *The Making of British Managers*, London: British Institute of Managers.

Management Charter Initiative, 1991a, *Occupational Standards for Managers, Management I and Assessment Guidance*, London: MCI.

Management Charter Initiative, 1991b, *Occupational Standards for Managers, Management II and Assessment Guidance*, London: MCI.

Management Charter Initiative, 1992, *Management Standards, Supervisory Management Standards*, London: MCI.

Manz, C. C. and Sims, H. P., 1993, *Business without Bosses*, New York: John Wiley.

Prahalad, C. K. and Hamel, G., 1990, The Core Competence of the Corporation, *Harvard Business Review*, May–June.

Tovey, L., 1992, *Competency Assessment: A Strategic Approach*, London: Harbridge Consulting Group Ltd.

7
Management Development

Competencies offer one route into business driven management development, but are neither the only option nor do they solve all the issues. The model described here assumes that a competency approach is not being used, but all stages are relevant in any case, except that some aspects of the approach will have been undertaken already. Those organisations which use the business driven competency approach will have already covered some of the steps in the first two levels of the model, although some new insight will be offered here.

The traditional way in which organisations have approached the task of deciding management development priorities, plans and programmes has tended to focus mainly on the development of the individual. Figure 7.1 illustrates this process in a general way, although of course there are variations on this theme. Corporate influence is exercised in two ways: the budgetary process limits expenditure, and budgets have tended to move up and down, with training treated as a discretionary item without great corporate impact. Good words are often said about the value of training, but the reality is that control is exercised on the spend, and not how the money is spent. In theory, line managers' assessments of individual development needs will relate to company needs: in practice the manager making the assessment may have only a narrow perception of these, particularly when situations are changing. The result of this approach is that the development

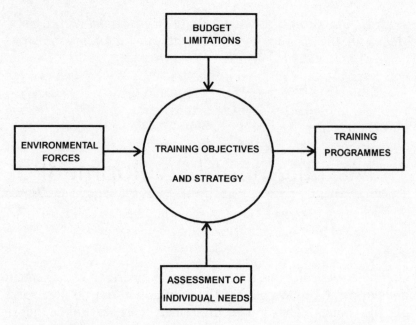

Figure 7.1   *The traditional approach to training strategy.*

initiatives available rarely meet the real priorities of the organisation, and even when the topics are right, their positioning and context may be wrong. Many organisations fail to ensure that those individuals, at any level of seniority, who need the training most actually receive it, and there is often an emphasis on training the lower levels, although it is those nearer the top who may be moving into, what is for them, uncharted waters as a result of strategic changes. Management development policy is often poorly defined, and in any case is not easy to formulate from the information available.

The Premier Foods case in Chapter 4 provides one example of how a different approach led to different management development outcomes, both in terms of the formulation of a credible policy that contributed to business success, and in the training and development actions that followed. Although it is possible, and sometimes worthwhile, to move to a business driven training initiative, such as that in the Otis Elevator case, a preferable position is to determine a business driven

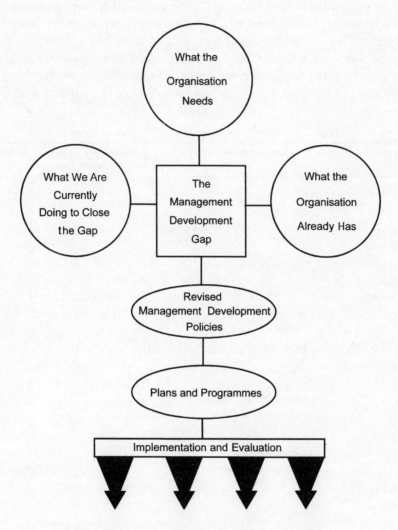

Figure 7.2   *Business driven management development.*

management development policy, which aids the setting of priorities and decisions on how specific needs will be met. Figure 7.2 illustrates this process, in a style which will already be familiar.

"What the Organisation Needs"

Once again the model starts with the needs of the organisation. The process for obtaining the necessary information about company vision, values, strategy and culture has already been described, and will not be repeated. Using that information to determine corporate management development needs is a different thing, and I should like to build on the matrix which

Table 7.1　*Getting to grips with organisational needs.*

Strategy	Corporate Need	Priorities by Level of Management		
		1	2	3
Euro Expansion				
	New Needs			
	Specific Country Knowledge		A	B
	Intercultural Differences	A	A	A
	World Class Manufacturing	C	B	A
	Market Planning	A	A	B
	Expanded Needs			
	Project Planning		C	A
	Visionary Leadership	A	A	C
Delayering	*New Needs*			
	Empowerment	A	A	A
	Career Management		A	
	Outsourcing Skills	A	A	B
	Internal Corporate Communication	A	B	
	Change Management	A	A	A
	Expanded Needs			
	Performance Management	A	A	A
	Situational Leadership		C	B
	Interpersonal Communication	A	A	A
Strategic Alliance	*New Needs*			
	Financial Assessment	A	A	C
	Managing Alliances	A	A	B
	Understanding Cultural Differences	A	A	A
	Expanded Needs			
	Evaluating Operational Performance	A	A	C
	Visionary Leadership	A	A	C

was presented in Table 6.1 (see page 116). This table began to develop the topics that could be determined from the various strategic drivers. In Table 7.1 I have developed the example further, taking three of the strategies, and looked at a few more of the topic areas which could be important. The three strategy headings might, in a more expanded form, appear in the format shown in Table 7.1.

- *European expansion*: the organisation has hitherto limited its activities to the UK. Over the past year it has completed a number of market studies, and now intends to set up operations, over a period of time, in all other major countries in Europe. The strategy will roll out over five years, and a priority order has been established so that the organisation can learn from experience. In this example, there are a number of corporate needs for knowledge and skills, which the organisation has not previously required. At the same time there are some topics where the organisation has some experience, but will be requiring many other managers to make this part of their day-to-day jobs. There are many other skills needed which could form a third category where the organisation believes it is fully experienced, but needs to check things out. Table 7.1 shows a number of key topics under the first two headings. The list is illustrative. In this example the top three levels of manager below the chief executive have been shown, level one being the most senior of the three. The ABC priorities are related to the role that people in these grades will need to play, and the importance of the topic at this level. This does not imply that every person on that grade will need to become fully competent in every area, and further work will be needed later to establish a functional and positional breakdown for each level.
- *De-layering*: the organisation plans to remove two layers of management, reducing managerial positions by 10%. It has not previously undertaken a shift of such magnitude. A little thought makes it clear that the list in Table 7.1 is very abbreviated. The way I would approach this list in a real situation would be to identify the critical success factors: what has to be done well in order to handle the downsizing in the most effective way, and ensuring that the organisation

can function effectively afterwards. Some of the requirements might be a short-term need, and involve only one or two people, such as the capability to design a redundancy package, and these would not necessarily lead to a training requirement. Others may be harder to think of, and more important because of this. One problem I have come across through research (described in Chapter 5) is that many organisations that considered training needs that arose from downsizing stopped at the communication and legal issues. The real problems begin when managers and those who they manage try to make the new structure work, and have to change the habits of a lifetime. These are some of the topics I have listed in my example, and the probability is that training here in an action-oriented manner would do a great deal to contribute to corporate success. If a reason for the delayering was to improve customer relations, a critical area would be the additional skills needed for this.

- *Strategic alliances*: our example organisation has decided that in some defined countries, entry will be through strategic alliances rather than attempting to set up their own new operations. Again the topics shown are only a fraction of the critical success factors, and again the hardest part in an organisation with limited experience of alliances would be to determine the critical areas. What is not known can be easily overlooked. It may be worth consulting people outside the organisation on this and any other new factor, to be sure that the key issues are known. For realism, one of the factors shown in the example, visionary leadership, appears elsewhere in the analysis. This of course is a likely outcome.

Table 7.1 could have been expanded to cover all the strategic elements of Figure 6.3, but although necessary in real life, it would have made the example more difficult to follow. Similarly, the topics which have been shown under corporate needs are broader in some cases than would be desirable in a real situation. We might want specific country knowledge only for France, Italy, Germany and Spain, and may not need every person at each level to be equally knowledgeable on each country. Do we mean knowledge of markets, the business infrastructure, law, or politics? World class manufacturing is itself an umbrella heading which covers many different manufacturing concepts, and other topics such as benchmarking. Sub-matrices might be desirable to probe some of these issues in greater depth. In a real situation, it may be necessary to develop several such matrices at different levels of resolution.

The matrix analysis will only give part of the answer to our search for the needs of the organisation. We will also need to draw from our overall assessment of future corporate human resource needs, what used to be called manpower planning, which is described in more detail in Chapter 10. This incorporates development needs arising from the expected development of the organisation, and the succession potential of people within the organisation. It is about using management development to ensure that the organisation's future requirements for motivated and appropriate people can be met. This does not mean that there is no connection between these issues and those revealed from the matrix analysis, but the link may be indirect.

Inevitably, much of what emerges from the matrix analysis will be related to the change areas in the organisation. Some thought should also be given to the preservation and maintenance of things that the organisation is currently doing well. An example of this is those management development actions that help ensure the continuation of the corporate culture, assuming there is no requirement to change culture.

"What the Organisation Already Has"

I have chosen to discuss this step of Figure 7.2 next, although it could be undertaken concurrently with the study of what the organisation is already doing to close the gap. It goes without saying that many of the skills needed to implement the strategies and attain the vision will already exist in the organisation. The difficulty is in identifying what is deficient. Because ultimately management development radiates to individuals, it is also necessary to develop a mechanism which identifies the development needs of individuals. These are likely to be deeper than the immediate business needs, as part of the aim of management development is to play a part in career management. An alternative label might have been the development priorities for employees within the organisation.

There is more to be said on this subject than has so far been raised in some of the case histories and the previous chapter on competencies. The methods shown here may be used individually, although it is often better to try a combination of approaches. The figures for the usage of these approaches are from Tovey, 1991 (large organisations surveyed in 1990) and Mason, 1993 (medium-sized organisations surveyed in 1993). These are referred to by the abbreviations (large) and (medium) below. The proportions should be taken as indicative, and refer to the organisations claiming to use them, not to the proportion of managers whose needs are identified in the manner described.

1. Annual appraisal of subordinate by his or her boss

This is the most common approach used by British organisations, and serves a useful purpose, but is rarely adequate. The training needs of individuals are assessed through the performance appraisal system by almost all large organisations and around 80% of medium ones. Given sampling and timing differences of the surveys, a fair generalisation is that almost all organisations of significant size rely on this approach. It was significant that in both surveys, many respondents were dissatisfied with the way in which this process worked.

One well-known problem is that when the performance management process also deals with remuneration and promotion, it may be behaviourally difficult for development needs to be raised by either the employee or the manager. To correct for this some organisations separate the development appraisal from the rest of the performance appraisal, undertaking them at different times.

In my opinion there are two main deficiencies of the annual appraisal approach. The first is lack of consistency in the quality of the appraisals, which can result in overemphasis of some needs and the understatement of others. This may be caused by lack of time by line managers to do the job well, lack of interest, and sometimes a belief that the process they have to follow is not relevant to their business. The second main deficiency has been mentioned before in this book. This is the fact that neither the appraiser nor the appraisee may be aware of a particular need. To some degree, the annual appraisal encourages cloning of junior managers in the image of their seniors, which may be fine in conditions of low rates of change, but can be harmful when the future is not going to be a repetition of the past.

The appraisal has some merit, because it follows the line of reporting, but there are better ways that can be used either separately or in conjunction with the annual appraisal.

2. Training needs assessment

The findings were identical for both large and medium organisations: around 60% made some use of separate training needs assessments, although this was usually a periodic rather than a regular activity. There are many different ways of conducting such assessments, but they usually involve some form of survey, either by discussion or questionnaire, with managers and/or the people to whom they report. This does not automatically remove the problem of a failure to perceive the real needs which occurs with annual appraisals. The same people are involved, and unless they are provoked by the approach into a different way of thinking, the probability is that their response will be the same as in the appraisal.

There are ways of enhancing managers' perceptions of what is needed. One approach, which is somewhat broader than an assessment of training needs, and may be biased to the strategic changes the company is facing, is to design a workshop for senior managers to work through what is needed to implement some of the strategic decisions the company has made. Part of this workshop would involve a consideration of the skills which are needed, against what they feel exists within the company. This can help managers to perceive needs which may otherwise be hidden to them, such as the many capabilities needed to manage strategic alliances, and the degree to which the managers who report to them have experience or knowledge that is relevant. Butler, 1992, described how strategic skills were improved at BAT through a workshop initiative which used work teams of managers to solve strategic problems. The aim was to develop the skills of those taking part and to solve the problems. Delegates were directors or senior managers with their immediate teams, usually of 4–5 people. There were three formal stages to the workshop. At a pre-seminar briefing lasting half a day, delegates discussed briefly an outline statement of the strategic problem defined by the team leader. All delegates were briefed to prepare personal cases of the people problems they had encountered in previous change situations, and to have these ready in time for the second stage, a one week seminar where delegates worked both on the issues of change management, with the help of a professional faculty, and on the strategic problem identified. The personal cases are an important part of the learning process. Emphasis was on both the solution of the problem and its implementation. Some time later the group reconvened, this time being joined by other managers who they had invited as being important for implementation. Progress was reviewed and actions were revised in the light of experience. This type of process can enable managers to see the issues more clearly, giving a sharper focus to any training needs assessment they may be involved with. The process can also be used to identify some of the major gaps in organisational capability, which have to be solved by training, recruitment, or the use of external resources such as consultants.

In the following example, Tovey, 1992, describes a survey approach to help assess training needs in an international automotive company. The case study is again of an organisation which I know, but which wishes to preserve anonymity. It uses the strategic approach to competencies described in the previous chapter, but the survey approach could be modified if competencies were not used. The extract is used with permission of Coopers & Lybrand, who now own the copyright.

COMPANY A: AN INTERNATIONAL AUTOMOTIVE COMPANY (Tovey, 1992)*

In 1989 the automotive industry was starting to experience the worst trading conditions for years. While downsizing and

---

*Reproduced by permission from Cooper and Lybrand.

restructuring were inevitable if Company A was to remain competitive, labour conditions meant that retention and development of high calibre people were essential. Managerial training therefore had to change in line with the new business situation, which meant a review of existing management training to ensure focus and relevance.

The following objectives were agreed for the assignment, which took place in 1990:

1   To identify and understand the key external factors impacting on the automotive industry, and Company A in particular, in the 1990s.
2   To establish the most important strategic areas of competence for Company A in the 1990s.
3   As a result of (1) and (2), to formulate the training initiatives required to address the key issues in the European Sales Operations.
4   To determine priority and other competency requirements by country, level and function, in terms of:
    —the organisation's need to respond to market conditions
    —individual training and development needs.
5   To assess the impact of organisational structure and culture on Company A's ability to implement change through management development and training.
6   To assess both the quantity and quality of training currently provided, by source, in order to identify the gap between current provision and future requirements.

The assignment focused on a specific group of Company A's employees, namely middle managers and potential managers in vehicle sales, parts and service activities in several European companies. The desired outcome was a comprehensive assessment of training and development needs against a set of strategically defined competency requirements.

The team for this assignment consisted of five consultants.

The Approach

The first stage of the assignment was a major review of strategic documentation relating to the automotive industry. This was analysed using Industry Structure Analysis and the issues facing the automotive industry detailed. A briefing pack was prepared, for each consultant to use throughout the assignment, which included:

- Company A—Company information, including background and history
- Industry Trends
  —Opportunities and threats
  —Other
- Strategies of international automotive companies
- Market data forecasts
- Industry map—European Automotive Industry
- Strategies of international automotive companies
- Company A—Strengths and weaknesses
- General information about the automotive industry.

In order to gain a deeper understanding of the business issues facing Company A in the 1990s from which strategic areas of competence could be identified, 85 face-to-face interviews were conducted with managers and staff at five different organisational levels. These interviews were conducted in Britain, Germany, Spain and the Netherlands as well as Company Headquarters. The programme included an interview with each of the Managing Directors of the four national companies.

To ensure consistency of information an interview guide was developed for use by the consulting team. Interviewees were briefed on the background to the project and the purpose of the interview. A summary of areas included is shown below:

- Background of interviewee (biographical data);
- Strategic and operating issues, including:
  —critical issues facing the automotive industry and prioritisation of these
  —the situation in the 1990s
  —current understanding of the issues
  —competitors;
- Strengths and weaknesses of Company A;
- Company A's knowledge of and response to marketplace issues;
- The contribution of training, including:
  —quantity and quality of training
  —impediments to training
  —sources of training;
- Individual training and development needs.

After the responses had been collated and subjected to content analysis seven strategic areas of competence were identified:

1 *Business knowledge and skills:* Areas of expertise and knowledge in core business functions (such as finance, strategic management, marketing) which help provide the Company A manager with a balanced commercial perspective.
2 *Managing the dealer network:* The organisational, business and "people" skills needed to develop relationships with, and provide more effective support to, a dealer network with rising expectations and increasing levels of professionalism.
3 *Europe and 1992:* A practical appreciation of the impact of 1992 on the organisation and the knowledge, skills and understanding needed to perform in the post-1992 era.
4 *Human Resources Management:* The "people" management and leadership skills needed to create and maintain a highly committed work force in an organisation facing tougher competition and increasing pressures for higher productivity and cost effectiveness.
5 *Information Technology (IT):* A clear understanding of how managers can use IT to contribute towards the achievement of business objectives supported by the necessary personal skills, knowledge and confidence to exploit this in current and future positions.
6 *Innovation and Change:* The capacity to create and implement fresh ideas and new ways of working so that the organisation can anticipate and adapt to external changes and competitive developments.
7 *Organisational Communications:* The effective flow of information up, down and across the organisation in order that individuals can relate their efforts to a common goal and have adequate information to perform their jobs.

Given the geographic scope of the assignment, and the large population to be covered, it was decided that a self-assessment questionnaire would be the most effective instrument to use. The questionnaire was subsequently structured around the seven areas of strategic competence listed above. Each area in the questionnaire consisted of a number of clusters with each cluster being subdivided into a series of individual competency requirements.

Strategic area of competence: Business knowledge and skills
Cluster: Marketing

Individual competency   —Understanding of present and
requirement: future customer requirements
                                          —Understanding the strengths
                                          and weaknesses of competition.

Respondents were asked to select the three strategic areas of
competence which they considered would be of most importance
to Company A in the 1990s and to rank them.

In the following sections they were asked to assess [for all
competences]:

1   Their existing level of personal competence in relation to their
    current position.
2   The level of personal competence required to perform in their
    position in the 1990s.

A further section of the questionnaire examined respondents'
perceptions of the impact of organisational structure and culture
on the way their company operated in Europe. This section
covered several areas, including:

·   The extent to which the structure of the organisation was
    considered to help or hinder achievement of certain factors;
·   The sharing of information across organisational boundaries;
·   Actions leading to success and failure in the company;
·   The treatment of individuals;
·   Leadership attitudes.

The final section of the questionnaire sought views about the
quantity and quality of current training provision in the company,
both at European and national levels.

The inclusion of a biographical section in the questionnaire
enabled a number of different data cuts to be made to allow
comparison between countries, functions and levels. As the
questionnaire relied on self-assessment, participants were strongly
recommended to score the questions after discussion with their
boss, colleagues and subordinates.

The questionnaire was completed by those individuals interviewed
in the four countries, and by an additional 85 respondents, ensuring
that positions and levels in each group were statistically represented
to maintain consistency and accuracy of information.

Tracking of returns was coordinated through contact partners in
each country. The responses were analysed by means of a tailored

computer programme, which was used to identify priority and other training needs.

In analysing the responses to the first section of the questionnaire (the ranking of the strategic areas of competence) a weighting system was used. A formula was devised whereby an area was awarded:

- Four points each time it was rated as the most important.
- Two points each time it was rated as the second most important
- One point each time it was rated as the third most important.

The scores for each area were totalled to produce an overall weighting and therefore priority ranking.

All data was computer analysed by total survey population and also by each of the population samples identified in the biographical data section of the questionnaire.

An assessment was then made, using a five-point scale, of each of the existing levels of competence and the level of competence needed for the 1990s. The difference between the ratings for existing levels of competence and the ratings for competencies needed for the 1990s for each strategic area of competence was used to gauge the level of training need using the matrix illustrated below.

Competencies	5		S	S	S	S	M
Possessed	4		S	S	M	N	N
	3		S	S	M	N	N
	2		S	M	N	N	P
	1		M	N	N	P	P
		1	2	3	4	5

Competencies needed

P = Priority Training Need, where existing level of competence is rated at 1 or 2 (none or very low) and level of competence needed is at 5 (high), or whereby existing level of competence is rated at 1 and level of competence needed for the 1990s is rated at 4.

N = Other Training Need: includes all other responses where existing level of competence is rated lower than the level of competence needed for the 1990s.

M = Match, where existing level of competence and level of competence needed for the 1990s are rated as being equal.

S = Surplus, where existing level of competence is rated higher than that needed for the 1990s.

Analysis of the questionnaire results produced a significant number of findings. These provided the client organisation with information about:

- Those *strategic areas of competence* perceived as most important to Company A in the 1990s.
- Perceived *priority* and secondary *training needs* for the population as a whole and for specific sub-groups.
- The impact of *organisational structure and culture* on Company A's ability to respond to changing business requirements.
- The extent to which current training provision was meeting existing needs. The italicised items are expanded below.

Strategic Areas of Competence

Innovation and Change and Human Resources Management were identified as the most important strategic areas of competence for Company A in the 1990s. These were closely followed by Business Knowledge and Skills.

Priority Training Needs

- Relatively high levels of training need were found for both Innovation and Change and Human Resources Management, with more than 50% of respondents identifying some competence shortfall in many of the individual competency requirements in these clusters. Very little of the training need was, however, identified as "priority training need". This is significant but not surprising given the weighting of the strategic areas of competence.
- Information Technology and Europe and 1992 were the areas regarded as the least important. They were, however, the areas for which the greatest training need was identified. On average, 40% of respondents emerged with some training need (competence shortfall) for the Information Technology cluster, while an average of 65% of respondents reported a shortfall in the Europe and 1992 cluster.

Perhaps more importantly, the levels of priority training need were significantly higher for these two clusters than any other.

Organisational Structure and Culture

Structure

- It was considered that the structure of the organisation was a considerable hindrance to risk taking and innovative approaches to problem solving.
- A clear majority considered the structure to be a hindrance to market focus and responsiveness to changes in the market place. About half the respondents also believed that the Company structure hindered customer focus and encouraged a reactive attitude towards the market.

There was a clear indication that, given the changes in business and market requirements, the structure of the organisation was likely to impede its effectiveness and act as a brake on remedial training efforts.

Culture

- There was a wide discrepancy between what respondents perceived to be actually needed to succeed within Company A and what they believed should be needed. Openness, teamwork, support for one's subordinates, creativity/flexibility, customer focus, quality and taking the long-term view were the dominant factors which respondents believed should be needed for success but which currently were not. They accepted that working hard, performing well and being loyal to the company were, and indeed should be, needed to succeed. However they also felt that success within the company depended too much on fitting the "company mould", supporting one's bosses, minimising mistakes and risk taking, and getting results at any cost.
- Over 50% of the survey population believed that senior management did little to promote openness, trust and teamwork. The majority, however, felt that they could rely on their immediate boss to support them, and to seek their ideas and opinions. Nearly half the respondents also felt their immediate bosses allowed them to explore and proceed with their own approaches and solutions to problems.
- Ninety per cent of respondents believed that the organisation's culture was one in which managers exercise all power and authority. Forty-eight per cent believed that other levels were

permitted to contribute information, but another 42% believed that the prevailing attitude was either that "managers exercise power as of right" or that "managers know best".

The findings concerning the organisational structure and culture were very significant, given that Innovation and Change and Human Resource Management were rated as the two most important strategic areas of competence to Company A in the 1990s.

---

3. 360° Feedback

Bottom-up feedback has become more popular in the last few years, although some of the methods have been in use for over 20 years. They have become more fashionable because they can be used in performance management processes, as a basis for personal improvement, and, as discussed here, to gain a more objective view of company capabilities and areas of management weakness. They are particularly useful for measuring capabilities in management and interpersonal skills; aspects of a manager's behaviour which are experienced by others besides a manager's boss; peers and subordinates; and in some cases customers and suppliers. All the methods take readings from one or all of these groups of people, as well as requiring the manager to undertake a self rating. One value is to close the gap between self perception and actual behaviour. The methods can be even more useful when the behaviours measured are those which have been determined as critical for the strategic success of the organisation. This gives a tool which enables the measurement of capability to be directly linked to strategic requirements.

The Premier Bank case study in Chapter 4 included an example of information collected through a feedback instrument. In this case the approach used was a refinement of the general concept, and measured those aspects of management behaviour which had been identified, through research and validation, as the factors which most influenced organisational climate. Other approaches commercially available are focused on such things as the behaviours needed in the exercise of transformational leadership. More commonly, questionnaires would be compiled around the specific sets of behaviours which research inside the organisation had shown to be important to that organisation. The descriptions of behaviours are not quite competencies, but are close to them.

In management development the feedback approaches have three main uses. The first is that they can provide objective information on areas where improvement is needed, and reports can be designed around any grouping inside the organisation which is large enough to conceal the individual responses. (In well regulated schemes individual reports are kept confidential, as are the ratings of individual direct reports on their boss, although disclosure rules might be defined differently when bottom up feedback is part of a performance management process.) General anonymity, often assured through the use of external agencies to administer the process, means that those making assessments have less fear of victimisation, and experience shows that this encourages most to give honest feedback. For management training needs assessment, the aggregate data is more important to the organisation than the individual data. It should also be stressed that subordinates are not asked to rate their managers as good or bad, but merely to complete the questionnaire to score how they manage through the various dimensions of behaviour chosen for the study. What is good or bad is often situational. That said, it is true to say that managers often receive surprises when they look at their own assessments, and as a result may use them as a basis for changing their own management behaviour. In the Premier Bank case such changes were an objective of the exercise and, you will recall, required new approaches to management processes as well as a collective modification of management behaviour.

The information collected can also be used in a management training course, so that the course is designed to fit the needs of the participants, and the aggregate and confidential individual reports show where the need for change occurs, thus facilitating personal action planning. Although the organisation does not record the individual ratings, and only the agency and the individual have access to these, in most cases those on a programme spontaneously share their results with others as part of the learning process. It is of course possible to use the feedback approach only in connection with training courses, surveying only those who are to attend each training event. This is a valid approach, but deprives the organisation of the wider information that would come from a more extensive survey. On the other hand there is a limit to the number of levels of management that should be included at any one time, as a situation could arise when every person is completing simultaneously questionnaires on a number of peers, subordinates and bosses, bringing a danger that thinking stops and the task becomes to get the forms back, regardless of the value of what is written on them.

The third management development use is in the evaluation of training. Value was added to the Premier Bank because the survey could be repeated after a reasonable interval, and after action had been taken to bring about changes. Objective data for evaluation is at a premium, and there are few other ways of collecting information with such relative ease.

I do not believe that it is possible to design valid feedback tools to assess functional and professional skills. The way a manager delegates can be observed through his or her behaviour: the marketing competence cannot be measured by subordinates in as objective a manner. This is a pity, as it means that feedback approaches can tell us a lot, but by no means as much as we usually need to know.

4. Assessment centres

The Tovey and Mason surveys referred to earlier showed a marked disparity in the use of assessment centres between large and medium-sized companies: around 80% in the larger companies but less than a quarter of the medium ones. The figures conceal that, in all companies, assessment centres are a much more selective tool, usually reserved for people in very specific situations, such as selection for promotion, or movement into a fast track grade structure, or as Bass used them to determine who to place on an extensive internal management development programme.

The big advantages of assessment centres are that it is possible to make objective observations of the strengths and weaknesses of the participating individuals, and it is possible to focus the process so that the assessments are business driven. Disadvantages are cost and the time it takes to assess large numbers of people.

"The Management Development Gap"

The information collected should enable an assessment to be made of the gaps between what the organisation needs, and the skills and competencies it already possesses. This is the next step in Figure 7.2. The assessment process will also have identified deficiencies which were perceived by the individuals and their bosses, but which did not appear on the requirements generated from the study of organisational needs. These may be in part things that individuals believe are desirable for the development of their own careers, routine things which line managers see as important to improve performance of an individual, and in some cases perceptions of needs which do not really exist, because of a change in the situation that neither the individual nor the line manager knew about.

To this we should add training and development activities which are important to the organisation, but which may not arise as a development need because the organisation has been attending to it rather well. An example might be induction training for new employees. The need for it might only show up in the assessments if the organisation stopped doing it.

The task here is to identify the gap, to classify it by level and category, and to attach estimates of the numbers of people involved. Categories might include:

- Immediate requirements driven by organisational needs;
- Longer term organisational needs (including such things as induction initiatives);
- Short-term remedial needs of individuals;
- Career development needs of individuals;
- Things individuals would like to do, but which have no direct corporate benefit;
- Other.

These could be further divided into three headings:

- The elements of the gap which are directly business driven, and have a fairly immediate business imperative.
- Elements which are indirectly business driven, which have a less direct benefit, and perhaps a longer term orientation.
- Elements which relate to individual desires, where the corporate benefit may be through a general encouragement of learning, rather than direct benefit to the organisation from that learning.

These cover the different policy areas which will be discussed in the next chapter.

For all these headings we are thinking about levels in the organisation and a grouping of topics that enables us to make policy decisions. The basis of good analysis and information discussed earlier is very important, but there is also room for judgement. The hardest task for those doing this work is to ensure that they are not blinkered by the past, and that they perceive the business needs and situations as they are, and not as they used to be.

"What We Are Currently Doing to Close the Gap"

This is a simple statement which summarises a complex exercise, and which hides an important element of this stage in the proceedings. In order to identify what we are doing that is appropriate, we must audit the management development activity, and also identify what it is that we are doing which does not help close the gap, or which does it less adequately.

My experience is that most organisations which audit their activities in this way will find that they are doing things which fall under all three of the policy headings, and almost inevitably will find it possible to redirect resources to give greater benefit to the organisation. This does not necessarily mean that what has been going on is bad, but is simply that the organisation could obtain more value if resources were more closely attuned what the organisation needs.

To simplify the discussion, the analytical process described here covers the management training activity, which of course is only one aspect of management development. The same sort of thinking should be applied to other management development activities, and also to training for people who are not managers.

In theory it should be easy to audit what is being done. In practice cost records are not always as good as they might be, and management accounts are often kept only on a global activity basis, and do not separate the projects that make up those spends. Typically it is possible to see what has been spent on hotels in total, but not always easy to break this down to specific courses. There is also the added complication that different elements of the cost of an initiative may fall under different budget responsibility centres: for example some organisations pay for the faculty, materials and meeting rooms from a central budget, but accommodation is picked up by the budget centres of the participants. This is only one of the numerous ways in which organisations keep the training accounts. In extreme situations I have found no control at all, in that although the training budget came under HRM, anyone in the organisation could code expenses to it, and once this was done accounts could not disaggregate the expenditures.

However, it is not only the costs which may give problems, as records of attendance are not always kept well, the aims of programmes may be obscure, and there may be no attempt to look at outcomes.

Although these factors may make it difficult to find the answers to some of the questions which will be posed here, and it may be necessary to reconstruct some of the costs, and supplement fact with estimates, there is value in finding out that training is not as well controlled as might have been thought, and is therefore not as carefully managed as it should be. Organisations which have all the information readily available will find little difficulty with the "audit", and probably already undertake much of what is recommended as a matter of routine.

The analysis should begin at the level of each initiative, although there may be several events within each; that is a training programme may be repeated many times to accommodate the target population. Because many initiatives have a horizon of several years, it is necessary to look at the statistics for an appropriate number of previous years, the current plan, and the intentions the year after. In some cases it may be desirable to choose an even longer horizon, as for example when a training initiative is broken into modules to be taken over, say, three years, and the planned roll out is for one new cohort of participants each year for the next three years. In such cases the only sensible horizon is to look forward over the time that will be taken to complete the whole programme for all participants.

An examination should be made of the rationale for each training initiative. This involves setting out information that explains the reason for the initiative, and includes:

- The purpose: what are (or were) the aims of each initiative?
- Which of the three policy headings discussed earlier does the initiative fulfil?
- Specific corporate goal, critical success factor, or strategy supported, or where this is not relevant to the initiative, the specific rationale for it.
- The target population for whom the initiative is intended.
- How the target population is identified.
- What is the basis on which people are selected to attend the initiative?

All these points are to enable the analyst to relate what is being done to what the actual need is, and to group the initiatives

Table 7.2   *Auditing current training activities.*

For Each Training Initiative:	
What were the aims?	**What has been achieved?**
Specific objectives of the initiative	When did the initiative begin?
How were the objectives determined?	Costs of events held/planned*#
What corporate needs were met?	Number of events held/planned*
What contribution to strategic success?	Number of participants attended/
Measurable targets of the initiative	planned*
Target population for the initiative	Participation as % of target population*
How was this population selected?	Results compared to specific objectives
Why was this target group selected?	How are benefits measured?
How are people chosen to attend?	
Detailed topics in each initiative	

*Period of 2–3 years history, 1–2 years future plan
#Full costs, not just out of pocket expenses

under the policy headings suggested earlier. There is a need for a critical examination of the detail of each programme. It can be very misleading to work only from programme titles, without finding out the detailed content and slant of the training, and assessing whether it really does fill the gap. Life being what it is, you will find that some programmes do not fit neatly into the categories, in that parts may slot into one or more headings, although the whole is not a good fit.

The next stage of the investigation is to collect the hard data for each initiative. For the past and future years determined as relevant, and for each initiative, the following information should be ascertained:

- Number of events held (or planned if for the future).
- Number of participants who attended (or are expected to attend planned events).
- Cost of each initiative, by main expense categories.
- Participants as a percentage of the target group.
- What can be stated about the results of the initiative. Under this heading we need to enquire how benefits are measured, and how the initiative has contributed both to the initiative's objectives and the real needs of the organisation that have been identified.

It is also useful to record when each initiative started, how it is integrated with other HR and management actions, and how the initiative is organised and resourced. We are left with another cost question, which is the residual cost of the training function, after charging the direct costs of initiatives to the right projects. These costs should be put under scrutiny, as it is likely that many of them relate directly to the initiatives, but have not been charged to them because of an inadequate project management system, and lack of a record of how time is spent. This issue will be returned to in Chapter 12.

At this stage of working through the model we should have accumulated a great deal of information. We know what the organisation needs in order to achieve its strategies, we have a good indication of individuals' needs, and we know what we are currently doing and not doing. We can assess all this information under various headings which will help us make business driven management development decisions. All this takes us to the policy and action elements of our model, and these will be discussed in the next chapter.

REFERENCES

Butler, J. E., 1992, Case History: Learning Skills for Strategic Change, *Journal of Strategic Change*, 1.1, January–February.

Mason, A., 1993, *Management Training and Development in Medium-sized UK Business Organisations*, London: Harbridge Consulting Group.

Tovey, L., 1991, *Management Training and Development in Large UK Business Organisations*, London: Harbridge Consulting Group.

Tovey, L., 1992, *Competency Assessment: A Strategic Approach*, London: Harbridge Consulting Group.

8
Management Development: Policy and Implementation

The previous chapter worked through a model of business driven management development, to the point where the facts needed to develop a response which fitted the business need had been identified. It took the discussion to where decisions had to be made, and detailed actions worked out and implemented. The final three stages of Figure 7.2 (see page 123) are described here, and deal with these decisions and actions.

"Revised Management Development Policies"

The label on this stage in the model assumes that the organisation already has a management development policy. In fact what I will concentrate on are those aspects which relate to the business driven concept, and which would form a nucleus of any policies, whether new or revisions of what already exists.

In this context *policy* really means the principles that determine how priorities will be determined and met, and is thus a key component of a strategic plan for management development. The information collected in the earlier stages is very important, because policy should be determined on the basis of the specific situation of the organisation. An organisation facing a major, discontinuous change situation will

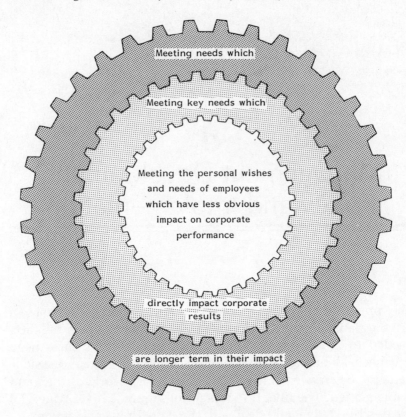

The size of each element shows a possible proportion of the spend on management development: the priority order of allocating available funds would be:

1 direct impact
2 longer term impact
3 personal needs.

The actual proportion of spend would reflect these priorities.

Figure 8.1   *Three policy areas which help drive management development.*

have very different management development priorities from one where the future is a smooth transition from the past.

The suggestions given here will help to identify some of the issues that should be considered by each organisation when making its own policies. It will not provide a universal solution which will immediately fit every organisation. In the previous chapter I suggested a number of headings under which the organisational need might be classified. For the sake of simplicity, I suggest using three summary headings here, although the classification could be expanded as desired. They are:

- Needs which are directly business driven.
- Needs which are indirectly business driven, which have a less obvious immediate benefit, and perhaps a longer term orientation.
- Needs which relate to individual desires and where the corporate benefit may be through a general encouragement of learning, rather than a specific benefit to the organisation from that learning.

The following checklist of points for consideration should be used for each type of need. In the notes below, I suggest some of the differences in policy which may be appropriate for each of the management development need categories. My general argument is that there should be differences, although the precise nature of these will vary with each organisation's specific situation.

WHAT PROPORTION OF EFFORT AND RESOURCES SHOULD BE APPLIED TO THE NEED?

In essence, the first point to consider is where the overall priorities of the organisation lie. There is a need to determine a balance between the short term and the long term, and there are issues of principle over the proportion of management development activity which should be devoted to each of the above categories. My own view is that the bias, which in many organisations is to the last two categories, should shift to the first two. However only in situations where the direct business needs are extensive and urgent, would I recommend doing nothing at all in the third category. If an organisation could achieve an equilibrium of something like 50% of resources for direct organisational needs, 40% for indirect organisational needs, and 10% for the third and more personally driven needs, there would be an undoubted increase in the effectiveness of management development and training activities, and the value of these to the organisation. But I should not be dogmatic about the figures, and I would argue for regular reviews to ensure that changes in the organisation's situation are taken into account.

The need is to reach a balance which is in the best interests of the organisation, which ensures that what is done adds value to the organisation, and that the best possible use is made of scarce resources.

POLICY FOR PROVISION OF MANAGEMENT DEVELOPMENT?

A policy should be decided for each of the three categories of management development. For example, it might be that the organisation will provide training courses for each of the first two categories, with the event taking place on normal working days, whereas in the final category, which is related much more to things driven by the individual, the organisation will establish a climate of self development, and provide resources to facilitate this, but will not run courses itself to meet these needs. One example of this policy might be to establish a facility where employees have access to distance learning programmes which can be borrowed from the organisation, possibly with counselling help, but which are studied by employees in their own time. Another is a scheme whereby the organisation will pay all or part of the tuition fees on external weekend and evening classes for certain types of professional and business courses that employees wish to attend.

For the middle category of management development, the indirect, longer term business needs, the organisation needs to decide the extent to which initiatives should lead to formal academic qualifications. If the acquisition of a diploma in management studies, or a master's degree in business studies is considered to be of importance to the organisation, in terms of ensuring consistent quality and increasing employee motivation, a specific policy is needed to achieve this. Although management development initiatives are not restricted to one per person, there are trade offs. For example putting a person on a three-year internal management programme which will lead to an MBA from a recognised university, may make it impossible to give that person a temporary development posting overseas. It is not only that time already spent on the internal programme could be wasted by such actions, but that the total number of participants have to be maintained at an educationally viable level. There is also the very real point that there are various levels of management, all of which have development needs, and one aspect of the policy should be to determine how each level is to be provided for, given that resources will always be limited.

Direct business needs also require policies to support the detailed actions. Should, for example, this type of need be met by training that cascades down the organisation, or should it be distinctly different for each level of management? Is it possible to meet some of the direct needs by inserting them into the second category of training, thus meeting two different objectives? For example, there might be a deliberate decision to ensure that all longer term development training should also meet some shorter term direct needs by changing the content of programmes, and by the nature of project work that could form part of the initiative. Where individuals need help to improve, so that they are able to perform well in current jobs, it may be appropriate to shift the bias from training courses to coaching by line managers.

HOW ARE PARTICIPANTS SELECTED?

In many organisations, training goes to those who ask for it, not necessarily to those with the greatest needs. Sometimes line managers may demand training for specific people, but often even this is a response to a coherent request made by the employee. I would suggest that there may be different policies on selection and attendance for each of the three categories.

Direct business needs, which have been identified from the study of the organisational situation might, as has been suggested, best be met in part by some form of training which cascades down the organisation. Selection in such cases is likely to be on a broad basis, because the judgement has already been made that most people need this training. Although there might be discussion with line managers, particularly on who should attend first, selection ultimately should be a central decision, and should be compulsory. Other types of management development to meet these needs could be on a different basis of selection: for example a secondment or transfer of someone to an area of the organisation which already has some of the new experience would be on the basis of choosing who is the most appropriate person. Again, the bias should be to the person who would be of most value to the organisation through this experience, which is not necessarily the same as choosing the individual with the greatest personal need.

Selection for the indirect, longer term, development programmes should perhaps be quite different. Here line managers might play a greater role, although for flagship management development programmes it may be of value to make the final choice through attendance at a development or assessment centre. One possible reason for this is to achieve fairness and consistency, in that a manager selected as best for the programme by one line manager, may not be better than someone not recommended by another manager. An approach that begins with recommendations by line managers for attendance at a development centre, the assessment itself, and final selection by a panel which includes line managers may be very appropriate for an internal MBA programme. At the other extreme, an induction course might well be compulsory for all new employees.

The final category of need becomes almost by definition self selection by the individual. There may be some counselling by line managers or HR, and a general encouragement to employees to develop themselves, but if individuals are disinterested there is a strong argument for not applying compulsion to any specific personal development that might be available under this category.

WHAT BUDGET ALLOCATION APPROACH SHOULD BE USED?

All organisations have an approach to management development budgets, but often this has developed as a solution to *ad hoc* issues, rather than as a coherent policy. For all initiatives it is recommended that as much attention is given to outputs as to inputs, which would avoid situations where an HR department switches to distance learning for management development, not because it is better for the particular situation, but because it can claim that more managers have received training for the same cost. The missing element in this type of decision is very often the effectiveness, and value to the organisation of the different types of training. Organisations have a mix of policies over to whose budgets training costs are charged. Some pick up the tab centrally, on the basis that this is the only way to ensure that training takes place; others operate an internal market system, whereby managers are charged when they use internally organised facilities, but can choose whether they buy from this source, or even at all. Other organisations charge management development costs to profit centres, either as a straight allocation, or on an "as used" basis. Then there is the decision as to what is a management development cost. Does it include the travel and accommodation costs of the individual? Does it include the salaries of participants? And the whole issue is complicated by the way HR is organised across large organisations, in particular the degree of devolvement from the centre to SBUs, and from HRM to line managers.

There is no single best solution which is right for every organisation and situation. However there is a need to think through what is right for the organisation at any given time, and this is related to management style, culture and top management's views of centralisation or decentralisation, and to the business situation faced by the organisation.

I should like to suggest a few principles that might help in the development of a specific policy for the organisation.

Firstly, no matter where costs end up in terms of budget centre responsibility, the system should enable the full costs of training to be ascertained.

Secondly, I would suggest that, where attendance on a programme is compulsory, the full costs should be born centrally by the organisational unit that has made this decision: this may be corporate HRM, or it might be the central headquarters of a business unit. This ensures that the training does take place, and that line managers are not aggrieved because they are forced to pay for things they did not decide, and may not agree with. This is even more important when bonuses might be reduced by such costs.

Thirdly, where line managers have full control over whether management development is "bought" or not, it is reasonable that the costs of what they "buy" should be charged to their budgets.

In most organisations, this would imply a need for different policies which are related to the purpose of the initiative, and the way participants are chosen for it. In deciding the policy the key issue should be what is best for the organisation.

A COMMITMENT TO EVALUATION

In my view a key element of any business driven policy should be a commitment to evaluation. One aspect of this should be that when the objectives are set for any management development initiative, there should also be a statement of how the results of that initiative are to be measured. Without this commitment, management development becomes a series of judgements and hunches, which are very difficult to defend. With it, it becomes possible for the organisation to measure progress, to abandon initiatives that do not work, and to be sure that money is being spent wisely. A commitment to evaluation implies more than simply measuring results: it also means a search for initiatives which will give the most value to the organisation. This may mean changing or giving up many of the management development initiatives already under way, in order to free resources for actions which give more value to the organisation.

Whatever the decisions made on the policies and priorities discussed so far, there are some overall concepts which, it could be argued, should apply to any management development effort.

A VISION STATEMENT FOR MANAGEMENT DEVELOPMENT PHILOSOPHY

It is worth spending a little time to define and agree what the vision is for management development in the organisation. This may take many forms. At various times I have discussed management development with organisations that have taken their vision of management development into widely different directions.

Some examples are:

- Every manager *must* have at least five days training every year.
- All training in this organisation must have defined bottom line objectives, and no training will be undertaken which cannot be justified in terms of expected contribution to the business.
- We are a learning organisation, so individuals are encouraged to learn anything that they may consider relevant to their role in the organisation.
- People are our greatest asset... (need I go on with this one?)

The point about these statements is not to state what is right or wrong, but to emphasise the need to think clearly about what management development should be doing for the organisation. A vision statement should be honest, and if not immediately believable should be made so through prompt action.

THE NEED FOR A REVIEW PROCESS

Management development which is seen only as an HRM activity has less chance of success than if it is owned by the organisation at large. One way of helping to ensure this, and ensuring that interpretations of business needs are as close to reality as it is possible to get, is to set up a top level review board, which will agree the management development plans and budgets, and particularly the priorities. Ideally, this should be chaired by the chief executive, and have senior line managers as members. In complex multi-business organisations this review process should be established at the level of each business.

PROJECT STEERING GROUPS

Each initiative should be managed with the aid of a steering group, to help design the objectives and scope of the initiative, to ensure relevance, and to decide how results will be measured and monitored. The majority of members should be drawn from levels of line management appropriate to the levels of the participants for whom the initiative is intended. A by-product of this is to help secure widespread management buy-in to the initiative, but the main compelling reason is again to help ensure that the initiative meets the real needs of the organisation.

"Plans and Programmes"

The next stage in the model is the design of plans and programmes to implement the policy decisions. In most organisations a careful analysis will result in a mix of current initiatives which should be abandoned, continued unaltered, or modified, and new initiatives which arise from the changed perceptions of needs and priorities. Being willing to abandon initiatives which, although they may be of good quality and well received internally, no longer meet the organisation's priorities and needs, is a key element of this planning, and why much of the earlier information was collected.

The plan element requires setting out the initiatives under the various priority headings of the policy, showing the objectives of each initiative, target participation, how participants will be selected, how benefits will be measured and monitored, the planned number of events, an outline timetable, detailed budgets, and an overhead budget. In effect they are the same sorts of headings under which information was collected as the analysis proceeded.

Programmes require a different sort of thought, and it is unlikely that they will, or even should, all be designed at the same time as the outline plan is prepared and the budgetary allocations secured. Having said this, it should be accepted that there will always be ongoing activities that should continue, and that many initiatives, such as an internal company MBA scheme, may be commitments for several years.

There is much to be said about one aspect of management development, the application and design of business driven management training programmes, which I have left until a little later in this chapter.

"Implementation and Evaluation"

The last stage of Figure 7.2 (see page 123) is the implementation and evaluation of the management development policies, plans and programmes. In theory implementation is a separate step from evaluation, for no one can evaluate a programme that has not been run. In practice, for many initiatives, particularly training where the initiative has to be repeated many times to accommodate the total population, evaluation of previous sessions and continued implementation of new sessions can be carried on simultaneously, and changes made to the initiative as a result of the findings.

Evaluation may be undertaken with different objectives in mind. The following quotation is taken from an earlier book of mine:

"Evaluation may have at least three objectives:
1. Is the training initiative fulfilling the objective for which it was established? Ideally this objective should be linked to a corporate rather than an individual benefit, although an intermediate step measuring individual changes may be desirable.
2. Is one method of training more effective than another? This is not the same as asking which is the cheapest. Such questions are becoming more important as companies experiment with computer-based learning, interactive video, or other modern distance learning approaches. Frequently these decisions are made on cost alone.
3. Is the training the most effective method for every participant? This ties into the concept of individual differences ..."

(Hussey, 1988, p. 166)

The most useful view of where to evaluate that I have come across was by Whitelaw, 1972, page 8, who derived his classification from work by Hamblin, 1968. Methods of evaluation have progressed since then, as the Premier Bank case illustrated, but the framework for thinking has stood the test of time. He suggests four levels for evaluation, which I have put in the order which stresses what I see as the importance of each.

The levels are:

- *Ultimate outcome*: the impact of the initiative on the bottom line success of the organisation. Certainly all initiatives which are business driven should have an outcome which can be measured and which has a direct relationship with profit. It may be a surrogate, such as increases in levels of customer satisfaction, reduction of costs, speedy integration of an acquisition, or increase in market share, but it should be something that ties directly with what it is the organisation is trying to achieve.
- *Intermediate outcome*: this is also an important measure, and sometimes we need evaluate no further if results are achieved here. It is the extent to which behaviour changed as a result of the initiative: in other words, did participants apply what we wanted them to learn? When culture change is the objective, this may be the most valid measurement, as it is hardly the fault of the training if the new culture defined by top management fails to deliver profit.
- *Immediate learning outcome*: this is useful theoretically, in that new concepts cannot be applied until they are learnt, but does not prove that what is learnt is used. For many situations our interest is in the application of knowledge, rather than the acquisition of knowledge itself.
- *Reactions outcome*: unfortunately this is the sole evaluation tool of most organisations, and it tends to measure enjoyment, rather than effectiveness. The measurement is taken from the view of the individual, who may not at this stage see the relevance of what has been learnt. Reactions level evaluation can give useful feedback for fine tuning parts of the programme where the learning method was not as successful as it should have been, but as an overall test of whether the initiative added value to the organisation it is incomplete and misleading.

WHERE TO USE BUSINESS DRIVEN TRAINING INITIATIVES

There are several situations where a training initiative may be the best way to achieve a bottom line result, because in addition to helping ensure that the organisation has the competence required, it provides an opportunity to communicate a change situation, involve people, and create a motivating environment. Some of the sections below were taken with minor modifications from Hussey, 1993.

Some strategic situations where training may be a key tool of implementation are described with examples. They include:

- Implementing a new policy
- Implementing a strategy
- Effecting an organisational change
- Changing the culture of an organisation
- Meeting a major environmental change
- Solving specific problems.

Implementing a new policy

There is not a great deal of difference in concept between using a training initiative to implement either a policy or a strategy, and in some situations the distinction between the two terms may become blurred. One difference may be the degree of precision with which quantified corporate objectives can be set as the desired outcome of the training.

> "One of the world's largest multinationals, always seen as one of the best managed, identified that more attention had to be placed on competitor analysis both at top level and in the development of marketing plans by each operating unit. This was after careful analysis had revealed that much of the company's recent growth was without profit, because of weaknesses in the market place where the competitors were proving more aggressive than the assumptions on which past plans had been based. Many companies would have issued a policy statement, in the form of an edict, that in future strategies should be formulated after more rigorous competitor analysis. Many would have failed to cause any change whatsoever, because:
>
> - most people would be complacent about their own approach, while accepting that others needed to do better;

- some would believe the issue was unimportant and only pay lip service to it;
- others would not understand the policy;
- a few might not receive or read the statement.

Aware of these probable outcomes the chief executive of this multinational personally directed a world wide educational initiative to bring the new thinking to life. He led top managers in a week long introduction to the theme of "what about competition", and insisted that several hundred senior people should spend two weeks on a strategic planning workshop. He introduced an 8 hour audio-visual presentation to thousands more managers as a basis for discussion of, and commitment to, genuine strategic thinking. Many week long implementation workshops have been held throughout the world, with practical training in competitor analysis which has led to the implementation of more realistic strategies.

Not surprisingly, this policy change has been made to work, and is enthusiastically endorsed by thousands of managers who are now convinced of its practical value."

(Hussey, 1985)

Implementing a Strategy

The right training initiatives can bring the understanding and commitment referred to earlier, and can ensure that the right skills are available so that implementation is possible. The four examples given below show what can be done.

- Lorenz (1986a,b,c) described how ICL used management training as a major means of implementing its strategy. Some 2000 managers were put through a programme which was uniquely designed around the company and its industry to improve competitiveness against American and Japanese rivals. The training programme, which cascaded through all levels of management, was held to have "...done at least as much as the company's new range of products and systems to give ICL an unexpected chance of prospering in the threatening shadows of IBM, Digital Equipment, and the Japanese computer giants" (Lorenz, 1986a). There were several tiers of courses, launched at the same time. All senior managers went through the top level course over an eighteen month period. Courses focused on key strategic concepts and industry issues, and were designed after a careful study of the company.
- Rose (1989) demonstrated that management training was the

key to the success of the strategic changes instituted in the retailers, Woolworths, in the UK. A lacklustre group underwent a change of ownership and management, which among other things resulted in a change of the group name to Kingfisher. The Woolworth store strategy was considerably changed: indeed some critics felt that until this happened it actually had no strategy, which was one of the reasons for its poor performance. However the new strategy involved much more delegation to local branch management, and at the time the strategy was formulated it was felt that branch management lacked the skills to operate in the way that was now essential for the success of the strategy. A training programme was developed for branch management, and was held to be a critical step in the implementation of the strategy.

• One of my consulting assignments with the British operations of an international insurance company was advice on the design and installation of a process of planning. The training workshops which were developed to launch the process were also used as the first in a series of strategy formulation meetings, when real issues were worked on. As an example, competitor analysis was not taught as an academic concept. Instead, dossiers were prepared on major competitors and used for real analysis by the planning teams who attended the workshops. Each workshop was attended by a team to whom one aspect of the planning task had been delegated. Much more work was done outside of the workshop, before strategic plans were put by each strategic business to top management for agreement. In this case training was used at the formulation phase, integrated with all the other actions the company was taking, and linked to a modest consultancy input. A result was considerable enthusiasm for strategic change, and a completely different understanding of the competitive environment in which the company operated. Many immediate actions were implemented by the SBU managers, as not all of the actions identified were strategic. Even some of the research subsequently undertaken among brokers, as a result of a new appreciation of the information needs of the company, brought immediate benefits in an increase in requests for quotations by many brokers who had not realised the firm's involvement in certain types of insurance work.

● In February 1996 the Institute of Personnel Development prize for excellence in training provision was awarded to European Gas Turbines (EGT) and the Engineering Training Authority. It arose from a new agreement between EGT management and the unions, which removed the demarcations which had been in force and which limited EGT's ability to compete. The new agreement made it necessary to establish a flexibility training programme to give workers all the skills needed, and including accrediting the new skills to recognised standards of competence. The design included the training of work-based assessors, the development of an assessment system, and the necessary training, much of which took place on the job. Incremental pay rises were given to those who gained new skills. The results were reduced manufacturing times, which gave an 89% fall in financial penalties for late deliveries, and a reduction in product costs. Although this example is not from management training, it makes the point that the concepts discussed here can be extended to cover all types of employee.

Effecting an Organisational Change

In both policy and strategy implementation there is the possibility that an individual may feel threatened because of lack of skill or knowledge to meet a new situation, or because his or her *psychological contract* has been changed. The concept of the psychological contract partly explains why changes are sometimes resisted. Although a person's salary or job title may not have altered, there may be a change in the unwritten expectations that the person has of the job. Perhaps previously certain decisions could be made without head office approval. Now the changes require that they be referred. This may take some of the job satisfaction away. The same thing may happen when authority is delegated to people whose psychological contract had included the comfort of a boss who has made all the real decisions. With an organisational change it is even more likely that "people" problems will emerge during implementation, and that these will frustrate implementation unless they are addressed. Training offers one way of approaching these problems.

"Delayering", "downsizing" and "rightsizing" (I do not believe there much real practical difference between them) are common responses to strategic pressures, both to reduce cost, and to take decision making closer to the customer. That at least is the theory, and many organisations have implemented it successfully. Some have achieved implementation merely by ripping out layers without changing individual jobs, or training people in the new skills needed. Scase and Goffee (1989) found in their research in the UK that many managers were frustrated by the extra pressures put on them, and felt they were on a treadmill from which few could see an escape, and from which they obtained little job satisfaction.

Handy et al, 1996, in their survey of managers which yielded a sample of 563 people, detected some slowing down in delayering, but found a heightened perception of stress, and high work loads which do often cause a conflict between day-to-day operational matters and the time that should be spent on strategic issues.

Organisational change often accompanies a new strategy, and both can be frustrated unless implementation is effective. L'Oreal in the UK used a training approach to secure the implementation of a new organisational structure. A new strategy was devised to increase market share for hair care products in the retail market. Because in the past distribution had focused on certain major retail outlets through which L'Oreal already achieved a disproportionate outlet share, it was clear that the new objective could only be achieved if distribution were extended to outlets where at the time L'Oreal were not represented or had a poor outlet share. The sales and merchandising teams had been organised to meet the previous pattern of sales, and it was apparent to the management that the new strategy would only succeed if these teams were to be restructured to meet the changed distribution strategy. Originally the company thought of implementing the structural change through announcement at sales conferences and supported by normal management action. Although this may have been successful ultimately, the fear was that it would take too long, during which time the success of the new strategy would be in jeopardy.

The changes in structure had an impact on the job of every

person in the sales and merchandising teams. For example the two teams were being amalgamated, so that every person would handle both tasks in the future. Different types of outlet would be called on, and transfer orders on wholesalers would be taken from many retail chemists. Again this was to be a new activity. The concern was that changes to the psychological contract would be perceived in a hostile way and that the turnover of sales representatives, which was already high, would increase. There was also a fear that many of the people would not have the knowledge or skills to enable them to cope with the new job requirements.

The training initiative took the form of a two-day workshop which was repeated on a regional basis so that all persons affected by the change attended. The new structure was announced in advance, but was not implemented until after the workshops. In the workshops there was immediate agreement with the new market share objective. A case study was provided, based on real market research, which required participants to work out a distribution strategy to attain the agreed objective. It was clear to all that whatever strategy was decided, the target could not be met without changes in the types of outlet through which the company reached the consumer. It was also clear to everyone that a change of distribution policy would require a change of structure. The new organisational structure was explained in the context of this shared understanding. The rest of the workshop provided training to provide some of the new knowledge that would be needed by participants, and identified the further training that participants themselves felt would be essential for them to become fully effective. This identification was done on the basis of an informed understanding by participants. The training element of the workshop included bringing in different types of retailer so that they could explain their requirements for merchandising and sales support.

This approach was reviewed by L'Oreal a year later, when the firm claimed that the workshops had enabled it to achieve the market share objectives. An unexpected benefit was a reduction in the turnover of sales representatives, presumably because of the greater feeling of commitment to the firm which had been built up in the workshops and subsequent management actions. It is doubtful whether so much would have been achieved by more traditional approaches to implementation.

Changing the Culture of an Organisation

Culture has been recognised increasingly as a factor in strategic performance, popularised in particular by Peters and Waterman (1982). Many organisations devote a considerable amount of effort, including a great deal of training activity, to maintaining a particular culture. The Peters and Waterman research, and a film based on this, showed how Disney uses training to develop the required consistent attitude to customers at Disneyworld.

There are many occasions when a strategic change also requires a change in company culture, and again a training initiative may be one of the most powerful tools that can be used. In this case the training programme must go hand in hand with the management process. Goshal et al, 1988, described how the change of strategy at Scandinavian Airlines Systems after 1981 required a cultural revolution (some mention of this was also made in Chapter 1). This was led by the president Jan Carlzon and owed much to his personal energy. The need was to change from a bureaucratic organisation that referred all decisions upwards, to a customer responsive entity where all reasonable decisions were taken by the person having point of contact with the customer. Management actions to change the process included "junking" the procedures manuals. "Education was considered necessary to reap the full benefits of the new organisation, and both managers and front line staff were sent to seminars" (Goshal et al, 1988).

Training initiatives could also be used more than they are to aid implementation in acquisition strategy, particularly where full integration takes place, and it is desirable to get both parts of the new organisation working together and to a common philosophy.

Globalisation strategies are causing many US and European organisations to introduce common training across geographical frontiers, holding the same courses but running them in appropriate languages. One of the reasons may be to build a similar culture across units of the organisation which historically had been run as separate companies.

Meeting a Major Environmental Change

The implementation need may be to bring awareness of the change, or the working out of detailed tasks in response to a change. Sometimes this sort of approach may also be used to formulate strategic actions.

Sometimes changes in the business environment can be seen only in the broadest of terms, yet the company has to begin to reposition itself to pressures that can only partly be forseen. In these situations the need might be to train people to be quicker in perceiving change, and helping them to be more flexible in attitudes.

Solving Specific Problems

Training works in the implementation situations described above. It is not surprising that it also works in some situations as a means of solving problems. For example one multinational engineering company used a training mechanism as a means of improving profitability at branch level. After careful research, a course was designed which included all the skills needed to improve performance, including planning, financial numeracy, marketing and teambuilding. A high level of project work was included, and many of the recommendations from the projects were subsequently implemented.

In another example a workshop was run for a unit of British Petroleum, which had been set up to supply high technology products and services for large ships. Ten months after beginning operations, losses had reached £500 000 without a single sale. The workshop resulted in solutions, and incorporated enough educational input to enable the managers to apply them. In a short space of time after the event sales of £1.5 million were achieved, which were accredited by the management of the business to the actions developed in the workshop.

TRAINING INITIATIVE OPTIONS

A training initiative which is intended to achieve any of the strategic changes described earlier requires skilful design, and in most cases should be tailored specifically to the requirements of the company. Although this costs more than a standardised training initiative, the value to the company may be immense. The successful implementation of a strategy, if it is the right strategy, may be worth millions of pounds.

There is some confusion among both buyers and suppliers over what is meant by a tailored course. To cut through this, I set out below what I mean by the different approaches to internal courses which are available. This will be followed by a more detailed description about what is involved in designing a tailored programme.

• *The standard course.* Although this may be delivered to a company audience, it is essentially the same course that the consultant will give to any other client. The client pays for delivery, and does not finance the development of the course. Often, when a course is put together by an in-house trainer, he or she will use various guest lecturers who employ standard material. Even if the course were completely delivered by internal trainers, it could equally well be given to another company, and includes nothing that is unique to the originating company. This is the cheapest type of course, and in the UK is one of the most common ways of approaching in-house training. It may have value in teaching generic competencies, but is rarely appropriate for the sorts of implementation and change situations described earlier.

• *The slanted course.* Here the provider uses what are basically standard materials, but spends some time trying to make the course more appropriate for the client. The activities undertaken may vary between merely learning the client's buzzwords to a genuine effort to make the course fit. When carefully approached with the overall objective, this approach may sometimes be appropriate for a particular change situation. There are many other implementation situations where the slanted course is not specific enough to bring about the necessary changes. Most UK suppliers who claim to offer tailored courses are in fact offering slanted courses. There is no common agreement on the meaning of words, and some suppliers do not know the difference anyway.

● *The tailored course.* This is a unique course built around the company situation. Concepts are translated into the context of the company, and a high proportion of the teaching material will be written especially for the situation. There are degrees of tailoring, but generally a course which is intended to implement a strategy, organisational change, or a new policy will be highly tailored.

It is possible for a company to design, develop and deliver its own tailored course using internal resources. Few organisations have the ability or objectivity to do this well, although sadly not all who try know this! Usually this sort of course will be better if experienced outsiders are used, possibly in partnership with some of the organisation's own managers. The reason for this becomes apparent when the main phases of work needed to develop a tailored course are considered.

DESIGNING A TAILORED PROGRAMME

A number of steps are suggested as essential for the successful tailored programme.

● *Define the objectives of the initiative.* Much care should be taken to determine the aims of the initiative and the target population to whom it is directed. Aims should be realistic, and should be related to other management actions needed or being applied. For example it is unrealistic to think that any training initiative can change the culture of an organisation, unless actions are also undertaken to alter the many other management practices and organisational policies which contribute to the culture. If the aim of the programme is to identify all these areas, this should be clear in the objectives. Thought at this stage should be given to how the organisation will know that the initiative has been successful, and how this will be measured and monitored.

● *Research.* The length of this phase will be affected by the objectives of the course, the complexity of the organisation, and the quality of diagnostic work that has already been undertaken. Whoever undertakes this task must be able to combine consultancy skills with a knowledge of what will work in a training situation. The purpose of this phase is to properly understand the issue around which the course is to be built, the priorities and weightings of the topics, the culture of the organisation, and the needs of participants. Thus it may involve a study of company material, interviews with key managers, group discussions with potential participants, and even surveys within the company.

● *Design and specification*. After the research phase, the course can be specified in detail. This should result in a document for agreement with the sponsors showing the aims of the course, each topic included (with reasons), the teaching method, the materials to be developed, and the objectives for each topic. Agreement at this stage is essential if wasted effort is to be avoided. The key skill at this stage is in course design, which requires a knowledge of both learning processes and the subject, and the ability to relate these to the organisation's business situation and the aims of the programme. Design may go beyond the confines of the course to post-programme projects, action plans and support mechanisms to aid implementation.

● *Development of the course*. This is usually the most time-consuming phase, since often the situation faced by the company has to be mirrored in the course materials. These materials have to be researched, written, approved, and prepared for teaching. In addition to the appropriate functional, and often multi-functional, knowledge, a mixture of consulting, training and writing skills are needed.

Course development may include the design of materials to aid post-course implementation.

● *Piloting*. After a full review has been made of the developed course, it is desirable to run the first session of the course as a pilot. When the course is to be repeated many times, this is easy to organise. There are practical difficulties if the course is to be run only a few times in a short period, and a full pilot may not be possible. In these situations it is important to leave an interval between the first and second sessions of the course so that amendments can be made if these prove necessary. In cases where a pilot is possible, it should be followed by a careful review followed by any necessary modifications of the course.

● *Evaluation.* The commitment to evaluation has been stressed previously, and is considered to be vital. Tailored programmes are expensive, and are often intended to be repeated many times. To continue a sequence of repeats over a lengthy period without taking time to assess results is irresponsible.

A tailored course may be the most effective way of converting the intention to use training for implementation into concrete action. If done well, it carries little risk of failure and can bring enormous benefits. But whether the course is developed and delivered internally or by outsiders, a professional approach is vital for success.

CHOOSING A SUPPLIER FOR A BUSINESS DRIVEN INTERNAL PROGRAMME

There are some 500–600 suppliers of in-company training courses in the UK, excluding those who offer tailored distance learning or computer based training. On top of this there are suppliers who offer packages which the organisation can deliver with its own trainers. Choosing a supplier is more complex than comparing prices and taking references, although both are relevant and important. What issues should be considered in order to ensure that you are matching the right sort of supplier to the particular need?

The points outlined below deal with choosing suppliers for programmes that directly relate to corporate needs, and for major management development programmes. The points need to be adjusted to the situation: for example point 5 may be very important to a multinational, but have no relevance to a single country organisation, and in any case may be important only when there is a need to run the same event in many different countries.

1 What concern is shown over how participants can implement the concepts of the programme?
2 What effort is proposed to make the programme fit the needs of the client?
3 How will they make the programme specific to the client situation and needs?

4 How flexible are the suppliers over the location, frequency and number of repeats of the programme, or in response to changes to the initial specifications of numbers?
5 What capability do they have to offer a global service, including language variations, to a global client?
6 Do they have any proprietary approaches that can add value?
7 How responsive are they to the client?
8 How creative are the solutions proposed?
9 What is the calibre, experience and business orientation of the people who will deliver the programme?
10 Are the suppliers able to understand the problems and issues the client faces, and to bring a consultancy skill into the course design?
11 What experience do they have on genuinely similar situations?
12 Are they willing to work in partnership with client managers to produce the best solution for the client?
13 Can they obtain academic accreditation for the programme should this be important?
14 Do they have a research programme which enables them to speak with authority about trends, methods and issues?
15 Are they fully up to date in the topic areas of the programme?

The ideal is to find a supplier that can exceed expectations and deliver real value to the organisation.

Hussey, 1988, p. 110, provided a case study of how Coopers & Lybrand selected a supplier for a major large-scale management development programme. The points shown below were each scored on a 0–3 scale, and five of the factors were given additional weightings of 2 or 3. This method was applied to each of seven suppliers who had been asked to bid for the work. The aim was to ensure that price did not become the main criteria of choice, and that attention was focused on finding the right supplier for the task.

The points were:

• previous experience in the market sectors;
• previous experience in delivering tailored programmes;

- design concepts offered;
- price competitiveness for a) development and b) delivery;
- commitment to delivering on time;
- willingness to develop tailored programmes (instead of selling what they already have on the shelf);
- client responsiveness.

Few organisations possess the internal capability to design and run tailored programmes for senior management, unless they do this with the support of external specialists. It is also possible to argue that, in these days of outsourcing and reduced numbers of core employees, the provision of a full time internal capability should not be a priority. The choice of an appropriate supplier becomes even more critical, and a poor choice can set the organisation back instead of taking it forward. However selecting a supplier does not mean that all aspects of the programme have to be passed over to the organisation: there are many opportunities for partnership initiatives which combine internal and external resources, and in any case it has already been suggested that there should be a steering group to manage and control the initiative.

The detailed approach described for competencies and management development illustrates in detail how the model described in Figure 3.4 (see page 46) can be modified for use in analysing specific aspects of HRM. To continue in this way for all HRM activities would become repetitive, and to avoid this a more general approach will be used to highlight some of the other activities in the next chapter.

REFERENCES

Goshal, S., Lefèbure, R. B., Jorgensen, J. et al, 1988, *Scandinavian Airlines Systems (SAS) in 1988*, Case Clearing House of Great Britain and Ireland, Cranfield, No 389-025-1N.

Hamblin, A. C., 1968, Training evaluation: a discussion of some problems, in *Organisational Necessities and Individual Needs*, R. J. Halcon, editor, A.J.M. Occasional Paper No. 5, London: Blackwell.

Handy, L., Holton, V. and Wilson, A., 1996, *The Ashridge Management Index*, Berkhamstead: Ashridge Management Research Group.

Hussey, D. E., 1985, Implementing Corporate Strategy: Using Management Education and Training, *Long Range Planning*, October.

Hussey, D. E., 1988, *Management Training and Corporate Strategy*, Oxford: Pergamon.

Hussey, D. E., 1993, Effective management training and development, in Hussey, D.E., editor, *International Review of Strategic Management*, Volume 4, Chichester: John Wiley.

Lorenz, C., 1986a, ICL: Metamorphosis of a European Laggard, *Financial Times*, 12 May.

Lorenz, C., 1986b, ICL: A painful process of change, *Financial Times*, 14 May.

Lorenz, C., 1986c, ICL: The power of saturation training, *Financial Times*, 16 May.

Peters, H. J. and Waterman, R. H., 1982, *In Search of Excellence*, New York: Harper and Row.

Rose, D., 1989, Woolworth's Drive for Excellence, *Long Range Planning*, Volume 21/1, February.

Scase, R. and Goffee, R., 1989, *Reluctant Managers*, London: Unwin Hyman.

Whitelaw, M., 1972, *The Evaluation of Management Training*, London: Institute of Personnel Management.

9
Strategy and Other HR Activity Areas

It would be possible to go through every area of HR activity in turn, modifying the models slightly, but effectively repeating much of what has already been covered in Chapters 3, 6 and 7, some aspects of which will in any case recur in Chapter 10. This would lengthen the book, without adding much except boredom for the reader. At the same time, to say no more about about the strategic implications of at least some of the other areas of HRM which are critical for strategic success, apart from what has been stated in the various examples given in passing and in the case examples, would unbalance the book.

The model in Figure 3.4 (see page 46) can be modified for use in all areas of HR activity, just as it was modified in the preceding chapter on management development to fit the particular considerations of that activity. We can simplify this even further, as a mental check as each activity is considered, to argue that as a minimum we need to ask the following questions:

- What does the organisation need from this activity in order to sustain the vision, and implement the strategies?
- How will the activity be affected by trends and events in the external environment?
- What are we doing at present?

- What do we need to do to change or supplement what is already being done?

As we have seen, it becomes more complex when these questions are applied systematically to a particular area, but the principles behind them hold firm for all areas.

Table 9.1 gives a short cut method for considering some of the other HR activities. It offers an indicative list, which can be expanded or contracted as needed, although the main risk in short-cutting the full approach is a failure to be totally objective. It is very easy to believe that something is doing what it should do, when there is no investigation, and this is what we should like to believe anyway. If you can be objective, and have deep knowledge of each area, the approach may be worth trying. It may also be useful to do it ahead of a more detailed study, to see whether there is a change of view. It may also be worth comparing what HR professionals in the company think with the views of a panel of line managers.

The idea is to rate each activity, as it is now, against whether it helps or hinders the corporate vision and the implementation of strategies. Does it help, hinder, or is it neutral? Should action be taken to change what is done? What obstacles might prevent such a change? In Table 9.1 I have expanded one or two of the headings to make the point that not every aspect of an HR activity may be operating with the same degree of success. Again, these expanded headings are meant to be no more than indicative, and they should be changed to fit the particular requirements of the organisation.

But these are still general concepts, and the observations below will attempt to put a little strategic flesh on the bones of some of the other HR activity areas.

THE LEARNING ORGANISATION

It is fashionable to talk of the learning organisation, but very easy to use the term as a reason not to think through the issues raised in the previous chapter. A learning organisation should not replace a management development strategy, but should be part of it, and should certainly not be used as an excuse for a

Table 9.1 *Contribution of HR activity areas to the business needs.*

HR Activity	Hinders 1	2	Neutral 3	4	Helps 5	What Could Be Improved?	What Obstacles to be Removed
Reward system:							
Managers							
Sales							
Shop Floor							
Other							
Culture:							
Internal							
Diversity							
International							
Internal communication							
Briefing Groups							
Co. Newspaper							
E Mail							
Other							
Recruitment:							
Managers							
Clerical							
Other							
Industrial Relations:							
Union recognition							
Works Councils							
etc							
Learning Organisation							
Performance management							

laissez faire approach to training, which assumes that what is done has to be worthwhile just because it *is* being done. Mayo and Lank, 1994, page 7 suggest that "A learning organisation harnesses the full brainpower, knowledge and experience available to it, in order to evolve continually for the benefit of all its stakeholders". In the lead up to this definition they stress that it should be a "business centred holistic approach" that looks at what makes it possible for continuous learning to take place both for the individuals and the organisation, and then relates the benefits of this learning to measures of success, such as return on assets, customer satisfaction, innovation, growth and employee morale. There is nothing in these observations which is incompatible with the approaches already advocated, although commitment to a learning organisation would change some of the policies and priorities.

A learning organisation requires at least two components which are not present in a more traditional approach. The first is a cultural dimension which fosters an interest in individual and organisational learning. This would include a philosophy of coaching right down the organisation, to the extent that it becomes the automatic way of doing things; a commitment to continuous improvement, so that every major activity is reviewed regularly by those involved, and the lessons identified; and an individual philosophy that enables people to respond to learning activities created by the organisation, but not to restrict learning to those opportunities. Handy et al., 1996, found in a survey of managers that personal development plans were a management development initiative in 65% of the organisations. However other initiatives that might imply a learning organisation were much less prevalent: coaching (28%), mentoring (19%), and a career resource centre/library (15%).

The second component is an information system which allows the results of organisational learning to be shared. The term "learning organisation" implies that it is more than the collective sum of random individual learning, yet few have found a method to dissipate the lessons of experience across the organisation.

The strategic dilemma is whether a commitment to be a learning organisation would do more to help the organisation achieve its aims than any other approach: the obstacles are whether it is possible for the particular organisation to achieve the cultural and systems changes needed to make it work. Nothing in the learning organisation concept precludes a business driven approach to development and training, but there may be an issue in determining priorities. The learning approach can help to change attitudes and behaviour in the organisation, but takes a great deal of effort, and is of necessity a concept for the longer term (although there may be random short-term benefits too). If the organisation is in a crisis situation, or faces massive changes that require immediate attention, much more specific and targeted HR responses may be better in the short term.

CULTURE

I do not know any organisation that has an HR department called culture, because by its very nature culture is shaped by a variety of events and actions, and is to some degree a legacy of the past. Nevertheless culture is of great concern to management, and therefore HRM, whether the issue is to maintain the current culture, or to change it. This point has been mentioned in several places in this book, and was partially illustrated in Chapter 4 by the Premier Bank case, and was certainly a feature of the Timex case. The strategic importance of company culture is clear, and HR has much to contribute to it through almost every other area of HR activity.

There are two other dimensions of culture which receive less attention in the UK than in some other countries, and both are of considerable potential strategic importance. They are *diversity* and *intercultural differences*.

Diversity

Although hardly discussed in the UK, this has become an area of great importance in the USA, and most large corporations have a very senior member of HRM whose title includes the word diversity. What is diversity? It is the removal of prejudice from the organisation and the individuals it employs, to ensure that all employees regardless of gender, ethnic origin, religion and life style receive equal treatment in the organisation. This is more than equality of opportunity for promotion, it is about creating an environment which encourages the creativity of all, and enables everyone to work without feelings of insecurity, and without insult. In the USA the drivers of the movement included legislation, and the realisation that the make up of the working population was changing, and that white Anglo-Saxon males would never again be the majority component of the working population.

Equal opportunities legislation in the UK is less stringent, but many of the pressures to ensure that everyone is treated with respect and fairness are becoming stronger. In the army and in many police forces diversity has become a high profile strategic issue. The policy about such issues may have been clear, but it is equally clear that it is not implemented by those with responsibilities for others. At peer level the treatment of some women and black males has been abominable, to the point where they have been forced to leave. Apart from the loss of talent to the organisation, there are increasingly the risks of expensive legal challenges, and high profile (negative) media attention.

Actions that may be necessary include setting appropriate policies, monitoring the effectiveness of these, training, and an effective system of receiving and dealing with complaints about discrimination. In the USA part of the training, which usually extends to all employees, is about understanding and being sensitive to cultural differences. This may not be enough to remove deep-seated prejudices, but can be effective in improving the situation among those who are merely thoughtless.

Intercultural Differences

For an organisation that has no significant operations or business outside of the country, intercultural matters may be of little or no importance. Organisations which have a multi-country operation or business should give some thought to how intercultural differences impede or enhance business success. This becomes of even greater importance when entering into strategic alliances with organisations in other countries; in acquisition situations; when departments in different countries (such as research and development) have to work closely together; when individuals of one country are sent to work in another; and when there is a need to have subsidiaries of various countries commit to a common vision, and common methods and processes.

There are at least three areas for consideration. Language is the first, for although most multinational organisations choose an official language, often English, local affairs are usually in the language of the country, and not all employees speak the official language. Attention to language skills in recruitment, and opportunities for employees to learn another language are commonplace solutions which need no discussion. One which is worth attention is the running of core management training programmes across all subsidiaries, but in the specific languages of the countries. Although not a representative sample, my experience is that British based head offices are less likely to consider this option than those in other countries, including regional European offices of USA multinationals. I established a service to offer this facility in most countries of Europe in the early 1990s, but was concerned that with only one exception our clients were not British, and this exception was one of the smallest international business units of a British multinational. The strategic questions for organisations are how they are achieving common understanding across borders, in order to achieve commitment to shared values and strategies.

The second area is important, but readily learnable, and is the understanding of manners in each country, so that the actions which can give offence are avoided.

It is the third area which is perhaps the most ignored and potentially most important: the national differences in culture which cause people to look at the same issue in different ways. The solution is to ensure that there is a shared understanding of these differences, and deliberate action to make choices in a way that enables all cultures to work in the most effective manner. This is both a total management issue, and of importance to HRM itself in the design of international HR processes and procedures. Because it is not something which figures significantly in as many organisations as it should, it is worth looking at this issue in greater depth.

The pioneer of ways of visualising cultural differences between nations, in a validated and reliable way, is Professor Hofstede who until recently was at the University of Limburg at Maastricht in Holland, and founder of an institute to continue the research, called the Institute for Research on Intercultural Cooperation IRIC. Commercial exploitation of the concepts is licensed to a Dutch consulting firm. Hofstede, 1991, builds on his past work, and provides five classifications that help define national differences. The differences have been quantified for a large number of countries. Neither Hofstede nor any of the other investigators of this subject would argue that every single person in a country conforms exactly to a pattern, but that the overall culture in that country follows certain definable characteristics. They are thus statements of prevailing national difference, not necessarily individual difference.

The five dimensions are:

1 *Power Distance Index (PDI)*: "the extent to which the less powerful members of institutions and organisations within a country expect and accept that power is distributed unequally" (Hofstede, 1991, page 28). Countries such as Great Britain, Germany and the USA have low scores which imply, among other criteria, low dependence needs, the minimisation of inequality, equal rights. In contrast a number of countries in Asia and South America have high scores, which imply the opposite.

2 *Individualism Index (IDV)*: measures a continuum. At the high extreme of the index the paramount concern is with looking after oneself and one's own family. *Collectivism*, where the group is predominant, is on the other and low extreme (see Hofstede, 1991, page 51). Not surprisingly we find the USA and many European countries lying on the high side, while many Asian countries, such as Japan, Singapore and Korea have low scores and lean towards collectivism.

3 *Masculinity Index (MAS)*: Measures (high scores) the extent to which the dominant values in society are assertive, tough and focused on achievement and success, and (low scores)

the extent to which society embraces the so-called feminine attributes of caring and concern over the quality of life (see Hofstede, 1991, page 82). In my opinion, the choice of name for this index is unfortunate and causes confusion (although Hofstede explains his reasons in the book), because the words have too many other emotive connotations. Austria, Japan, Switzerland, Italy, Great Britain and Germany, in descending order, have high scores: The Netherlands and the Scandinavian countries have low scores.

4 *Uncertainty Avoidance Index (UAI)*: is "the extent to which the members of a culture feel threatened by uncertain or unknown situations" (Hofstede, 1991, page 113). A high score indicates intolerance of ambiguity, and a low score tolerance. Great Britain has one of the lowest scores found, considerably lower than many of its fellow members of the European Union. Does this help explain why we see many of the rules that come out of the EU as bureaucratic nonsense, while France and Germany see them as an essential way to bring order out of chaos? If we are quite comfortable with uncertainty, we have no need to try to resolve it. Perhaps it also explains why as a country we face no great internal pressure for a written constitution.

5 *Confucian Dynamism Index (CDI)*: is a "long term versus short-term orientation and can be interpreted as a society's search for Virtue" (Hofstede, 1991, p. 171). Not surprisingly Asian countries, such as Japan and Taiwan, which have a base of Asian religions, score highly. Pakistan and Western countries have low scores.

Trompenaars (1993) offers an alternative research-based approach, although based on a smaller sample than that of Hofstede. He suggests seven orientations of culture: five based on the ways human beings deal with each other, another on attitudes to time, and the seventh on attitudes to the environment. The examples in his book give considerable insight into intercultural differences, and offer practical advice for various specific circumstances.

Hall, 1996, discusses what she describes as the "compass model of culture". A useful aspect of her concept is that it enables organisational cultures and country cultures to be plotted on similar criteria, which offers a way of looking at organisational fit in various country environments. A gross simplification of the approach is the plotting of cultures on a diagram with four quadrants, created by the intersection of two lines representing variables. The variables are responsiveness and assertiveness, both measured on a high to low scale.

The four quadrants formed are:

- Low assertive/low responsive—*North style*
- Low assertive/high responsive—*East style*
- High assertive/high responsive—*South style*
- High assertive/low responsive—*West style*.

Example countries quoted are:

North Style: The Netherlands; Great Britain
East Style: Japan; Italy
South Style: France
West Style: Germany; USA.

No author would claim that his or her approach covers everything there is to cover about intercultural differences. But what all of them do is offer a mechanism that allows differences to be examined and considered, without confusion with stereotypes. The danger of trying to think about culture without such a vehicle is that it is too easy to fall back on cartoon type pictures of individuals from various countries. The fact that these have no value is demonstrated when a collection is made of the stereotypes that people in a number of countries have of themselves and each other: good for a laugh, but not much else.

Attention to intercultural issues can make a significant contribution to the business. This may become even more important when the organisation's strategy is taking it into new countries, or different forms of alliance and collaborative ventures. An organisation that has operated stand alone subsidiaries in different companies for years may expect to encounter new problems if its aim is to draw these businesses closer together, to operate common marketing strategies, and to rationalise manufacturing and services. These things are hard enough to achieve within a national culture, and can be made even more difficult once cultural borders are crossed. HRM can contribute to the success of such plans by ensuring that national differences are considered when common policies are defined, that announcements are made in a way that is most effective for each culture, and that managers who have to operate across country borders understand the nature of the cultural differences, and adjust their own behaviour to obtain the best result.

COMMUNICATION

In many organisations responsibility for the media of internal communication may not lie with HRM, although in many others it will have responsibility for at least some of the internal media. The official media, such as the company magazine or newspaper may be important, but may not have as much impact as the day-to-day communication activities of managers. If the journal preaches the organisation's vision, but the immediate superior puts across a quite different message, it is probably what the superior says that will have the most impact. A major part of every manager's job is internal communication, which means that we are once again in an area where HRM has to be both proactive and reactive.

It has to take a lead in pointing out where the style, method and content of communication might be affected by a new organisational vision or strategy, but has to follow the lead of top management once decisions have been made. Many aspects of communication are closely bound up with culture, and if the culture is appropriate for the organisation all aspects of communication should aim to reinforce it. The Timex case in Chapter 4 showed weaknesses in communication that were closely linked to the culture of the organisation.

Caldwell, 1995, suggests that "Effective communication is one of the most direct forms of 'employee involvement'". Hubbard, 1996, argues that communication plays a large part in managing employee expectations in times of change (Chapter 11 deals with change management at greater depth). Table 9.2 summarises the four communication styles defined by Caldwell.

Table 9.2 Styles of communication.

Communication Styles	Closed	Informing	Listening	Open
Orientation towards employees	AUTOCRATIC Manager makes decision	PATERNALISTIC Manager presents decision as in best interests of employees	CONSULTATIVE Manager seeks input before making decisions	PARTICIPATIVE **Manager facilitates decision making by employees**
Communication tools, media, approaches	# written codes # instructions # formal meetings	# newsletters # notice boards # employee reports # one way briefing	# focus groups # employee surveys # informal discussion # two way briefing	# self managed teams # joint problem solving groups
Communication goals	Command and Control	**Disseminate information: Sell decisions: raise awareness**	Test and validate decisions	Build autonomy and commitment

Communication pattern

← One-way, mainly downward flow, low feedback

Two-way, greater upward flow, high feedback →

Source: Reproduced by permission from Caldwell, R., 1995, Closed or open? Four styles of employee communication, *Journal of Strategic Change*, 4.1, Chichester: John Wiley & Sons.

It is not my purpose to argue for a particular style, but to offer this as one way of thinking about this issue in relation to what the organisation is trying to achieve, and also to begin to relate some of the communication tools and media, which may fall directly under the control of HRM, to the style which is appropriate to the organisation.

I do not believe that there is only one right style for all organisations, but that the appropriate approach is highly situational, affected by the culture of the organisation, its intended vision and values, and the skills and capabilities of employees. However it is an issue which deserves careful consideration, and which should not be allowed to emerge by accident and without forethought. Caldwell offers another chart in his article, which is not reproduced here, which places his communication styles—closed, informing, listening and open—in a matrix, one axis of which is the degree of employee involvement, and the other the degree of employee commitment. The reason I have not shown this here is that I am not sure how much is cause and how much is effect. For example, the closed style has low involvement and low commitment. If commitment is low, a high involvement style will not work: however, a low involvement style may cause the low commitment. I think this shows that the issue is complex, as well as important, and well worth considerable attention by HRM if it has ambitions to be business driven.

In contrast to these complex issues the working tool shown in Table 9.3 is almost mundane. However it is an approach that I have found useful when thinking about a communications strategy, if only to ensure that there is a common base from which to start. The table has been simplified for demonstration purposes, and in reality there may be many more target groups of managers that the tools and media are trying to reach. My example has no middle managers, but this is not to suggest that organisations should not communicate with middle managers!

The two arms of the matrix are the main things that are (or should be) communicated, and the methods. Initially the matrix will show what the organisation is now using, but as the analysis develops the list should be extended to other methods it could use. The numbers in each matrix are keyed to the target employee groups, and the particular positioning should not in

Table 9.3 Communication—what, how and to whom?

What to Communicate	Conference	Briefing Groups	Method of Communication Training Prog	Memos	Newspaper	Notice Board
Company values	1–3	1–6	4		4–6	
Growth strategy	1–3	1–6			4–6	
Specific problems	1–3	1–6	1–3		4–6	
Competitive situation		1–6	4		4–6	
Quality initiatives		1–6	5	4–6	4–6	
Strategic changes		1–6	3	1–3	4–6	1–6
Need to change		1–6			4–6	1–6

Types of employee
1 Business unit managing directors
2 Business unit directors
3 Other senior managers
4 Sales force
5. Direct skilled workers
6. Clerical employees

any way be taken as a recommendation. In practice I should add another refinement to the matrix, by using different colours when employee groups are placed on the matrix to indicate how effective the method is. Ideally the effectiveness should come from some objective survey, and not from management opinion. The fact that senior managers or HR professionals rate an approach in a particular way does not mean that this is how it is perceived by other levels.

Actions that may result from such an analysis may include adding new methods and tools, making what is done more effective, but above all ensuring that the methods fit the desired communication style, and that the style is related to the business needs.

REWARD SYSTEMS

It is possible that there may be no existing HR activity in some of the issues discussed so far in this chapter. This is not so for reward systems where every organisation has an existing system in place. The important thing for a business driven approach is to ensure that the existing processes are indeed the best response to the needs of the organisation. As the general model in Figure 3.4 (page 46) shows, it is not just what the organisation is trying to achieve which should impact on HR policy, but also the trends and forces in the external environment. This is true of all aspects of HR, but particularly true of reward, where the levels of pay set, and the way in which reward is managed must be appropriate to ensure that the organisation can attract and retain the numbers and types of employee that it needs.

There is no perfect way of managing reward, for anything that encourages behaviour to move in a direction that the organisation sees as positive may also trigger behaviours which is the organisation might see as negative. Apart from the issue, mentioned in an earlier chapter, that a reward system which is based on individual success may encourage selfish behaviour at the expense of teamwork, there may also be a much wider concern among employees over equity and fairness. Bonus schemes and performance related pay may be capable of being related explicitly to organisational strategies, but can bring two other problems: how do you decide the contribution that each person has made, and are we absolutely certain that we have captured all the key elements of a job in the reward structure? On the first point there is a danger that the larger the element of reward which purports to be related to individual performance, the greater is the propensity for others who do not do so well to feel that the system is unfair. On the second point, there have been high profile situations where a top manager has achieved a performance bonus for the year's work, only to be dismissed shortly after, over a performance issue which relates to that year but was not one of the bonus performance criteria.

Handy et al, 1996, page 13, report on their survey of managers that

> "... organisations are criticised for playing too great a reliance on performance related pay (PRP). Relatively few managers are motivated by this type of reward and incentive system, although many report that their organisation uses PRP to motivate staff."

Much depends on what we mean by motivation. I believe that a pay system can direct behaviour in a certain direction, without building any positive feeling towards the organisation. It can reinforce positive motivation that comes from other sources when the reward policy and systems are designed to do this, and everything pulls in the same direction. There is still much truth in the view of Herzberg, 1966, that removing feelings of dissatisfaction around a hygiene factor such as a reward system does not create satisfaction.

There are many different pay systems to choose from, among them competency based pay, profit related pay, flexible pay systems, as well as those already mentioned. The strategic HRM task is to make the pay system fit not what the organisation has been in the past, but what it is trying to be in the future, and to remove conflicts between the reward system and other management processes. It is not an easy task.

SUMMING UP

It has not been the intention of this chapter to ensure that every aspect of HRM is mentioned; neither is it meant to imply that things not mentioned are of lesser or no importance. The business driven approach requires consideration of every aspect of HR, both as an individual activity, and as part of an integrated and coordinated approach to HRM.

The questions suggested at the front of this chapter are a critical starting point. The model in Chapter 3, Figure 3.3 (page 43), is also important as a reminder of the integrated nature of the components of HRM.

What was apparent from the chapters which looked in detail at competencies and management development, and which also emerged in this chapter, is that the business driven approach needs objective information if it is to be effective. Not only do we need to know what we are doing now, which can be difficult to find out sometimes, but we need to know the results of what these actions are. Although this need emerges through the discussion of how to achieve business driven HRM, it is in fact a straightforward requirement of good management. The next chapter will take us more specifically into some of the quantification aspects of HRM, and we will return in the last chapter to aspects of performance of the HRM function itself.

REFERENCES

Caldwell, R., 1995, Closed or Open? Four Styles of Employee Communication, *Journal of Strategic Change*, 4.1.

Hall, W., 1996, *Managing Cultures*, Chichester: John Wiley.

Handy, L., Holton, V. and Wilson, A., 1996, *The Ashridge Management Index, 1966*, Berkhampstead: Ashridge Management Research Group.

Herzberg, F., 1966, *Work and the Nature of Man*, Cleveland, USA: World Publishing.

Hofstede, G., 1991, *Cultures and Organisations*, London: Mcgraw-Hill.

Hubbard, N., 1996, Managing Employee Expectations in Times

of Organisational Change, *Journal of Professional HRM*, 1.4, July.

Mayo, A. and Lank, E., 1994, *The Power of Learning*, London: Institute of Personnel Development.

Trompenaars, F., 1993, *Riding the Waves of Culture*, London: The Economist Books.

10
The Numbers Game—
Planning HR Needs

So far we have largely ignored the core of what was known as manpower planning, which was concerned with forecasting the future needs of the organisation by skills and numbers, relating this to the expected availability, and developing plans to ensure that the organisation could obtain and retain the people it needed. Manpower planning was always more than a forecasting game, and would have included certain areas of policy, albeit in a somewhat different manner than the business driven approach which I have advocated. I have always preferred the term personnel planning, because of the somewhat narrower confines of the word manpower.

Although much of the emphasis in this book is very different from that of the manpower planning texts of the mid-1970s, such as Bramham, 1975, there is much of value in the old approach which we have not yet discussed. We do need to try to understand the future employee requirements of the organisation, and areas where there are likely to be shortages of supply. Confidence in forecasting ability may have been undermined by some of the published forecasts: the statement made just before the depression of the early 1990s that this was the best time ever to be a new graduate, because of the overall national reduction in the number of school leavers, seemed somewhat hollow as organisations plunged into depression and reduced staff. Graduates found that they did not have the promised wide choice of jobs, and many were lucky if they found any job within a reasonable period of graduating. But this sort of error does not remove the need to try to get a fix on external supply and demand, and the organisation's own requirements. Some assumptions are needed for sensible planning, and the assumptions are likely to be more helpful if they are underpinned by some rational analysis. This is what this chapter is about.

A FRAMEWORK FOR PLANNING FUTURE HR NEEDS

The framework shown in Figure 10.1 should be thought of in the context of Chapter 3. It is not competitive with the approaches suggested there, and should be seen as an essential expansion to provide the organisation with the data it needs to plan effectively.

The top three boxes of the model could be rephrased in more simple terms as three questions. What do we want the organisation to be? What people resources do we have now? How easy or difficult will it be to bring in any resources we need from the labour market? What we are trying to do is to move from the current position to see what we will need at some future state. How far forward we should be looking is a matter of judgement, but whatever period we choose for our detailed forecasts, we should think about the trends for an even longer period, so that there is a context for the figures. There should be no need to discuss every aspect of the top box in the model again, as it has appeared in almost all the strategic thinking so far, and the focus will be on a few matters which are additional to the earlier discussions. There is a lot to say about the current internal and external situations, and both will be discussed in much more detail later in this chapter.

The first three boxes of the model would enable us to make some forecasts, but there are other things going on as the business driven strategies begin to emerge from the various areas of HR, and from the overall HR policies. Our interest is

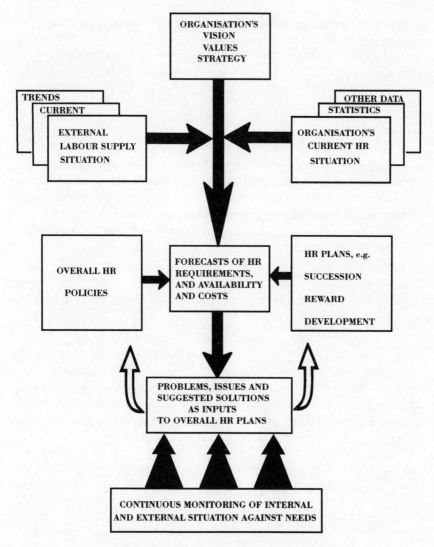

Figure 10.1 *Framework for planning future HR needs.*

not really in the forecasts that are generated, but in the implications that arise from them, and this takes us to the next box in the model. Nothing is straightforward, and there is a potential reiteration here, as the findings from this work cause a reexamination of the plans and policies that have been provisionally developed in the various components of HRM. In real life these other areas would be drawing statistics from the same organisational database, so many of the issues will have already been identified by the various HR specialists. In real life, too, there is much to be gained from a process which has the whole HRM senior team meet, possibly also with line involvement, to examine and discuss the factors that go into the forecasts, and the implications, at several stages before final conclusions are reached. The intent should not be for whoever does the forecasting to surprise the organisation with his or her brilliance, but to share and use information as work progresses. Reality would suggest many more interactions between the players than the step by step diagram implies.

It is also worth emphasising the need for an integrated plan to deal with the various issues, as suggested in Chapter 3, and the aim should be for all the areas of HR to coordinate and work together to produce the best possible solution for the organisation. There are comparatively few solutions that can be applied by one area of HR in isolation from other areas. For example, a retention problem which jumps out of the forecasts may require a solution which addresses remuneration, training, communication, culture, career management, and others. This is self-evident, but worth stressing, because although we need to bring specialist skills to bear on the HR issues, they are only of value if put in the context of all the other specialist areas.

The final box in the diagram is a reminder that neither the internal nor the external factors will be as we have assessed them. Apart for potential errors of omission, important factors can change quickly and dramatically. Hindsight might tell us that we should have foreseen some of the changes. The reality is that we never will foresee them all. The next best thing is to keep the organisational antennae twitching, so that the organisation is in a better position for quick reaction.

No further discussion will take place here of the boxes in the diagram covering overall HR policies and HR plans boxes, as these have been aired in great detail elsewhere and little would be added by going over old ground, even in a slightly different context. The focus will be on those boxes of the model where there is something new to add.

SPECIFIC ISSUES FROM THE ORGANISATION'S VISION, VALUES AND STRATEGY

As has been discussed at great length, almost every aspect of HRM should be impacted by what the organisation is trying to do. In the context of this chapter, the main interest is in those aspects of strategy which will alter the human resource needs of the organisation, and the costs of those resources. The choice of words is deliberate, as it is not essential for all the requirements of the organisation to come from employment, and other options should be explored, such as contracting out or alliances. An intent to have a more flexible cost base would feed through into not only the forecasts of numbers of people, but the nature of the relationship.

There are factors which tend to increase the numbers and different types of employee that the organisation will need, and these must be balanced against other factors which will decrease requirements. The degree of certainty around the impact of the various factors will vary: some things can be estimated with a fair degree of precision, while others may lie between a fairly wide band of possible impacts. Seven questions should receive attention:

1 *What totally new activities does the organisation plan to undertake?* Anything that will be added to the organisation's activities represents a potential increase in the numbers of employees. If the plan is to expand by acquisition it may be possible to assume that the extra numbers will come with the acquired organisation. Often this will be a superficial assumption, as acquisitions frequently bring changes to both organisations. Incremental expansion, such as opening a marketing office in a country where none exists, will usually be fairly easy to see in both organisational and numerical terms. A green field expansion into a different business is usually more complex, because its scale may depend on the degree of success, and lack of knowledge may mean that all the employee implications cannot be foreseen without seeking advice outside the organisation.

2 *What activities will cease?* Cessation of an activity may take many forms, each of which may impact HR requirements in

a different way. The intention may be to close an area of the business which is neither delivering results, nor contributing to the strategy of the organisation: the Timex case is an example. This has very different implications from when a business is intended to be sold as a going concern. Often the planned changes are concerned with a function or department of the organisation, such as the closure of an internal printing organisation, or the contracting out of the IT function. In the former case the people and their associated overheads will not be required. In the latter, the same people may still work in the organisation's premises, but as employees of another organisation, so there will not be the same knock-on effect on the numbers of people needed to provide security, safety and certain welfare services. The different types of situation need to be carefully identified, so that the various impacts on HR needs can be estimated.

3 *What activities will change?* Often the organisation will plan to perform an activity in a different way. For example, an investment in new technology can change both the numbers of people required, and the competencies required from those employees. The activity is not closed, and may even expand, but how it will be undertaken will change. The impact may be across the whole organisation, or just in a few areas of the organisation. Examples can be found in insurance, where clerical jobs are reducing and knowledge workers increasing, and in manufacturing where automation may reduce the overall numbers of people, but increase the requirement for those with the new competencies.

4 *What changes will take place in the location of activities?* There can be situations where the total employee requirements are constant, but there is still considerable turbulence in the situation. This could occur if, for example, production was transferred from the UK to a new plant in South East Asia. In reality it is more likely that there would be changes in how the activities were undertaken in parallel with the shift in location, so both types of change would need to be considered. Relocation does not have to be to other countries to impact the organisation's termination and recruitment activity, and a similar, though perhaps less widespread, effect

follows the relocation of an office or factory to a different area of the country.

5 *What increase or decrease is expected in the volume of current activities?* So far we have looked at a number of circumstances that may be planned for in a specific way. Frequently the plans of an organisation will be based on growth or decline of current activities, which can be looked at as incremental changes. The volume of product X is expected to increase at 10% per year: sales in country Y will increase in real terms by 15%: there will be a decline of 5% in product Z. This does not mean that employee numbers will change pro rata, and the implications need to be examined by broad job categories. Will the changes take up unused capacity? Can the current overhead departments meet the changes from existing employee resources? Will the variable labour requirements of production be met by new employees, or by overtime? Does the sales force have to change in any way because of the planned changes?

6 *What productivity increases does the organisation expect?* It is unwise to assume no change in productivity when considering the conversion of a business plan to employee requirements. Some specific and major productivity initiatives have been mentioned under the other headings, but it may be desirable to go a step beyond foreseeable events to looking at the expected impact of things that cannot be seen as clearly. Benchmarking studies against other firms (see Chapter 12) may for example demonstrate that the organisation is lagging behind the industry leaders, and that a sensible forecast should take into account the sort of productivity increases that others have already achieved. A recently entered activity may be expanding very fast, and the principles of the experience curve may apply: this holds that costs will fall by a steady amount as the cumulative output doubles. The learning effect was first observed in the air frame industry, where production workers were found to take a reduced amount of time as their experience increased. The second air frame took less time than the first, the fourth less that the second, the eighth less than the fourth, the sixteenth less than the eighth. Further, the percentage reduction held firm each

time cumulative output doubled. Cumulative does not mean annual change, but over the whole time since production began. There are limits to the experience curve, and certain activities may reach a plateau beyond which the concept does not work, particularly those which are in the nature of personal services. However, the argument that one should not calculate future needs by doing no more than extrapolate current ratios is valid.

7 *What seasonal factors should be considered?* Not all activity follows an even monthly pattern. It is important to identify the seasonal peaks and troughs which will occur, in businesses where there are significant variations over the year. Failure to identify these factors will mean that any forecasts of employee requirements will underestimate needs at peak times, and overestimate them in the low season.

Finding the answers to these questions will give some of the raw materials for the requirements forecast. However, we are not dealing with a stagnant pool of employees, but a lake with outflows as well as inflows, which means that we have other factors to consider before we can prepare forecasts which are meaningful.

THE ORGANISATION'S CURRENT HR SITUATION

Most organisations know how many people they employ, but even that is sometimes an easier question to ask than to answer, because of definition problems and timing issues. But there are legal reasons which demand that these figures are available for at least some points in the year. For a detailed understanding of the organisation we need to have much more good statistical data than just total numbers. In fact the use of totals without an underlying depth of knowledge can mislead. A simple example is that a bald employment total gives us no idea of how many people we might expect to have to recruit next year, just to maintain the same numbers. And the real life situation is much more complex than this.

Many organisations are well aware of the types of statistics that are needed to support HR management. Some readers may wish to skip the description of the minimum statistical needs, on the grounds that they both know what is needed, and could expand the list. In all cases the statistics are more helpful if in a time series, so that a run of several years can be compared and, where there are seasonal factors (if relevant), lesser periods, such as by month or by quarter, can also be compared.

Detailed Analysis of Actual Employment Numbers

Employment numbers should be broken down by business areas, country, location within the country, and departments. The reason for this group of headings is obvious, and can be related directly to some of the strategic factors discussed in the preceding section. If you do not know how the employees are dispersed by location and organisational unit, it is not possible to assess the impact of some of the changes in activity which are intended to take place.

This is a starting point, and there are other headings that should be investigated. It is also necessary to get an understanding of the types of employee in the overall totals. Traditionally many organisations have kept statistics on the basis of direct and indirect employees; hourly paid and salaried; productive and non-productive. In the USA there is also normally a breakdown of exempt and non-exempt, which is a legal requirement related to terms and conditions of service. These breakdowns take us a little further forward, although they mostly emerge more from accounting needs for costs, than for HR actions. The separation of direct from indirect workers is less meaningful than perhaps it once was, because of the replacement of numbers of direct production employees by automation, which requires the support of more indirect experts.

The next level of resolution is concerned with seniority and skills. The first point can be more easily covered if the organisation has a grading system, because there is at least some chance that every employee has been put into a grade. This gives us some good information to build on. However, information on level in the organisation does not tell us what people do, and it is not really meaningful to combine a sales manager, when sales managers are easy to recruit or promote from within, with a scientist on the same grade, when there are few others in the organisation with the same disciplines, and of which there is a world shortage. In this example, we could double the number of sales managers without a problem, but this may not be true of the scientists. So we need to have access to some statistics which describe jobs in a broad but meaningful way that is suitable for aggregation. It is possible to go further, to try to break down employees by skills and competencies, and such data bases can be very useful but also extremely difficult to establish and keep up to date. It is also harder to keep the information in the same way as the other statistics, as each employee may fall under several headings in the analysis. A simple example is that when I used to analyse the saleable skills of employees of a consultancy which I managed, I always had more skills than people. When we added language fluency the list extended again. This was a useful and simple exercise in a consultancy employing 20 full time people and about 10 part time associates, where all the people knew each other, but would be very complex and more difficult to apply to a very large business.

The final level of resolution is certainly gender, and possibly ethnic minorities. The main purpose is to ensure that the organisation's anti-discrimination policies are operating in a satisfactory way, although the statistics are not the whole answer to this question. However, they will give a preliminary indication of whether the organisation operates a "glass ceiling", with few women or people from ethnic groups able to move beyond a certain level. Such statistics have to be read with care, as the fact that a plant in Bradford has more employees from minority ethnic groups than another in Pulborough, West Sussex, may be more to do with the make up of the population in the area than any policies applied by the organisation. The gender statistics are also helpful for various areas of HR policy, varying from the provision of special conditions of service to enable more women with children to remain in employment, to consideration of the costs of company insurance policies

Table 10.1 Number of managers by grade, age and gender.

Age	Grade 1			Grade 2			Grade 3		
	M	F	Total	M	F	Total	M	F	Total
61–65	2		2	1		1	4		4
56–60	3		2	2		2	5		5
51–55				18	1	19			
46–50	12		12	12	2	14			
41–45	38	8	46	11	2	13			
36–40	49	40	89	15	5	20			
31–35	7	3	10						
26–30	21	25	46						
21–25									
Total	132	76	207	59	10	69	9		9

Grade 3 is the highest grade: managing director not included.

Age and Length of Service

Other statistics are needed to give more insight into potential human resource issues and problems. A starting point is an analysis of age of employees by grade and by length of service. Table 10.1 has been compiled to indicate the type of problem that can be revealed by age analysis. It is deliberately kept simple, and assumes that the organisation has three grades of manager plus a managing director. Grade three is the most senior grade. and these are the executive directors. If we relied only on the bottom line of totals by grade, we would see that there is an issue, in that the proportion of women moves from just over a third in the lowest grade to nil in the highest, but it would not give any insight into where to look next, nor would it have given any indication of the other problems that can be seen from the age analysis. What the detail shows is that the organisation seems to have done something about achieving a measure of parity in the entry level grades, but there it ends. It also suggests that unless particular attention is given to this issue, it will be many years before there is a more appropriate proportion in the next grades. A companion length of service analysis would bring more insight. If, for example, it showed that in Grade 1 75% of the 36–40 year old males had at least 10 years experience, but that 50% of women had less than five years, it would indicate that either the organisation has greater difficulty in retaining women, or that when vacancies have arisen it has taken deliberate efforts to have a fairer recruitment or promotion policy. In Grade 2, we would make different deductions if the length of service analysis showed that most of these managers had spent their whole careers with the organisation, than if there were a healthy mix of service periods which showed that not all promotion was from within.

The main strategic problems revealed from Table 10.1 are around management succession, impending changes at the top, and the potential career management issues for those in Grades 1 and 2. Length of service statistics would give further understanding.

Apart from the insight such analyses give to the organisation, they provide a basis for calculating retirements, which will influence how many people have to be recruited, as well as being essential for succession planning.

Labour Turnover Analysis

There are two elements to labour turnover statistics: how many people leave and why they leave. Statistics should be capable of being presented under all of the headings discussed so far, so that it is possible to compare areas of the organisation, grades, and age/length of service. For forecasting and for policy purposes it is important to know the broad reason for leaving, such as death, retirement, health, redundancy, other organisational initiative, and resignation. It is also useful to be able to add those who have left a grade or area on promotion (or for another reason) to elsewhere in the organisation, an analysis which might have more complexity in a multinational enterprise that moved people into different businesses and countries.

The cause of the turnover is very important. Projecting historical ratios of all turnover is not safe when there is an abnormality in the situation. The retirement pattern of the past few years may not continue because the organisation has had a policy of early retirement and there are now few people left who are over 50 years of age; there may have been major redundancies in each of the past three years, but the organisation is now slimmed down. Such "one-off" events may not be expected to recur.

What is revealed about resignations at different levels or areas of the organisation can be important for the designing of actions to change the situation. Often this will mean further investigation, such as surveys to find out why people resigned.

Turnover by grade and age can be particularly revealing, in that an apparently healthy rate for the whole can conceal major problems in certain areas. An overall turnover rate of 10% might hide the fact that in some areas it exceeded 100%. While turnover rates should be expected to vary across the organisation there are limits to what should be seen as healthy.

Overtime

Overtime has been a long-standing way of giving some flexibility of resources to the organisation and boosting the income of employees. Typically, figures will only be available for overtime for which the organisation pays and therefore excludes most management and much clerical and secretarial time. For forecasting purposes the main need is for figures on paid overtime working, although there may be other HR reasons for a check on the unpaid hours that other employees are putting in, as this can contribute to stress and morale problems. Extra time, willingly given, to deal with a particular problem or project, may be a sign of a motivated organisation. A situation where people stay at their desks, regardless of whether there is work to do, so that they are seen to be there long after closing time, is a sign of low morale and an unhappy, distrustful atmosphere.

Lost Time Analysis

Time may be lost for unavoidable reasons. However sometimes it can be as a result of either low morale, or the working situation itself. For forecasting purposes it is important to know the patterns of time lost in different areas of the organisation, and whether these can be changed. Because there may be large differences by location, grade and type of job, it is not appropriate to assume that overall ratios can be universally applied. The information may be important in highlighting problems that can be cured by management and HR actions, and monitoring the success of those actions. Categories under which information might be analysed include days lost because of:

- Industrial disputes
- Accidents
- Occupational illness
- Other health and illness
- Time off in lieu of overtime (where the organisation has such a policy)
- Other approved reasons (eg unpaid leave, or education)
- Absenteeism.

Holidays have not been included in this list because they are an entitlement. However it is important to know the various entitlements so that allowance can be made when forecasting different types of employment needs. Further breakdowns of the headings may be helpful for considering HR policies.

Non-employees

Most organisations have people working on site who are not employees, but for whom some services have to be provided. The sources may be temporary staff, who are the employees of an agency; contract staff, some of whom may be self employed, but where the organisation has responsibilities to collect tax and national insurance; and contracted out services, such as security, internal auditing and IT operations. It would be wrong to ignore these categories of people, and I would suggest that the minimum information needed is the total hours they provide, and the maximum and minimum numbers of people each month.

The information discussed above is directly related to the focus of this chapter, although indications have been given of the wider value of much of this information. It should not be seen as a description of all the information needed for business driven HR management. Earlier chapters have already shown some of the other information needs, and the case histories have illustrated others. As with all planning activity, the universal rule is that more information will be needed than is normally available! A flexible HR information system makes life much easier.

EXTERNAL LABOUR SUPPLY SITUATION

However much we try, our view of the future is too often conditioned by what we are experiencing today. In a period of high unemployment it is hard to accept that there will ever be a problem of adequate availability of people to meet the organisation's needs, and at a time when organisations are going through redundancies, it is even harder to get managers to think of recruitment as an issue. The reality is that the organisation does not exist in a vacuum, and its ability to obtain and retain employees depends partly on its own actions, and partly on the external supply and demand situation. If the external elements are ignored the organisation may find that its strategies are frustrated for lack of the right people.

The components are those of any market: supply, market demand and price, and as with any market the interest is both on how it is today, and how the trends will develop in the future.

Supply

At any one time, the national workforce is a finite resource, although it has elastic edges, in that if national demand for labour increases, people who are not currently available for work may be tempted into the system: examples are people who have retired but are still capable, and self employed people with portfolio careers who have gone this route by necessity and not choice. At any one time there is an existing level of unemployment, when demand for labour is less than its supply. There is a flow of school leavers and new graduates into the system, and a flow out of the system through death, ill health and retirement. Immigration and emigration are factors which will add to or reduce the national workforce.

The national supply situation is important for the individual organisation, but in many situations the local area supply, or the supply of a particular type of employee may be more important. Mass migration of people from one part of the country to another to meet the needs of a factory expansion is possible, but expensive and unlikely, although managers and skilled specialists are generally more mobile than factory and clerical workers. Availability of the labour may be a key factor in deciding whether to expand a plant, or where to open a new site. Specialists may be mobile, but if the whole specialisation is in short supply, it may be necessary to look beyond the borders of the country.

Demand

In general terms, the demand for employees is a factor of economic growth, influenced by world competitive trends which put continued pressure on costs, and cause a never-ending search for ways to reduce labour costs. To some degree, supply affects demand. A pharmaceutical company, for example, is unlikely to establish a major research and development function in a poor Third World country that produces no scientists and medical practitioners. Expansion may be curtailed in any organisation if people of the right quality cannot be obtained at the right time. Demand also affects supply, particularly for skills that require specialist pre-employment education and training. If the demand for teachers falls away, fewer will train and the supply will reduce. At any one time unemployment gives a crude measure of the gap between supply and demand, and these figures are available at a regional level so that some indication of local variations is available.

Price

The price of labour is its wage or salary, plus any fringe benefits that are paid for it. (The cost of labour to an organisation will be more than this, and will include national insurance contributions, training and various administrative costs.) A shortage of labour leads to increased wage levels as fewer people compete for each job and firms increase what is offered to attract new recruits, and also have to examine existing remuneration policies in order to retain employees. The bargaining power of labour increases, while that of the organisation reduces. In times of high unemployment, the opposite is true and organisations can hold remuneration down, and can have a greater control over employment terms and conditions. It is interesting to speculate how many of the flexible pay schemes of the early 1990s would survive were there to be a return to the high employment levels of the early 1970s.

Practical Implications

Organisations cannot afford to ignore the national supply and demand for labour, although few will find justification for compiling their own forecasts from the economic statistics. Fortunately there are reputable organisations which research supply and demand on a global basis, and in respect of specific skills and problems. Most HR departments have a fix on the current situation, even if it is a general awareness rather than specific numbers. Organisations such as Henley Forecasting Institute and Institute of Manpower Planning offer services which help establish the trends.

It is also sometimes worthwhile to commission research of a collaborative basis with others in the industry who have an interest in the same issues. Two examples which have been published and are thus available to an even wider readership, are Rajan, 1990a and Rajan, 1990b. The first studied the supply and demand for employees on a Europe-wide basis. The second examined the changes from clerical to knowledge workers which were taking place in the financial services industries. This study was partly financed by the London Human Resource Group, an association of large organisations which were either in or associated with the financial services industry.

The ability to look forward, even if it is only to establish possible future scenarios, is critical. The one certainty is that current situations will change.

FORECASTS OF HR NEEDS, AVAILABILITY AND COSTS

By this stage a great deal of information has been amassed, and the next step is to use it. The easiest way to show how the information might be used is to work through an example. The example organisation was invented for the purposes of this book and is simpler than might occur in real life. The outcome will not be typical of all situations, but will show how the strands of information are brought together. Some of the key figures appear in Table 10.2, but this table does not make sense without the narrative which appears below.

The task is to forecast supply and demand for the manufacturing employees of an organisation. To simplify the number of calculations, only forecasts for next year are shown, next year being now + 1. There are 1500 shop floor employees

Table 10.2 Example of human resource forecasts.

Type of Employee	Now	Now + 1	Change	Retirement	Resignation	Retrain	Retrain gain	Problem Area
Grade 1 (Unskilled)	600	450	−150		75			−75
Grade 2 (Semi-skilled)	450	300	−150	30	10	35		−70
Grade 3 (Skilled)	300	450	150	25	5	10	35	150
Grade 4 (Technician)	150	300	150	15	5		10	160
Totals	1500	1500		70	95	45	45	

directly engaged in production, and there are four grades of employees. The example does not cover managers, supervisors and support services. This is to simplify the descriptions and to save the reader from wading through too many schedules. Currently the plant produces 1 500 000 units per year.

- *Step 1*: The plan is to increase production by 50% next year. The initial temptation is to gross the employment figures up by 50%, pro rata across the grades and forecast a labour force of 2250 people. Prudence, however, intervenes, as the analyst knows that such pro rata effects rarely occur. In this case detailed conversations with production management reveal that new plant has been ordered, and will be installed by the start of the next year. This will mean that the increase in output can be produced by the same number of people as are currently employed. Unfortunately this does not mean no change, as the new plant requires fewer lower skilled people, and more with higher skills.
- *Step 2*: The current and next year's figures are set out in the Now and Now + 1 columns of Table 10.2 and give a first stage forecast of labour needs. The change column shows how some grades will increase in numbers, while others will decrease, giving a potential redundancy and recruitment situation.

Our age analysis tells us that there will be 70 retirements next year. This is potentially helpful in that it could reduce the redundancies, but unhelpful in that it increases the numbers of higher skilled people we must recruit. The turnover analysis gives us a basis for estimating how many resignations there would be in a normal year. Both the retirements and resignations are important elements, but we would also need to look at the pattern through the year. If 75 unskilled people were to resign between the date of the forecast and day one of the new year the problem area would reduce considerably, and this is the assumption in the table. However, even if the assumption is correct it leaves another HR problem in its wake: can we find a way of maintaining output without taking on more people? Solutions may include the use of agency people, or recruitment for defined short-term periods. In any event, in real life we would have to look closer at the monthly phasing of the figures.

- *Step 3*: The next question is the extent to which we have employees who we could retrain to move to the higher skilled jobs. This is not just a question of the skills needed, but is also of the abilities of the employees themselves, and their willingness to undergo extensive training. In this example the assessment is that 35 of the semi-skilled workers could be retrained to move them up to the skilled grade, and 10 of the skilled workers could move up to the level of technician. Two columns of the table reflect these increases and decreases of personnel. Note that in this element of the forecast we are in fact proposing an option which has implications for management and the training area of HRM, and which has costs and benefits which can be identified.

  If everything worked out as the table suggests, we would need to recruit 150 people in grade 3 and 160 in grade 4. In grade 4 this is more than the net increase over the forecast of total employment need because of the impact of expected retirements and resignations. At the same time we have a redundancy problem to deal with in grades 1 and 2, although if the assumptions are right this is not as big an issue as it appeared when the exercise started.

- *Step 4*: The forecasts predicate even production throughout the year. A further stage would be to explore this premise in some depth, and to look at the impact of overtime hours. The answers will affect the sorts of solutions that can be produced to solve the problems. It may be that there is capacity to cover some of the extra jobs through increased overtime working, so that recruitment can be phased to some degree. If there is no such flexibility, or if the start of the year is the busiest period, the recruitment problem may become more urgent.

- *Step 5*: So far the figures appear to assume that new employees can be attracted to the organisation as required. This is a dangerous assumption to make without investigation, in that the whole plan could falter if there were shortages of some of the workers needed. To take this further we would need to break down our grade 3 and 4 workers into skill areas and look at the labour market to assess the chances of attracting the right people. If we are recruiting more people who are skill clones of those that we already employ, we may already have a good fix on availability, and our low turnover rate suggests that our organisation is attractive to these types of people (or it could be that we are the only employer in the area that requires some of these skills, and our demand is roughly equivalent to the local market supply). It may be that the new investment requires skills that we have not used previously, and our plans could be upset if there were likely to be difficulty in recruiting them. Assessments of the labour market might also indicate that we cannot recruit the new specialist people at our current remuneration package. This would bring another set of HR issues to consider, which could affect the forecast costs.

The loop effect shown in Figure 10.1 (see page 195) is important here, as the problems thrown up by the various stages of the forecast will require examination of policies and these in turn will affect the forecasts. For example, if the costs of retraining are thought to be too high, the numbers in the forecasts will change.

The final stage would be to cost out the various elements of the forecast.

There are four more points to make. The first is that we are dealing with a dynamic, and the forecasts are means to an end and have value only for this purpose. The second is that in a well ordered organisation, this particular example would have been a part of the decision to buy the new plant and equipment, and not be undertaken for the first time, as the example implies, after the decisions had been made and the plant ordered. HRM can hardly claim to be business driven if the sort of analysis described here is unable to influence the decisions and their implementation.

Thirdly, many of the options require management decisions, and the sort of closeness of HRM and management which has been described elsewhere is important.

Finally, we should never forget that forecasts are just that. They may be based on issues that are by their nature uncertain, and may be affected by the assumptions that are made. For this reason, assumptions should always be clearly defined (even if everyone knows what they are), and consideration should be given to sensitivity analysis around a series of "what if" questions. What if the delivery date for the new plant is wrong? What if we cannot recruit the new people to the required timetable? What if economic circumstances change and we have more resignations than we expect? These are but examples. The danger of well presented forecasts, particularly if printed out from a computer, is that they carry an air of accuracy which may be greater than they deserve. We are dealing with an essential and important process, but one that will often carry errors, and we should always be aware of this possibility.

The forecasts themselves are only important if they are used.

PROBLEMS, ISSUES AND SUGGESTED SOLUTIONS

The example discussed above illustrated the sort of issues that emerge from the analysis. There are various ways of reaching a set of agreed forecasts, but probably the most effective would be to achieve the feedback into the various elements of the HR strategy through a more dynamic mechanism than passing pieces of paper around the organisation, which is one way that Figure 10.1 could be applied. The disadvantages of a formalistic system of passing information and ideas are that there is reduced opportunity for real debate and exploration of the problems, and an increased risk of each area acting in a way that is not coordinated with the others. There is also the issue of how to bring line management into the equation, and in my view it is usually better to do this at a problem formulation stage, because it strengthens involvement, adds new knowledge and insight, and thus is likely to lead to better solutions.

A sensible approach would have included one to one discussions, where appropriate, during the stage of building up the first draft of the forecasts. My preferred approach to the final stage of ensuring a coherent and coordinated response to what the analyst sees as the forecast would be to have the key members of HRM coming together as a group to discuss and agree both the forecasts and the HRM actions that result from them. Such a working meeting, for which adequate time should be planned, is even better if membership is extended to key managers from outside HRM. The intention should not be to agree a total HRM business driven strategy at this stage, but to ensure that there is a quantitative underpinning to the final HRM strategy. Teamwork at this point aids the ultimate task of ensuring an integrated business driven HRM strategy. Chapter 3 showed the overall approach, and although discussion of various elements of HRM showed that each required specific attention, success will only result if the whole is drawn together as a response to the overall situation. By necessity, the various heads of specialist HRM sections will be working on the strategy in parallel, and the approach of this chapter offers one of the ways of achieving congruence in the various parts of the process.

REFERENCES

Bramham, J., 1975, *Practical Manpower Planning*, London: Institute of Personnel Management,
Rajan A., 1990a, *1992: A Zero Sum Game*, London: Industrial Society.
Rajan A., 1990b, *Capital People*, London: Industrial Society.

11
Managing Organisational Change

The common factor which every organisation faces is the need to manage organisational change effectively. The HR function has a dual responsibility, in that it not only has to manage the changes which it initiates itself, but it should be in a position to act in a consultancy and facilitation role in the organisation at large. Indeed it is difficult to see how the elements of a business driven HRM can work if they are treated in isolation, and are not integrated with other relevant initiatives: a point that was made in Chapter 3.

As we have seen there is a real need for HRM to have a role in the strategic processes of the organisation, but in terms of HR work volume most effort will always be directed to the role of aiding the implementation of those strategies. Neither role is of greater importance than the other: the organisation can sink because it has a poor strategy, or because it has a good strategy that it does not implement effectively. Implementation of a strategy that requires a fundamental change within the organisation is rarely the sole responsibility of HR, but it is often a situation where there are many HR issues, and HRM is in the best position to look at the behavioural aspects of the change.

This chapter will examine four aspects of successful change management: the integrated organisation; resistance to change;

a way of managing change; and situational factors in change management.

THE INTEGRATED ORGANISATION

It is difficult to begin to contemplate anything more than the smallest of incremental changes without a total picture of what makes an organisation work. Figure 11.1 offers a view of the key areas which are affected by change, and which themselves will affect other areas if they are changed. This view of an organisation is a long way from seeing the organisation only in terms of its structure. Although structure is an important element of the organisation, it is not the only element, and changing structure without at least thinking about the other factors is courting disaster.

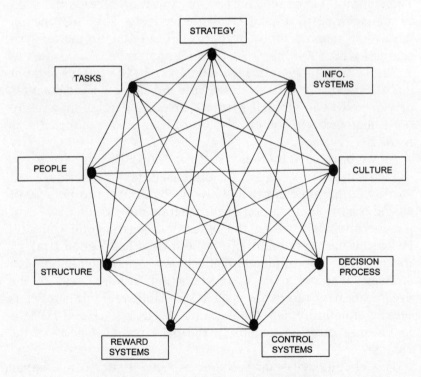

Figure 11.1 *An integrated view of organisation.*

The thinking that led to Figure 11.1, and concern about the integrated nature of the organisation began with Leavitt, 1970, although this was based on an earlier publication, Leavitt, 1964. He argued that organisations were multivariate systems, in which there were at least four interacting and significant variables. These were described as Task, People, Technology and Structure, and appeared in diagram form as what some call the Leavitt diamond. The key argument was not just about the variables, but that he saw them as interdependent, "... so that change in any one will most probably result in compensatory (or retaliatory) change in others" (Leavitt, 1970, p. 364).

The definitions attached to the words in Leavitt's diagram are broader than the definitions in Figure 11.1, but the overall concept is the same.

Variations of the Leavitt diamond, with added layers of complexity and usefulness have been published by a variety of sources. It is not always clear whether these were arrived at from independent work, or were developed from the original ideas of Leavitt. Perhaps the most well known is the McKinsey 7S model, which has influenced thinking at least as much as the Leavitt diamond itself. Among other places it appears in Peters and Waterman, 1982, page 10. The interrelated nature of the components is clear in the McKinsey view: the seven elements of this model are Structure, Systems, Style, Staff, Skills, Strategy, and Shared values, and these bring culture very clearly into the thinking.

Another version, Galbraith and Nathanson, 1978, envisages a model which is driven by strategy with the aim of achieving performance. The organisation which the strategy drives consists of Task, Structure, Information and Decision processes, Reward system, and People. No doubt there are many similar models in the literature. Figure 11.1, which has nine elements, owes a debt to the works quoted, but also brings in my own experience. Its value is that it aids thinking on the total impact of any change in any one or more of the variables on all of the other variables. I suspect it was the absence of such an approach which led to the rather shallow view of the impact of change by organisations which should know better, which emerges from the findings of some of the research described in Chapter 5.

Change is often about altering normal mental patterns, and to make this point the labels in Figure 11.1 will be described working in an anti-clockwise direction. In fact they could validly have been taken at random, since there is a potential interaction of any element with any other element. In order to sharpen the description of the figure, I will take the imaginary situation of a grocery products company which has operated across Europe on a country by country return on investment centre basis, but has now decided to take a more global approach with an overall European view of manufacture and marketing.

• *Strategy*. Under this heading I would include both what the organisation is trying to become, as well as how it is setting out to achieve this. The label therefore embraces vision, objectives, and the strategies being applied, but also needs to take account of the degree of flexibility needed because of the degree of turbulence in the organisation's environment, and the uncertainties in the situation. In the grocery products example the strategy is to gain both cost advantages from European rationalisation, and to improve the organisation's competitive position in the marketplace. The reader may find it worth pausing for a moment before reading further, to think about the sorts of changes this strategy will have to bring to the other elements in the model if it is to succeed.

• *Tasks*. Under this heading I mean those things which have to be done across the organisation in order to make the strategy work, which in turn takes us to the additional or changed competencies that will be needed. Although the heading covers the unique (to the organisation) things that may only be done once, such as the handling of an acquisition, considerable emphasis should be placed on the continuing tasks that will go on even after the strategy is considered to be implemented. In the grocery products example, there will be major changes to what is required from people at the centre who will take on wider responsibilities, and it may well be that the organisation does not currently have the competencies needed to set up and run some of the new Europe-wide operations. At the same time, the requirements from country managing directors and their managers will drastically change, in that they will no longer be responsible for running local businesses which are fully integrated within the country. Much more cooperation and teamwork will be needed across borders, which creates a different set of requirements. And some tasks will completely disappear as factories are combined into fewer, larger units.

• *People*. We know what we have to do, but do we have the right people to do it? Even more important is whether they are willing to make the necessary changes to how they do their jobs. What can easily happen when the nature and scope of a job is changed is that the psychological contracts are destroyed: although job titles and pay may remain the same, something that the particular employee values may disappear. In the grocery products example, the managing directors of the country companies could well value the role of being responsible for every aspect of an integrated business. Now much of that responsibility is transferred away, and the new job, however important it may be, is no longer the one they had signed up for. HR management has a clear role in helping to identify and deal with such situations, as it does with helping to ensure that those filling the jobs are competent to operate in the new way.

• *Structure*. This is the way tasks are divided between jobs, and jobs are clustered into reporting relationships. A shift of strategy may well cause a change to the structure. The grocery products example would require a change in the structure at both local company and head office levels, because of the shift in emphasis of where responsibilities lie, and how many activities will now be carried out. Some companies in the group will lose functions, such as production and research and development. Some new tasks will have to be accommodated. And in line with the flavour of the times, we will probably want to do everything with a smaller, flatter organisation. When considering structure, it makes sense to look at alternative ways in which the required tasks might be undertaken. It is not necessary for an organisation to do everything internally. Outsourcing, flexible employment operations, and alliances might all be considered.

• *Reward systems*. The issue is not whether the organisation has a reward system, but whether this supports or inhibits the strategic changes the organisation is trying to bring about. Changes in individual competencies needed might well call for a review of how people are rewarded, as it is possible that the reward system is now encouraging behaviour which is different from what is required. In the grocery case, country managing directors may have had a bonus system based on annual profit and return on investment targets for their spheres of operations. In the past they were totally responsible for what went on in their businesses. Now we have transferred some functions away from them (they can no longer control production costs for example), and we have a European strategy which means that we may transfer resources between countries in order to meet a marketing threat. In the old days the local managing director might have let market share slip in the country, as long as he or she could meet profit targets. Under the European approach the marketing supremo might decide to fight an aggressive competitor in a particular country, making up the loss here with profits from other parts of the European operation. The job of the local managing director is so different, that to reward it in the same way would encourage the wrong actions. It is possible to observe reward systems in organisations which may have been based on competencies which are now the wrong ones, or on results which are no longer the results sought. As people generally tend to behave in the way the reward system encourages them, intended actions can be frustrated if the reward concepts are not changed. Management exhortation will rarely be enough to overcome the pull of a misdirected reward system.

• *Control systems.* The control system, too, can either aid or hinder. There are both formal and informal dimensions. When Scandinavian Airlines decided to empower those closest to the customer to make decisions which affected that customer, they had to dismantle many layers of bureaucratic control, which would have prevented these decisions from taking place. The managing director who insists that his managers delegate, but phones frequently to ask questions on the minute detail of things in the department that happened only a few hours ago is, by his or her informal control system, saying "do not delegate, because if you do you will not be able to answer my questions". In the changed responsibilities of the grocery products example, it is clear that control systems must also change: not to do this would result in people being held accountable for actions for which they are not responsible, and other critical areas might escape any form of control. These issues are not only pertinent to the rest of the organisation but also apply to HRM itself. If management development activity were to be re-focused so that it is business driven, would this not challenge the traditional (and often inadequate) way in which this activity is currently controlled?

• *Decision processes.* There are two aspects to this element of the model: who is empowered to take what decisions, and the process by which they are taken. An organisation in a highly turbulent environment would be ill advised to have a bureaucratic decision process, which slowed down responses in a volatile situation, where success depends on fast movements. Dealers in the money market, for this reason, are usually able to make on the spot decisions of great magnitude. As already mentioned, a change to a more customer responsive organisation may change where decisions are taken. The grocery products example implies many areas where decision making responsibilities must change. The process is also important. Decision making can be extremely bureaucratic and formal, as is the case in many universities. Little is possible that does not follow the appropriate procedures. It may be autocratic, with all decisions taken by one or two people: old hands at a company I once worked for used to remember the founder of the company who even took such basic decisions as whether they could draw a new pencil from stores: the old stub had to be inspected before this decision could be made. Decisions also can be made in a very democratic way that involves many people in the organisation. The process moves us towards the next box, as the way power is exercised is a component of culture. The message here is to confirm that both aspects of decision making fit with what it is that the organisation is trying to achieve.

• *Culture.* The McKinsey 7S model uses the terms *shared values* and *style* in place of culture. Although culture is more than this, shared values are a good viewpoint from which to start the exploration of this element. When the whole organisation shares a common conception of vision and values, it is much more likely to be successful in implementing its strategy. The problems come when a change in strategy means that the old culture of the organisation is out of tune with what is needed to be effective in the changed circumstances. We saw this from one aspect in the Premier Finance example discussed in Chapter 4, and it was also a key element in the changes made by Scandinavian Airline Systems to make itself a more focused, customer-oriented organisation. It is easy to see how lack of attention to culture could frustrate the new strategy in our grocery products example. Previously the organisation operated in a way that allowed considerable deviation in the cultures of each country company, although inevitably there would be some overlay of culture from the parent company. Now we are telling people to think Europe, and that although their particular job may focus on a specific country, overall the key is cross-border cooperation and the common good. If cultures do not change, we may find behaviour at variance with requirements, and cause stress among many employees as they are compelled to act against what has become their instincts. Instead of cross-border cooperation, we can easily breed a degree of mistrust that can frustrate the strategy.

Culture is of course more than shared values. It springs from many things, not least of which are the traditions of the organisation, pride in its history, role models from within the organisation, and the climate caused by the way in which people manage their subordinates and work with their peers. There have been many high profile organisations which have declared that their old culture is no longer right for the situation they are now in, and have set about changing it: British Petroleum and British Telecom are prime examples. The judgement that has to be made is whether the culture can be changed to enable the new strategy, or whether it is set so hard in concrete that the strategy should be altered.

• *Information systems*. It may seem a truism to argue that the way information is collected and disseminated should fit not only the strategy, but also all other elements of the integrated organisation. Unfortunately there are many organisations whose information systems do *not* fit the needs of the present situation, and their ability to adjust to changed needs may be very low. I had one client, a large company which could only produce its financial results against budget on a quarterly basis, and this did not appear until more than three months after the end of the period. Their planning and budgetary processes meant that managers had to prepare a forecast of the full calendar year against budget during August, at which time the only figures available to them were for the quarter ending in March. Usually the problem is not such a horror story, and is a question of the system's failure to adjust to new circumstances. The reasons can be as diverse as managers not communicating changes to the information systems people; a failure by those who should know better to think through the new requirements, so that not even the managers knew what they wanted; or inflexibility in the systems so that it is impossible to produce information in a different way without considerable investment of time and cost. But without the right information it may be impossible for managers to take the right decisions, or even know the outcome of those decisions they do take.

In all aspects of Figure 11.1 the key word is "integrated". The requirement is not to get some of the elements right, but to get them *all* right, and this requires, firstly, deep understanding of the current situation and the impact of any change, and secondly, a willingness to make the necessary changes in every element so that the organisational machine becomes tuned to what the organisation now needs. This should be the starting point of any significant change.

RESISTANCE TO CHANGE

It is misleading to think that people always resist change. If this were so we would probably still all be living in caves. In fact the amount of change that many living people have experienced and contributed to in the last fifty years alone is enormous. Yet often change in an organisation does meet obstacles, and identifying these and developing ways of dealing with them is an essential part of change management. HRM is often in a good position to help management with this task, and should be able to point out areas where the enthusiasm for the new state shown by those at the top is unlikely to be matched by those at the bottom of the organisation.

Hubbard, 1996, argues from her research that success in change situations is largely affected by the way the expectations of employees are managed, which has many implications for the nature, style and frequency of communication, a subject which will receive more attention later in this chapter. Rumour and misinformation may cause resistance which would not have arisen if the process had been better managed.

There are many reasons why change may be resisted, some of which will not necessarily be consciously known to those who resist it. Obvious reasons may not be the only ones, and there may be more to address than these.

• *Fear.* In many situations fear is totally justified. It may take many forms, some of which can be dealt with by actions from within the company to support the change, while others are much harder. Fear that I may not be able to do what is now expected of me may cause me to try to frustrate the change whenever I can. This is an area where training and counselling can help considerably, as is an answer to the question of what will happen to me should I no longer be able to cope. Fear of losing one's job accompanies many changes such as delayering, the closures and relocations which would come from the change in strategy such as in the example of the grocery products company, and acquisitions and mergers. Often this fear is justified, as people will lose their jobs. Pretending that they will not can be more damaging than facing up to the situation. In straightforward circumstances, such as the closure of a factory, it is often easier for management to be frank about job losses. In an acquisition situation it may be harder, because the decisions have not been taken at the time of the acquisition. It is situations like this where the temptation to make statements about having no intention to make any changes can be misleading and dangerous, and if found later to be false can make the next stage of the situation much worse.

• *Breaking the psychological contract.* The psychological contract was mentioned earlier, and in my opinion is one of the major causes of why managers resist a change which top management see as clearly beneficial to the organisation. Because the psychological contract is specific to the individual, the problem may not be the same across the whole organisation, and may be harder to diagnose. However even a minority of key people can frustrate or delay certain types of change. Their behaviour is likely to be all the more damaging because much of it may spring from the subconscious, and they may not be aware that they are in opposition to the new policy or strategy. Senior managers who make the major change decisions are often too single minded, and sometimes too insensitive, to see behind the overt reasons for resistance. Often it will be rationalised to another cause, and therefore not be dealt with in the change process. Sometimes the result is that people whom the organisation does not wish to lose leave of their own accord, and in some situations this may be the only option. In the grocery products example, some country managing directors might feel so concerned about losing elements of their job that they see as important to them, that this will be the final outcome. Others may take actions that slow down the pace of the change, while a number will inevitably find a new equilibrium in the new circumstances. Change is likely to go much more smoothly if time is taken to understand these underlying issues, and as far as is possible ways found to deal with them. At the very least, an understanding of why a person behaves in a certain way may make it easier to reach the right operational decisions during the change process. The most dangerous thing is to concentrate efforts on the wrong symptom. Recently one of the European Business Schools brought in a new Dean, and this was followed by a haemorrhage of senior faculty personnel over the next 18 months. I was told that 18 people left in a one year period. I have a lot of sympathy with the Dean's dilemma, in that he took steps to prevent the faculty from competing at a personal level for the type of business that the School was now trying to obtain: consultancy and in-company management education programmes. Until this point faculty were entitled to seek this business privately, and historically the Business School itself had been interested only in academic and open programmes. Programmes which were specific to one company were not seen as the mainstream of its activity. But of course the market changed, and clearly it would have been intolerable for employees of the Business School to run their own private businesses in competition with that of the School itself, both in terms of the moral dilemmas that would face everyone, and the confused market identity which would have resulted. The obvious reason for the faculty to leave was that they were hit in the pocket, and would lose present and expected income, and of course this was a factor. However, there were more hidden issues to deal with: the psychological contract, the importance they placed on being able to work independently of the business school, their freedom to choose who worked with them on the assignments, and the personal satisfaction that clients came to them because of their individual skills, and not just because of the reputation of their employer. Those who have discussed this with me have said that the way the change was handled meant that the psychological contract was never addressed, and that if it had been, and solutions found, the Business School could have achieved its aims without the loss of so many people, although some would have undoubtedly resigned. This of course is speculation, but would certainly have been worth trying.

• *Lack of understanding of the change.* There is likely to be more resistance to change when people either do not understand what is going on, or do not know why it is happening. One could argue that one of the problems of the Timex case, discussed in Chapter 4, was that management never got the message through to the employees at large, and tended to speak to the Union representatives and not directly to their employees. In the hypothetical grocery products example in this chapter, it is easy to see how good or poor communication could each affect the speed and success of implementation of the new strategy. Communication to ensure a full understanding of the change, and pre-empting damaging rumour, is one of the lessons identified by Hubbard, 1996, from organisations which successfully manage major change. It was certainly one of the most noteworthy features of British Petroleum's Project 1990, where massive effort was directed to help the whole organisation understand the direction of the desired changes to structure and culture, the reasons for them, and their implications on how the organisation would operate. However communication is not everything, and BP also had a reputation for fair financial treatment of those who had to leave the organisation, and this reputation was not diminished by the treatment given to the "casualties" of Project 1990.

• *The head and the heart.* One problem that I have found in my consulting work is resistance which occurs after managers have agreed that a certain course of action has to take place. In these cases, the emotions around a situation and the logic behind the decision are at loggerheads. They agree because they cannot disagree, but there is no emotional commitment. This became very clear to me in a consulting assignment with one of the old established names in British engineering, where I worked with the top management team in a knowledge transfer style of consulting, helping the executive directors to identify the problems and some of the options, but they themselves reached the conclusions and decisions. In simple terms their problem was that they had about 60 businesses, most of which were successful, but could only muster the resources to compete on the necessary world scale for a fraction of these. Consequently they were losing their competitive position in many businesses, and this would get worse.

In fact they became one of the first British companies to start what became fashionable as a strategy to revert to the basics, or core, of the business, and to sell off the peripheral activities that had been acquired during a period when diversification was seen as the essential corporate philosophy. It proved to be a very effective strategy for my client, but was not implemented as speedily as expected. The businesses were clustered under group managing directors, and it was these people, plus the chief executive and some functional directors, who made up the executive committee where the decisions were taken for ratification by the main Board. There was genuine agreement on the general strategy, and those businesses which were to be divested were agreed after a lot of debate and questioning. There were also some businesses where judgement was reserved for later. Some of the debate was over definition, and whether some businesses, if looked at on technology grounds, might be said to be more closely related to each other than a market analysis would have suggested.

The result was that each group managing director was charged with the task of selling the surplus businesses which reported to him, and managing them for the best results in the period up to the sale. Twelve months later, little progress had been made. The reason was that commitment to the concept ran into difficulties when it came to the specific businesses, where emotions overcame logic. In this situation the team was clear sighted and frank, and defined the problem. Basically it fell into two parts: individuals had an emotional commitment to some of the businesses. One group managing director, for example, had made his name in the early years when he joined the company and successfully turned around one of the weaker businesses, which was now listed in those up for sale. He felt that presiding over the sale was like denying his past success. All found it difficult, after having discussed the impending disposals with the management teams of the businesses, to work with those teams on strategies and business improvement, while at the same time looking for a buyer. The emotional commitments pulled in two different directions. The solution they came up with was to delegate all aspects of divestment to one senior colleague who was not involved directly with the management of any individual businesses. Over the next twelve months most of the strategy was implemented, and the financial resources released were, as planned, put into the expansion of the core businesses.

AN APPROACH TO MANAGING CHANGE

So far we have looked at one way of thinking through the impact of a strategic change on the various components of an organisation, and have examined some of the reasons why there may be resistance to change. Knowing where the problems are likely to arise, and getting all components of the organisation to change in harmony, is an essential first step, but there is more to successful change management than this. One generalised approach is shown in Figure 11.2, which I have termed the EASIER approach, not because it is easy, but because the acronym helps, and because although still complex, the model helps to structure the things that should be done. The various elements of this approach, which will be described below, can be said to apply to every situation. The style with which each is approached, and the degree of emphasis given to each component, are matters which are to some degree situational. A major transformational change, for example, would require much more emphasis on each element than an incremental change. However, the urgency with which the change must take

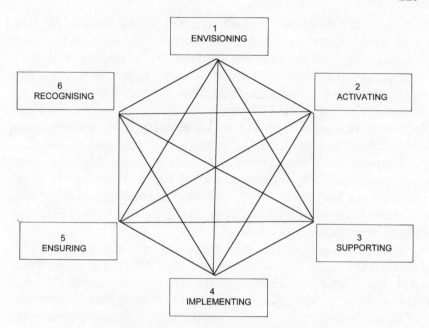

Figure 11.2   *An approach to managing change.*

place, and the amount of resistance within the organisation, will affect whether the style is one of involvement or is dictatorial. It is often true that the involvement of people in the change process at all levels can be a key force for success: but it is not universally true. It is doubtful whether the major changes that took place in the newspaper industry in the 1980s could have happened other than by dictatorial means; there were too many forces fighting against the change. One critical element in deciding style is how important it is that the organisation goes into its new future with the same people. It is possible to argue that one of the factors in the way the Murdoch organisation fought the battle over the use of new technology in the newspaper business was that they did not care whether the existing workers stayed or left, because the changes were so fundamental that the numbers and skills needed in the future would be quite different from those needed in the past. Figure 11.2 will be described on the basis that the circumstances allow a measure of participation in the change process.

An advantage of the model is that it can be applied at any

level in the organisation where change has to be led and managed. It can be used by the chief executive of a major organisation, or it can be applied by a middle manager managing the introduction of a new innovation into the organisation. It works equally well for an HR director to manage change in the HR area itself. The scales of the tasks are all different, and will influence exactly what is done under each heading of the model, but the concept itself is sound.

There has been much written on change leadership. The main inspiration for this particular model comes from a variety of sources, in particular Tichy and Dervanna, 1990, Nadler and Tushman, 1989, and Dinkelspiel and Bailey, 1991, leavened by experience with many clients.

Two points should be made about the model as a whole. The first is that every step is important, and ignoring even one can put the change process at risk. The second point is that although the model shows a reasonable starting sequence, most of the six stages will continue until the change is implemented. Thus you do not stop step 3 because you have moved on to step 4. As with some of the other models I have used, there is a recycling element, in that experience of going through each stage may influence all the other stages.

● *Envisioning*. This is the process of developing a coherent view of the future in order to form an over-arching objective for the organisation. The vision may cover such things as size, scope of activities, economic strengths, the relationships with customers, and the internal culture, including the values of the organisation. The vision may be to be the best in certain fields: the best innovator; the most effective producer; the best employer. It does not necessarily have to be of a future that is radically different from the past, and will often not be radically different in incremental change, but it becomes a much more important part of the implementation process when it is inspired by a realisation that a significant change is necessary.

Defining the vision clearly is an important element in the implementation process. The leader that cannot articulate the vision in a way that has meaning to others, will find it harder to ensure that everyone pulls in the same direction.

Vision is an appropriate first step for implementation at various levels in the organisation, and will be as critical for the leader of a business unit, or the head of a section. Effectively it will provide a reason for the various strategies. The content of the vision would be different at different levels. For example, downsizing of an operation may be accompanied by a vision which is concerned more with a future cost position and internal culture, than a view of products and markets. The vision of the manager of a business unit will be constrained by what the overall organisation is trying to do, but may be focused on the needs of the specific group of customers which that business unit serves.

An inappropriate vision can frustrate the implementation of the strategies. A key change management/leadership task is to think through the vision to ensure that it is both desirable and sound.

• *Activating.* Envisioning is a difficult process, because the borderline between empty platitudes and meaningful descriptions is very narrow. Activating is even harder. It is the task of ensuring that others in the organisation understand, support, and eventually share the vision. The vision cannot be understood unless it is communicated, and it cannot be communicated unless it is defined in a coherent way. Initially the task is to develop a shared vision among the key players in the task of implementation, but in most organisations there are benefits in reaching deep into the organisation, so that there is a wide belief in and commitment to the vision at all levels and functions.

A widespread commitment to the vision makes it easier to see the relevance of the strategies, and underlines the importance of coordinated efforts. Even when implementation causes people to lose their jobs, this is more likely to be acceptable to them and to their surviving colleagues, when they support the underlying vision that has led to this situation.

• *Supporting.* Good leadership is not just about giving orders and instructions. It is much more about inspiring others to achieve more than they might have believed possible, and providing the necessary moral and practical support to enable this to happen. The envisioning and activating steps in implementation are about sharing and sustaining inspiration.

The supporting step is about helping others to play a key part in the implementation process.

To achieve this the person leading the change has to have a strong empathy with the people he or she is trying to inspire, and the imagination to see things from their point of view. There needs to be an understanding of both their present capabilities and their potential. While giving support to help a subordinate reach a tough new goal, the leader has to be able to recognise the problems the person faces, without ever implying that there is the slightest doubt that the person will succeed.

There is a parallel with the principle of situational leadership, where the way each individual is managed is adjusted to his/her level of capability and degree of motivation.

There is always a danger when the person leading the change lacks integrity or is insincere. A manager who pretends to give encouragement, when it is clear that he or she does not really care and is merely performing a ritual, is likely to be counter productive. Supporting needs a base of respect, trust and integrity, and fails when these essentials are lacking.

● *Implementation*. The first three components of the model have a strong bias to dealing with the soft behavioural issues. With implementation we begin to look at three, predominantly "hard", aspects of managing the situation. In this context, the implementation box is about the process of developing detailed plans to enable the strategy to be implemented and controlled.

The nature and shape of these plans will vary with the complexity of the strategies, and their nature. Only in rare circumstances will it be a task that should be totally undertaken by the centre, and in most cases the process would benefit by the involvement of the key people who are expected to carry out the actions which will implement the strategy.

The instruments that may be used will also vary, depending not only on the complexity of the strategies, but also on the time-scale for implementation: however, the basic reason is constant. It is to:

—ensure that all the consequences of the change are understood, insofar as they can be foreseen. This includes the impact on the organisational variables discussed earlier;

—identify all the actions that have to be taken to bring about the change. This usually requires more attention to detail than would be appropriate for any formal strategic plan or boardroom presentation. It also has to be accepted that in some cases only the initial actions are clear, and that what happens subsequently will depend on the results of these. The more complex the strategy, the more likely will be the need for several phases of this detailed planning stage;

— allocate responsibility for the various actions that have to be taken;
— establish the priorities of the various actions, in particular those that will hold up the whole process if not done to time;
— provide the budgets needed to ensure implementation of the plans;
— set up the teams and structures needed to implement;
— allocate the right human resources to the tasks (if necessary recruiting additional people or using consultants);
— determine any policies that are needed to make the implementation process work.

There is nothing unique or special about any of these individual requirements, nor the instruments such as plans, budgets, critical path analysis, Gantt charts or other tools which have to be developed to ensure that nothing is overlooked, and everything is coordinated. These are all the regular instruments of management.

It should be recognised that when the strategies take the organisation into new situations, past experience may be little help in this process, and the planning of many large and small actions needed to ensure success may be much more difficult than expected. The organisation should not be too proud to supplement its implementation skills from consultancy or other sources where it lacks experience of what it is about to do.

● *Ensuring.* Plans, structures for implementation, and policies may be formulated, and on paper the organisation may have covered everything. But this is not enough to be certain of success, and consideration must be given to monitoring and controlling processes that will ensure that:

— all actions are taken on time, unless there is a conscious, justifiable decision to change the actions or priorities;

— where actions are changed, there is both a good reason for
the change, and a re-planning for the new circumstances;
— the results of the actions are as expected and, if they are not,
that corrective action is taken;
— plans are still appropriate if the situation has changed.

All organisations have monitoring and controlling processes,
but those that currently exist may be inadequate to monitor the
new strategies. One of the actions in the implementing phase,
therefore, might have been to establish supplementary controls,
so that timely information is made available on a regular basis.
When considering controls, attention should be given to the
qualitative issues as well as the quantitative. It may, for
example, be as important to survey periodically the morale in
the organisation, as to measure whether a new strategy has
brought the expected reduction in unit costs.

Monitoring and control processes also provide a reason for
the various players in the implementation game to meet, thus
providing another way of reinforcing the commitment to the
vision.

● *Recognising*. This is giving recognition to those involved in the
process. Recognition may be positive or negative, and should be
used to reinforce the change, and to ensure that obstacles to
progress are removed.

Although recognition may include financial reward, this may
be the smallest part of what is needed. Public recognition
(among peers and senior managers) of the part played by a
particular manager may show that what has been done is
appreciated. Promotion of someone who has played a major
role may be a consequence of his or her performance in helping
to implement the strategies. That small word "thanks" may
have great motivational value when expressed sincerely by a
leader who is respected by the person.

The negative aspects of this box may include the transfer of a
valuable person who opposes the strategies to a role where it is
not possible to damage the process. In some cases it may
include the dismissal of a particular person who is frustrating
the change or causing the pace to slow. Strategies that cause
fundamental change often bring this type of casualty. It would
be unrealistic to suggest that there will never be management

casualties, however much attention is given to the first three steps in the implementation process.

The approaches described offer a blueprint for implementation. They should be used with good sense. It has already been stated that the situation will affect how the concepts should be used, and the more fundamental the change, the more effort will be needed to apply all aspects of the approach. Where the changes are incremental, effectively bringing little difference to what the organisation does, and hardly affecting the organisational variables, some elements of the approach may not be as important as suggested here. The danger often is that we do not know what we do not know, and it is human nature to assume things about the impact of the strategy, without really thinking them through. At the very least, the approaches described should be used as a checklist to stimulate thinking, so that an implementation process can be defined. The underlying message must be to give attention to both the hard and the soft aspects of management. Neglect of either may cause failure in implementation. All readers will have realised that the key words in the model were selected to make up the acronym. By all means change the headings, if you think other words would work better in your organisation, but do not change the underlying concepts.

Again I should like to stress that managing change can be a complex and difficult task. There are many published recipes for success, and all of these look very logical away from the hurly-burly of the real situation. Time spent to understand fully all the implications of a proposed change is never wasted, and may remove many possibilities of failure. The EASIER model should be used as a starting point for thinking, interpreted against the realities of the situation, and seen as a process rather than a series of discrete steps which can be ticked off when done. Each component of the model will require the development of a detailed course of action, and will repay thought in the context of the change itself, and the particular organisation. Continual monitoring is critical: if one method of communication does not appear to be creating a sense of shared vision, try something else. Flexibility within each component, and in relation to changes through the overall implementation process, is critical.

The final plea of this chapter is: *do not be tempted to be superficial.* Do not consider that a delayering exercise has been implemented because the new organisation has been announced, and X% of employees have been made redundant: it is only implemented when the new organisation is able to work effectively, and to fulfil the tasks that are essential for long-term success. An acquisition is not implemented because the purchase agreement is signed: it can only be counted as done when the new combined organisation is able to achieve the vision and the strategy that lay behind the decision to buy the other organisation.

REFERENCES

Dinkelspiel, J. R. and Bailey, J., 1991, High Performing Organisations: Aligning Culture and Organisation Around Strategy, in Hussey, D. E., editor, *International Review of Strategic Management*, 2.1, Chichester: John Wiley.

Galbraith, J. R. and Nathanson, D. A., 1978, *Strategy Implementation: The Role of Structure and Process*, St. Paul: West Publishing.

Hubbard, N., 1996, Managing Employee Expectations in Times of Organisational Change, *Journal of Professional HRM*, 1.4, July.

Leavitt, H. J., 1964, Applied Organisational Change in Industry: Structural, Technical and Human Approaches, in Cooper, W. W., Leavitt, H. J. and Shelly, M. V., editors, *New Perspectives in Organisational Research*, New York: John Wiley.

Leavitt, H. J., 1970, Applied Organisational Change in Industry: Structural, Technical and Human Approaches, in Vroom, V. H. and Deci, E. L., editors, *Management and Motivation*, Harmondsworth: Penguin.

Nadler, D. A. and Tushman, M. L., 1989, Leadership for Organisational Change, in Morhman et al, editors, *Large Scale Organisational Change*, San Francisco: Jossey-Bass.

Peters, T. and Waterman, R. H., 1982, *In Search of Excellence*, New York: Harper and Row.

Tichy, N. M. and Dervanna, M. A., 1990, *The Transformational Leader*, New York: John Wiley.

12
HRM and Added Value— A Health Check

No senior human resources manager can afford to become complacent about the contribution HRM is making to the organisation. It is very easy to assume that anything which is worthy will also add value. Unfortunately, worthiness and added value are not necessarily the same thing, and in any case the never-ending task is one of seeking improvement to the contributions made by HRM.

This chapter is about ways of assessing whether, in the particular organisation, HRM is making a real contribution to shareholder value, whether it is truly business driven, and ways in which it might seek to become more cost effective. It is about trying to avoid complacency.

Preceding chapters have shown how to develop a business driven approach. It was found from the research that not all organisations who claim to practise business driven HRM are fully living up to their claims. One of the topics of this chapter will be a self auditing of HRM, to help organisations explore how deep their business driven approach really is. Although I am not starting the detail of this chapter with this topic, I should like to take what might be the first two questions of any audit as a means of provoking thought.

- Is HRM business driven in your organisation?
- How do you know?

The first question is merely a lead in to the second. I know from experience that an almost automatic *yes* is given by most organisations. It is the second question which causes people to think about whether unfounded assumptions are being made, and whether the commitment is more than skin deep. The questions could be modified to replace "business driven" with "value adding". But let us not take the audit further at this stage, and instead begin with some thoughts on customers.

SERVING A CUSTOMER

It can be argued that shareholder value begins to be created by the way in which organisations give primacy to customers. HRM rarely has customers outside of the organisation, but has internal customers, and where an organisation has a customer responsive culture, internal suppliers will respond to internal customers in much the same way as they would to external customers. At least that is how the theory goes. It can get twisted. In one client organisation with which I had extensive dealings, line managers were perpetually annoyed by the HRM response, "you are the customer, what would you like?", when what they wanted was some leadership and positive direction over an HR issue. Of course the clients of HRM are critical, and ways should be sought to add value through the way they are served, but this does not mean that the customer is always right, or even always knows what the needs are. This is true of all products, but particularly true of much of the advisory/consultancy role that many HR functions now play. HRM has to deliver what the organisation and the internal customers *need*. A line manager who wishes to sack a senior manager may feel that he or she should have complete freedom to act. The reality may be that the manager needs advice, that he or she does not want, to prevent further problems from arising. I speak from experience, having many years ago gone through the trauma of giving advice to top management of the subsidiary company in which I worked in a way that could not be ignored. The company planned certain strategic moves dictated by the majority shareholder which involved the transfer of assets and overseas businesses without payment to other, wholly owned companies in the group. Apart from defrauding the minority shareholders, the moves would have fallen foul of the Inland Revenue, and (at the time) contravened exchange control regulations. They did not want my advice against this move, but they needed it, as subsequent discussions with their lawyers proved to them. However they made sure that they did not get my advice again, and I was sacked.

Giving customers what they need is, to me, part of providing a value adding service, and is much more customer focused than delivering just what they want to hear. There are various ways of looking at how value is given to a customer. Johansson et al, 1993, page 4, suggest that there are four value metrics: quality, service, cost and cycle time. Some of the components of each metric, which are relevant to an intangible "product" are:

- *quality*: meeting customer requirements, fitness for use, process integrity/minimum variances, and elimination of waste;
- *service*: customer support, flexibility to meet customer demands, and product service;
- *cost*: administration, quality assurance, and distribution;
- *cycle time*: time to market, response to market forces, and lead time.

The last two metrics listed require some modification to fit them to HRM activity, but it is not difficult to apply the ideas to the HRM situation. The issue for HRM is how to increase the value added by attention to these metrics. This requires a closeness to the customers on a continuous basis, and an understanding of the business imperatives which drive them. Only in this way is it possible to ensure that HRM acts in a creative and proactive way. Hiltrop and Despres, 1995, page 201, refer to an internal study among all the subsidiaries of United Technologies, which include Otis Elevators, Sikorsky Helicopters, and Pratt and Whitney, of the value adding contribution of HRM to the internal customers. A task force was convened for this purpose. Describing it, Dailey, 1992, himself a senior member of the HR team, wrote:

"HR professionals stood up for the HR perspective, which is good, but did it quite traditionally. They were fairly competent, but didn't measure themselves very rigorously. They did their homework and came to meetings prepared, but were not seen as very innovative or risk taking. In short, the message from this survey was, 'You're not really a strategic partner'."

Another finding was that the HR professionals put a higher value on each other's contribution than did the line managers.

The method used by UTC is one way of establishing the degree to which the HRM function is perceived as adding value, and being business driven. Of course the reality may not match the perceptions, but if it does not it implies a need for better communication and closer working with the line. The questionnaire which UTC used contained 18 questions to be scored on a 1–4 rating (1 is high), and for the most part covers the value metrics of quality and service. Eight of the questions explored aspects of the HRM behaviours which were directly related to the needs of the organisation: in other words, they were business driven. The questionnaire used for this survey is published in the sources quoted, although it would not be difficult for a small task force of managers and HRM specialists to design something similar which was geared to the situation in a specific organisation.

The real message of this section about serving the customer is that attention must be given to each of the metrics, with the aim of finding ways not only to improve the quality and service levels, but also to do it at lower cost, and in a timely way. HRM has moved beyond the era when claiming to be worthy is enough. One of the steps to improvement is to establish economic performance standards so that results can be demonstrated.

LEVELS OF PERFORMANCE

Earlier I referred to the reluctance of HRM to establish effective ways of judging success in areas such as training. The reluctance is partly that some aspects of HRM are very difficult to measure, and it is always easier to measure inputs than results. This means that some statistics, although they may be useful for planning purposes, measure activity rather than value. Hiltrop and Despres, 1995, page 210, compiled a list of performance indicators from selected published sources. They included, for training and development, the ratio of trainee days to number of employees, and the total training budget as a ratio of total employment cost. Certainly these are useful figures, and certainly it would be possible to set targets and measure against them. The problem I have with them for measuring value added performance is that they relate to quantity and not quality, to what is spent, not what is gained. There is also a hidden assumption that spending more is better than spending less. It might be, but is not necessarily so. In my view a better way to establish performance levels for training would be to add a quality dimension to the input figures. Chapters 7 and 8 cover part of this, but there is another dimension which comes from Mayo, 1995. He suggests that in an organisation where the ownership of individual learning plans is seen as important, three measures of HRM effectiveness might include the percentage of learning plans compiled, the percentage achieved, and average increase in competence levels in key skill areas. These measures extend beyond HRM, as line managers are also involved, and imply that there is a good process behind the learning plans which means that they are worthwhile. This sort of new thinking does help get a fix on what is important.

Other quantitative measures in the Hiltrop and Despres list go closer to effectiveness, such as the proportion of vacancies filled internally by each of promotion, transfer or demotion, or the number of long-term vacancies as a ratio of the total number of jobs (although as a ratio of all vacancies might be a more useful measure of the effectiveness of HRM). Not in the list, but possibly as important at measuring effectiveness, might be performance measures on the costs of recruitment of different grades, and the number of new recruits who leave in less than a given period, such as a year. These begin to get to the heart of the cost effectiveness, timeliness, and quality of recruitment activity.

Hiltrop and Despres also paraphrase a conceptualisation of Bernadin and Kane, 1993:

- *Quality of delivery* (in terms of conforming to some practice ideal, or fulfilling the intended purpose).

- *Quantity* (expressed in terms such as dollar value, number of units, or number of completed HR activity cycles).
- *Timeliness* (the degree to which an HR practice is completed, or a result produced, at the earliest time desirable).
- *Cost effectiveness* (in the sense of optimising the gain or minimising the loss from each unit or instance of use of human and financial resources).
- *Need for supervision* (the degree to which a person or unit can carry out an HR practice without requesting assistance, or requiring intervention to prevent an adverse outcome).
- *Positive impact* (the degree to which an HR practice promotes feelings of self esteem, goodwill, commitment, satisfaction, and cooperation among co-workers and subordinates).

This conception relates more closely to the value metrics discussed earlier.

There is an undoubted difficulty in measuring some of the results of HRM actions. A measure can be defined, but is only of value if it can be measured. Since some of the measures deal with values and attitudes, it will be necessary to undertake special investigations from time to time. The Premier Bank case in Chapter 4 offers an example of one such method. It is not easy, but it is no harder than the periodic surveys that organisations make to establish the market share of their products.

Unfortunately, many HR managers cannot know the cost effectiveness of specific activities which they provide, because they do not track the costs. Mention was made in earlier chapters of organisations which have no sound information on, or control of, management training expenditure, but this is the tip of the iceberg of the problem. It is not new. Peel, 1984, page 24, for example found that most of the organisations which had a cross-charging system for training services did not make a charge for overheads. "This being so, a rational decision, on the grounds of costs, as to whether to 'buy out' management training or to use internal resources must be difficult. The dice can be loaded against the external provider." But it is not only training. How many HR departments know the full costs of any recruitment that is handled in house, or of the design of a remuneration system, or the development of a succession plan?

While cost is only one part of the equation, and there are other considerations such as timeliness, knowledge of the organisation, and quality, an HR department that cannot measure how its time is spent, and the cost of that time, will never truly understand whether or not it is cost effective, and whether the organisation would be better off by outsourcing more of what it does.

The components of such an economic evaluation are the ability to properly cost time, and some sort of time sheeting system that enables time to be charged to projects. This may sound a tall order, but it is done by many other professional people, such as accountants, solicitors, management consultants and engineering consultants, and in many of those organisations is extended to secretaries and administrative staff who are working on those projects. While there may be many small activities every day that are not worth booking time to, there are many others where such information would be invaluable.

The costs of time are a little more complex, in that there is a short-term and long-term aspect. Firstly let us deal with expenses which are directly attributable to a project, such as the hire of a seminar room at a hotel, or the costs of a function to launch a new appraisal system. These can be booked directly to the project they are for, and this is indeed done by a majority of organisations. But what is the cost of a professional human resource executive? Often when looking at the daily charge rate of an external consultant, managers make the mistake of comparing it with a quick calculation of their own daily salary. But the daily salary is not the right figure. Firstly the prime cost of a person is all the employment costs (salary, fringe benefits, national insurance, etc) of that person divided not by the number of days in the year, but by the number of effective days when work will be done. So as a general rule we need to deduct weekends, public holidays, and paid vacation. Just to keep the calculation simple let us assume that of a 52 week year, 5 weeks are not available for work because they are either holidays or public holidays. This means that the employment costs, which let us take as £15 000 per year, are really £15 000 ÷ 47, or just over £319 per week, and not £15,000 ÷ 52, or just over £288, an increase of more than 10%.

This is only a beginning. The employee uses secretarial and other support, occupies office space, is sometimes ill, and does not always work on the activities that are the prime reason for which he or she is employed. By the last point I mean that there are internal staff meetings, appraisals, administrative tasks like claiming back expenses or compiling budgets, all of which consume time which cannot be attributed directly to any specific project or activity. All these things are overheads of the individual, and typically we might expect the total weekly cost of that individual to go up by a factor of 2 to 5. Thus the £288 with which we started has become something between £638 and £1595. The calculations are crude, but make the point.

Having got our costs, we need to be sure that time is properly charged. As an example let us look at the temptation of a training manager to consider only attendance time as the basis of the cost of running a 5 day programme. Using the figures above it might be argued that the cost in money is the £1595 for a working week of five days. However, the true time will always be higher. There is administration, to ensure that the course materials are prepared, videos obtained, and the like. Time may have been spent in developing the course. The trainer also has to prepare and rehearse. So the real cost of running a programme may be much higher than is assumed.

However there is both a short- and a medium- to long-term position. It is only in the latter that benefits can be gained from changes to the economic structure of HRM, and these benefits require a change of some sort. To outsource a programme, or any other activity, without removing the costs the organisation is already incurring on its existing internal resources, or finding an alternative economic use for those resources will not bring a saving, even though the outside supplier may be cheaper. Similarly overheads such as secretarial support are only saved if the number of people giving this support is reduced. Nothing is saved if the cost of these resources is merely spread across a lower number of activities.

This knowledge of economic costs is essential for the development of an effective business driven HRM function, and for establishing meaningful performance measures. It requires HR managers, who aspire to a stronger advisory and consultancy role in their organisations, to take on some of the disciplines of a management consultant.

STRATEGIC AUDIT OF HRM

One way of finding out whether HRM has a business driven approach in a particular organisation is to find out what other managers think. This was illustrated by the UTC example mentioned above, and is a very useful idea. It is also possible for HRM to undertake an audit of itself, which is a useful supplement to information from line managers, providing the questions are answered with honesty, and wishful thinking is not allowed to hide the truth. It is difficult to be totally objective, and there is an argument for suggesting that the audit might be more useful if it drew views from the whole of HRM. The perspective from the middle is often very different from that of the top. The aim of such an audit is, of course, to see whether improvements are needed and where they can be made.

A starting point is the two questions raised at the start of this chapter, perhaps phrased a little differently, and the discussion of Chapter 3 is also relevant, particularly Figure 3.6. In a situation where HRM is allowed to take no part in anything strategic, and has no access to any information, there is really no great point in proceeding with a more detailed audit. But let us assume, and this is the situation in most large organisations, that HRM has reasonable access to top management thinking, to line managers, and to formal planning documents.

Table 12.1 sets out a few questions which might help guide an examination of whether HRM is truly business driven. The scoring set against these questions is somewhat tongue in cheek, intended to attract attention and stimulate thinking, so please do not take the interpretation of the scores at the end as more than this. The questions themselves are serious, and going through these, with some attention to the possible answers on the scoring scale, will leave a clear impression of how deep the concept goes in the organisation: if, that is, it goes at all.

Table 12.1   *How business driven is your HRM activity?*

		Score		
		1	**2**	**3**	**4**
1	Is HRM consulted while strategies are being considered?	Never	Rarely	Often	Always
2	Does this advice have any impact on the decisions?	Never	Rarely	Often	Always
3	Is the HR role proactive?	Never	Rarely	Often	Always
4	Will risks be taken to give unpopular advice?	Never	Rarely	Often	Always
5	How many specific examples can be given where HRM has contributed to the strategic success of the business in:				
	5.1 Overall HR	None	1 or 2	3–5	Over 5
	5.2 Remuneration	None	1 or 2	3–5	Over 5
	5.3 Recruitment	None	1 or 2	3–5	Over 5
	5.4 Management development	None	1 or 2	3–5	Over 5
	5.5 Training	None	1 or 2	3–5	Over 5
	5.6 Succession	None	1 or 2	3–5	Over 5
	5.7 Others?	None	1 or 2	3–5	Over 5
6	Is there a clear strategy and policy for each HR area?	No	Some	Most	Yes
7	Does this derive specifically from business strategies, etc?	No	Loosely	Partly	Totally
8	When were all HR policies and strategies last reviewed?	Don't know	Years ago	Last year	This year
9	Are such reviews made regularly?	No	Infrequently	Periodically	Yes
10	Do top management play a part in such reviews?	No	Not much	Informally	Formally
11	Is line management involved in such reviews?	No	Not much	Informally	Formally
12	Have performance criteria been set for HR?	No	A few	Most areas	All areas
13	Are the criteria derived from the business needs?	No	A few	Mainly	Totally
14	Do you know the costs of activities in HRM?	No	A few	Some	All
15	Do you measure HR time spent on key projects?	No	Roughly	In part	Fully
16	Are HR actions such as training evaluated?	Never	Rarely	Sometimes	Often
17	How are priorities decided when setting the HR budget?	None	Whim	Gut feel	Corp need
18	Are HR actions in different parts of the organisation coordinated to give priority to business needs?	No	Rarely	Sometimes	Always
19	Are your HR policies comparable with best practice in world class organisations?	Don't know	No	Some	Broadly

Table 12.1 Continued

		Score		
		1	2	3	4
20	How do the HR performance measures compare with:				
	competitors?	Don't know	Badly	Same	Better
	world class organisations?	Don't know	Badly	Same	Better
21	Do line managers think HRM is a good strategic partner?	No	Sometimes	Mainly	Yes

Maximum score 27 x 4 = 112
Minimum score 27
Under 50 : Not business driven
  51–75   : A long way to go
  76–85   : Improvement possible, but mainly business driven
  85+   : Probably business driven
  112   : Probably wishful thinking!

Question 1 explores an issue that has received much attention in earlier pages. This is the extent to which HR is in at the beginning of a new strategy (or other change action) so that a proactive role can be played. However, it is possible for the senior HR manager to be on the board and present at all key discussions without being in any way proactive (question 3). The danger is in confusing the opportunity to play such a role, with how the individuals in the organisation actually work. Any failure to be proactive could be because of unwillingness of the HR person to take risks, or because other managers have a closed mindset and will not allow a proactive role. Question 2 is another way of thinking about the effectiveness of HR as a proactive force. How often is any advice given allowed to influence the decision and how it is implemented? The question of personal risk is taken up in question 4, and can be related to a similar question in the UTC survey. It is a difficult question for any person to answer about him or herself, but is usually one where the answer is clear to peer managers and HR subordinates. It is very easy to fall into a trap of saying only the things that people want to hear, particularly in modern times when redundancies are in the air. A dissenting voice is often taken as hostility, and it is easier to go along with the tide. But doing nothing to challenge thinking which will not give the best HR results for the organisation would hardly justify any claim of having business driven HRM.

In question 5 attention is focused on bringing to life any broad statements that might have been made in the preceding questions, although this question deals with both the proactive and the reactive roles of HRM. The number of areas of HR could be expanded: those shown are meant to be indicative. Finding honest examples of how HR actions have been specifically moulded to the needs of the business is easy to do in a superficial way. Again the plea is not to confuse something which is worthy, because it follows sound, generally good professional practice, with something which is specifically geared to adding value to the business. The best way to answer the question may be to start with a change situation of significance, and work through how each area of HR sets out to help make it work. Another caution is not to oversimplify these issues, but to remember how some of the research in Chapter 5 showed how many organisations were looking at the HR implications of a strategic change in a very superficial way.

Questions 6 and 7 explore the existence of clear HR policies and strategies, and whether these derive specifically from business strategies, vision and objectives. Mere existence of a policy does not indicate a business driven approach, which is why thought about where the policy came from is important. Questions 8 and 9 assume that the organisation is dynamic, and that changes are taking place regularly. It is therefore relevant to enquire how old the HR policies and strategies are. This question should be adjusted to the business situation of the organisation, or to use the Ansoff terminology discussed in an earlier chapter, the degree of turbulence the organisation faces: the need for frequent policy review would increase as turbulence increases, whereas a static organisation facing little change may have no real need to change HR policies.

The issue of reviews is taken further in questions 10 and 11, which seek to explore whether management is involved in HR policy reviews. I should find it hard to accept a claim that HRM was business driven, if only HR people were involved in reviewing and agreeing HR policies.

Questions 12 to 15 echo some of the earlier discussion on performance criteria. It is not just a question of whether HRM has performance criteria, but how close these are to the needs of the business. The line of thinking goes on to knowledge of the economics of HR departments. There is a hidden attitude that may emerge here, because one of the reasons for failure to have performance measures in place in HR is because some HR people are afraid of what will be revealed. Sheltering behind such phrases as "not relevant", "cannot be done", or "too costly" should be recognised as signs that the HRM is not business driven. Evaluation of the benefits of HR actions has been discussed in many other chapters, and in Chapter 4 it was demonstrated that the research showed that, in training at least, evaluation was a neglected, and often rejected, art. It may be hard to do, but again an intent to ensure that HRM is really contributing can only be taken as serious when actions are evaluated. The question could be rephrased to look at each area of HR, as was done in question 5.

The difficult issue of how HRM determines its priorities is explored through question 17 about the annual budget. A number of related questions could have been developed, as the real issues are where the priorities come from, and how they are supported through the provision of resources. The ideal is close to a zero based budgeting approach, where expenses can be looked at both in terms of categories (for example, salaries, travel, etc), by responsibility centres, and by projects (grading system for managers, new performance management process, senior management strategy programme, etc).

Question 18 may require modification to suit the needs of the organisation. It assumes a central HR department consisting of groups of specialisations, such as remuneration, recruitment, industrial relations and training. In large organisations there may be a measure of decentralisation by business unit, and geography. It is not always true that all aspects of HR fall under an HR department, and there may be some aspects that are handled by line managers. The issue of achieving a coordinated policy which gives priority to business needs can be complicated, but is nevertheless an important aspect of a successful business driven approach.

There is a danger in taking too parochial an approach, and questions 19 and 20 try to give a wider perspective. It is easy to dismiss questions such as this as irrelevant, but it may be interesting to ponder whether Timex might have taken a different path had they made comparisons of this nature early enough. Benchmarking is the next topic of this chapter, so further discussion will be reserved until then.

The final question, 21, is not of great value unless companion research is undertaken of the opinions of other managers. It comes into its own when a contrast can be made of what HRM believes managers think, and what the actual opinion is, as in the UTC example.

No doubt other questions could be added to this list, and another way of proceeding could be to compare the various models suggested in earlier chapters with what goes on in the organisation. However such an investigation is undertaken, it is worth remembering that the enemies are complacency, wishful thinking, superficiality, and lack of objectivity.

BENCHMARKING

One aspect of business driven HRM is to help the organisation to continuously improve performance. There are two dimensions to this for the HR manager. The first, and most important, is the processes and policies that impact on bottom line results, and whether these can be improved to increase cost effectiveness. The second is the operations of HRM itself, the degree to which HR is decentralised to the line, and the performance of the HR department. One way of aiding this improvement is through benchmarking.

Most HR managers would claim to do benchmarking, and most would be wrong. What is often construed as benchmarking is one of its possible first steps, a comparison of ratios, or other facts, such as salaries. These are very useful, and have been used by HR departments for decades, and I should urge their continued use. But this is not benchmarking.

What benchmarking does is to study the *processes* which lead to the ratios or other results, by comparing your own with those of organisations who are achieving better results.

There are various ways of applying benchmarking. The first may be applied in an organisation where it is possible to benchmark against other areas inside the group. This has the advantage that cooperation is easier to obtain, and confidentiality is not a problem, but has the disadvantage that although improvements may be gained, it may be possible to do better by looking outside the organisation.

There are three broad areas from which benchmarking partners may be chosen, and these relate to the ambitions of the organisation: is the aim to be the best in the industry, best in the country, or best in the world? If the first, attention might be placed on benchmarking against other members of the industry, who may or may not be direct competitors. The second accepts that better performance can often come from studying what goes on in other organisations in other industries, and that for most aspects of HR much can be learned from the best performers in that process or activity in the country, regardless of industry. The third takes the thought further, and argues that to be world class performers, you have to learn from those organisations wherever they are in the world who are themselves the leaders in that particular area.

Of course benchmarking is not restricted to HR, and is applied to a variety of processes and activities. HR is particularly well suited to benchmarking because there is such a wide choice of possible people to benchmark against, and many fewer processes which organisations might wish to keep secret.

There are many complexities in a benchmarking study, and the six steps shown below are a simplification. More complete information will be found in Watson, 1993 and Karlöf and Östblom, 1993. Watson writes with experience from Xerox Corporation, who were early pioneers of benchmarking. Karlöf and Östblom relate benchmarking to the learning organisation through a concept they term *bench learning*.

The six steps are:

1 *What to benchmark*

The initial task is to decide what to benchmark. The selection might arise from a comparison of performance ratios, or from recognition that there is an area which could benefit from some different thinking. The area needs to be carefully defined, and although it may encompass a number of related processes, it should not be so broad that it becomes

impossible to benchmark. A profitability ratio might show
that the organisation was lagging, but there are too many
processes contributing to profitability for it to be a
meaningful subject of one benchmarking exercise. The
process of changing products on a production line, with the
aim of reducing the time taken would be narrow enough to
do something about.

2   *How do we do it?*

Before even thinking about benchmarking partners, the
organisation should study its own process. It is not possible
to learn from benchmarking until you know exactly what
your organisation is doing. For example, one study
Harbridge Consulting Group made for a client was on the
career progression and utilisation of newly qualified MBAs.
The first stage of the assignment was to collect information
from the client organisation, in quantitative and qualitative
terms, to identify the processes used, and to compare what
was found with the progress and utilisation of other
graduate recruits. Only at this stage did it make sense to find
out what other organisations of a comparable standing were
doing. This first stage took a great deal of time, as it meant
defining what actually happened in the organisation.

Unfortunately it is a step which is often neglected.

3   *Who should we choose as a benchmarking partner?*

Benchmarking implies an exchange of information. It should
not be seen as a one-sided exercise whereby the organisation
can somehow gain benefit without giving anything in return.
There is also a need for trust, since some of the information
exchanged may be confidential. Although it is possible to
benchmark against competitors, it is usually easier to work
with organisations who are not in the same industry, or are
not competing in the same arena. Watson, 1993, quotes a
General Motors quality benchmarking exercise against 11
companies, none of which were competitors. Any dealings
with benchmarking partners should be made with integrity.
Watson, 1993, page 217, offers a code of conduct for
benchmarking.

There are many reasons why the best organisations to
benchmark against may be outside of the industry, and
every reason why attempts should be made to find partners

who have an outstanding reputation in the area being benchmarked. And it is worth trying to think creatively. If the HR department believes it is in a mainly consulting role, then perhaps a good benchmarking partner might be a leading management consultancy offering HR skills.

4 *How do they do it?*

We already know what we do. The next step is to make a parallel study of what each of the benchmarking partners does. This in fact is another reason for studying your own process in detail, because in effect it is a rehearsal for when, with less time and reduced opportunity for follow up visits, a study is made inside another organisation. Part of the code of conduct means that there is an exchange of information, and also that anything learned is used only for the purpose of benchmarking. It would also mean that no use is made of any other information one might come across which is not part of the benchmarking exercise.

Finding out how others do things is about detail. On paper two processes may look the same, and only careful study of how they are applied will reveal the reasons why one brings better results than the other.

5 *What are the lessons, and can we apply them?*

The aim of benchmarking is to learn so that improvements can be made, or reassurance can be obtained that the process as applied is as good as it could be. The lessons emerge from a careful comparison of what they do with what we do. However, although this may give the clue to action, there is need to think about how to apply the lessons. Sometimes this means modifying the change so that ideas are better fitted to the culture and activities of the organisation. Often it is the clue to a better way of doing things that is needed, and much more effort has to be made by the organisation to make it all work.

There may also be a composite of experiences to compare. If around 10 benchmarking partners are involved there will be a need to see what practical approach can be derived from what is learned from all of them. Five may achieve better results than your organisation, but you cannot introduce five different ways of following the same process. One solution has to emerge from all this work.

6   *How can we implement the change?*
A new procedure or changed process means nothing unless it can be implemented, and this phase also requires very careful thought. Some of the comments from the previous chapter on managing organisational change are relevant here. In particular the advice has to be to think through all aspects of the change, and not to make unfounded assumptions that what works for them will automatically work for you. If their success depends on the attitudes of employees rather than the way a system is designed, effort may have to be devoted to developing the right attitudes among your employees.

Until the change is implemented, there is no return on the effort, usually extensive, that has gone into the benchmarking exercise.

FURTHER STEPS TO IMPROVING HRM'S COST EFFECTIVENESS

Much of this chapter is about the cost effectiveness of HRM, and the point has already been made that HRM is not business driven until it reaches a state when it regularly reviews the cost effectiveness of its own operations. In these days of continuous competitive pressure, the ability of HRM to do the things that need doing is dependent on its ability to scrap those that do not, or to find ways of delivering more benefit for less cost.

Benchmarking can be very helpful, and is a good first step for the application of Business Process Reengineering to HRM. Unfortunately BPR as a concept became corrupted very quickly, and the name was applied to numerous cost improvement activities that organisations were already doing, thus at a stroke bringing the organisation up to the latest fashion without the inconvenience of doing anything differently. That is also the same mechanism by which many personnel departments suddenly became HR departments, without taking on board the extra things that HRM implies. BPR is not about tinkering with the edges, it is about organisation-wide examination of processes, with a view to their radical redesign. Often HR processes are only part of something wider, and BPR should look at the whole, and not just that part which falls under HR control. Johansson, H. J. et al, 1993, is one of several good books which explore the total concepts of BPR. The basic steps in BPR make it seem much easier than it really is: select the process; define the process; challenge all assumptions about the process; think creatively; redesign the process; implement. It is possible to gain benefits by studying a process, and taking steps to eliminate waste and duplication, but the real rewards come to the organisations that are willing to break the china and reassemble the pieces in a dramatically different way.

HR has always used consultants and other suppliers to do some of the work that in theory could have been undertaken by internal resources. For example, although there may be an established training facility, an external specialist organisation might be contracted to run certain courses: a recruitment organisation might be hired to advertise and prepare a shortlist of candidates for a vacancy, even though the organisation employs some people who are expert in recruiting. There are good reasons for this sort of action, and although selection may have been adversarial, often a strong working relationship develops and the same suppliers are used for many years. In fact it is possible to argue that what often happens is not a genuine partnership, but a form of lethargy, which means that the *status quo* continues. This was certainly a finding of the Harbridge Consulting Group researches into management training and development which were referenced in Chapter 5. What is beginning to be a sensible action to consider in HRM, as in other areas of the organisation, is outsourcing.

One area which has been outsourced in many organisations for many years is the running of the "hotel" aspects of company training colleges. This had many benefits, as it is an area where few organisations have first hand experience, and there is added value in working with an organisation that, because it serves several facilities, can offer back up staff in times of illness or holidays.

In other areas of the organisation, outsourcing has embraced many operating activities previously thought of as sacrosanct, such as internal audit and information technology. It is a concept which could be applied to all but the policy and strategic tasks of HRM. For example, all training activity, parts of the recruitment process, and the implementation of internal communications activities could all be outsourced. The main benefits are saving in overheads, access to a wider base of knowledge and skills, and the flexibility of only having to pay for something when you need it. Outsourcing makes it easier to adjust the size of the organisation, and can increase the cost effectiveness of a service.

The difference between outsourcing and buying in services in the traditional way is summed up by the word partnership. Two, or more, organisations work together to achieve a common end, acting more as an alliance than as separate organisations. Some of the employees of the outsourcing supplier may work inside the premises of the host organisation: others may serve several clients, and be drawn on as needed.

McHugh, Merli and Wheeler, 1995, take the concept of BPR outside of the borders of the firm to the whole process across all the different organisational links to the customer. Even after an outsourcing decision, it is possible to work with the partner to gain improvements in the total process. This needs flexibility on both sides, as it may be better to move activities from one organisation to another in order to achieve a better overall result.

CONCLUSION

The overall messages of this chapter are: never assume that improvement is impossible, be willing to review what is done on a regular basis, and really work at the business driven concept.

This seems to be a fitting place to end the book. I hope that it has helped to shed light on what is an essential and complex aspect of HRM, and that at the least it will help people to work out their own methods and approaches, and at best will set some on a path that they may not previously have travelled. I have not tried to minimise the difficulties in achieving a business driven approach, but I believe that the effort is worthwhile, both for the good of the organisation, and for the continued health of HRM. Try it.

REFERENCES

Bernadin, H. and Kane, J., 1993, *Performance Appraisal: A Contingency Approach to System Development and Evaluation,* (2nd edition), Boston, MA: PWS-Kent.

Dailey, L., 1992, United Technologies Corporation, *Human Resource Management,* Spring and Summer, 15–17.

Hiltrop, J. M. and Despres, C. (1995), Benchmarking HR Practices: Approaches, Rationales, and Prescriptions for Action, in Hussey, D. E., editor, *Rethinking Strategic Management,* Wiley, Chichester.

Johansson, H. J., et al, 1993, *Business Process Engineering,* Chichester: John Wiley.

Karlöf, B. and Östblom, S., 1993, *Benchmarking,* Chichester: John Wiley.

Mayo, A., 1995, Economic Indicators of HRM, in Tyson, S., editor, *Strategic Prospects for HRM,* London: Institute of Personnel Development.

McHugh, P., Merli, G. and Wheeler, W. A., 1995, *Beyond Business Process Reengineering: Towards the Holonic Enterprise,* Chichester: John Wiley.

Peel, M., 1984, *Management Development and Training,* London: British Institute of Management/Professional Publishing

Watson, G. H., 1993, *Strategic Benchmarking,* New York: John Wiley.

Index